THE NEW INTERNATIONAL WEBSTER'S VEST POCKET THESAURUS

PRESS
INTERNATIONAL

Published by
Trident Press International
2003 EDITION

ISBN 1582792208

Printed in Peru

aback *adv.* **BACKWARD:** back, behind, rearward; **UNEXPECTED:** suddenly, unawares, unexpectedly

abandon *n.* **ENTHUSIASM:** impetuosity, spontaneity; **IMMORALITY:** shamelessness, wantonness

abandon *v.* **GIVE UP:** forgo, forswear, quit, relinquish; **DESERT:** forsake, leave, resign, vacate

abandonment *n.* abdication, renunciation, repudiation, resignation, surrender

abase *v.* debase, degrade, disgrace, dishonor, humble, humiliate

abased *adj.* degraded, disgraced, dishonored, humbled, humiliated, lowered

abasement *n.* degradation, deterioration, disgrace, dishonor, groveling, humiliation, lowering, shame

abash *v.* confound, confuse, disconcert, embarrass, humble, humiliate, mortify, shame

abashed *adj.* ashamed, chagrined, confused

abasing *adj.* abusive, insulting, offensive

abate *v.* **LESSEN:** decline, decrease diminish, ease, ebb, fade, lower, moderate, slacken, relieve, slow; **DISCOUNT:** allow, deduct, rebate, remit, subtract

abatement *n.* **LESSENING:** alleviation, decrease, mitigation, slackening, subsidence; **ENDING:** cessation, remission, suppression, termination

abbreviate *v.* abridge, condense, contract, cut, reduce, shorten, truncate

abbreviation *n.* abridgement, brief, compendium, condensation, shortening, truncation

abdicate *v.* abandon, cede, disavow, disclaim, disown, relinquish, renounce, resign, secede

abdomen *n.* belly, breadbasket, gut, midsection, paunch, potbelly, stomach, tummy
abduct *v.* capture, kidnap, seize, shanghai
abecedarian *n.* beginner, novice
aberrant *adj.* **DEVIATING:** divergent, errant, irregular, straying; **ODD:** abnormal, peculiar, queer, strange, unnatural, unusual, weird
aberrational *adj.* curious, odd, peculiar, strange
abet *v.* advance, aid, assist, back, condone, favor, further, help, promote, sanction, support
abettor *n.* accessory, accomplice, ally, associate, cohort, confederate, conspirator
abeyance *n.* cessation, deferral, discontinuance, hiatus, moratorium, suspension
abhor *v.* despise, detest, hate, loathe
abhorrence *n.* aversion, disgust, dislike, distaste, hatred, loathing, horror, repugnance
abhorrent *adj.* abominable, despicable, detestable, disgusting, loathsome, offensive, nauseating, odious, repugnant, repulsive, revolting, shocking, vile
abidance *n.* compliance, continuance
abide *v.* **DWELL:** inhabit, live, reside, stay; **WAIT:** attend, await, remain, stay, tarry; **ENDURE:** allow, bear, remain, stand, suffer
abiding *adj.* enduring, lasting, permanent, steadfast
ability *n.* aptitude, bent, capability, capacity, competence, dexterity, expertise, facility, faculty, knack, proficiency, qualification, skill, skillfulness, talent
abject *adj.* base, contemptible, degrading,

despicable, disheartening, ignominious, miserable, poor, sorry

abjection, abjectness *n.* churlishness, degradation, humiliation, meanness, nastiness

abjuration *n.* abnegation, denial, disavowal, rejection, renouncement, renunciation

abjure *v.* forswear, recant, recall, renounce, retract, withdraw

ablaze *adj.* **BURNING:** aflame, blazing, fiery, flaming; **FERVENT:** ardent, eager, excited, exhilarated, intense

able *adj.* **CAPABLE:** adequate, apt, competent, efficient, fit, qualified; **SKILLFUL:** accomplished, adroit, dexterous, expert, gifted, ingenious, proficient, talented

able-bodied *adj.* fit, healthy, robust, strong

abloom *adj.* blossoming, flowering, sprouting

ablution *n.* cleansing, purification, purging, washing

abnegation *n.* abjuration, denial, disavowal, rejection, renouncement, renunciation

abnormal *adj.* aberrant, anomalous, curious, deviant, irregular, odd, peculiar, unnatural

abnormality *n.* anomaly, curiosity, irregularity, malformation, nonconformity, peculiarity, perversion

abode *n.* domicile, dwelling, habitat, house, residence

abolish *v.* abrogate, annul, cancel, eliminate, end, eradicate, extinguish, nullify, obliterate

abolishment *n.* annulment, cancellation, elimination, eradication, nullification

abolition *n.* annulment, cancellation, dissolution, elimination, eradication, repeal, revocation

abominable *adj.* abhorrent, contemptible, despicable, detestable, disgusting, hateful, horrible, loathsome, offensive, repugnant

abominate *v.* abhor, despise, detest, hate, loathe

abomination *n.* **HORROR:** loathing, revulsion; **WICKEDNESS:** amorality, depravity, evil, immorality

aboriginal *adj.* domestic, indigenous, local, native, original, primitive

abort *v.* annul, cancel, destroy, fail, interrupt, miscarry, nullify, scrap, stop, terminate

abortion *n.* **CESSATION:** cancellation, interruption, termination; **MONSTROSITY:** abnormality

abortive *adj.* fruitless, futile, ineffectual, unavailing

abound *v.* overflow, pour, swarm, swell, teem

abounding *adj.* abundant, lavish, luxuriant, plentiful

about *adv.* **CONCERNING:** referencing, regarding; **APPROXIMATELY:** almost, around, close, near, nigh

above *adv.* **HIGHER:** atop, beyond, over, overhead; **GREATER:** preeminent, superior, surpassing

aboveboard *adj.* candid, frank, guileless, honest, open, overt, sincere, straightforward

abrading *adj.* annoying, harsh, nasty, offensive

abrade *v.* **WEAR:** chafe, corrode, erode, grind, rub, scrape; **IRRITATE** : anger, annoy, bother, gall, irk

abrading *n.* abrasion, attrition, erosion

abrasion *n.* blemish, bruise, cut, scrape, scratch

abrasive *adj.* annoying, exasperating, grating, harsh, jarring, nasty, offensive, rasping, shrill, strident

abreast *adj., adv.* **BESIDE:** against, aligned; **INFORMED:** apprised, familiar

abridge *v.* abstract, compress, condense, curtail, cut, decrease, diminish, lessen, reduce, restrict, shorten

abrogate *v.* abolish, annul, cancel, invalidate, nullify, repeal, rescind, revoke, void

abrupt *adj.* **SUDDEN:** quick, sharp, unexpected; **CURT:** blunt, boorish, brusque, discourteous, hasty, impatient, rude; **STEEP:** craggy, hilly, precipitous, sheer

abruptness *n.* brevity, curtness, shortness, terseness

abscessed *adj.* inflamed, painful, ulcerated

abscission *n.* deletion, eradication, excision, removal

abscond *v.* bolt, depart, escape, flee

absconder *n.* cheat, charlatan, rogue, swindler

absence *n.* **LACK:** dearth, default, defect, deficiency, need, want; **AWAY:** nonattendance, truancy

absentee *n.* defector, delinquent, deserter, fugitive, escapee, runaway, truant

absent–minded *adj.* forgetful, oblivious, preoccupied, unmindful

absolute *adj.* **PERFECT:** certain, definite, faultless, ideal, sure, unconditional, unquestionable, utter, whole; **AUTHORITARIAN:** autocratic, despotic, dictatorial, imperious, peremptory, strict, tyrannical

absolution *n.* acquittal, clearance, exoneration, vindication

absolvable *adj.* excusable, forgivable, inconsequential, justifiable, minor, pardonable, permissible, venial

absolve *v.* acquit, clear, discharge, excuse, exonerate, forgive, free, justify, liberate, pardon, release

absorb *v.* **INCORPORATE:** amalgamate, assimilate, consume, devour, engulf; **ENGROSS:** engage, employ, occupy; **UNDERSTAND:** grasp, assimilate, learn, sense

absorbed *adj.* **INCORPORATED:** assimilated, digested, dissolved, permeated; **ENGROSSED:** enthralled, immersed, intent, involved, preoccupied, rapt

absorbent *adj.* permeable, penetrable, porous, spongy

absorbing *adj.* engaging, enthralling, exciting, fascinating, interesting

absorption *n.* absentmindedness, preoccupation, reflection, reverie

abstain *v.* avoid, decline, eschew, forgo, refrain, shun

abstinence *n.* avoidance, forbearance, moderation, self–denial, sobriety, temperance

abstinent *adj.* abstemious, continent, moderate

abstract *adj.* **THEORETICAL:** conceptual, ideal, hypothetical; **ISOLATED:** apart, separate, special, unrelated; **COMPLEX:** complicated, deep, difficult, obscure

abstract *n.* abridgment, brief, compendium, condensation, digest, distillation, outline, summary

abstract *v.* **REMOVE:** disjoin, dissociate, isolate, separate, withdraw; **CONDENSE:** abbreviate, abridge, digest, distill, edit, outline, summarize

abstruse *adj.* complex, difficult, intricate, involved

absurd *adj.* asinine, foolish, irrational,

inane, ludicrous, preposterous, ridiculous, silly

abundance *n.* bounty, extravagance, fullness, profusion, prosperity, wealth

abundant *adj.* copious, abounding, flowing, fruitful, opulent, profuse, plentiful, prodigal, prolific, teeming

abuse *n.* misuse, defilement, desecration, mistreatment, profanation, subversion, violation

abuse *v.* **MISUSE:** attack, desecrate, harm, hurt, injure, maltreat, mistreat, wrong; **BERATE:** assail, denounce, disparage, insult, malign, reproach, revile, scold

abusive *adj.* **AGONIZING:** insufferable, intolerable, painful, unbearable, unendurable; **DISCOURTEOUS:** rude, sarcastic, slanderous, truculent, vituperative

abut *v.* adjoin, border, touch, verge

abysmal *adj.* bottomless, deep, immeasurable, profound, unfathomable

abyss *n.* chasm, gorge, gulf, hole, perdition

academic *adj.* **SCHOLARLY:** collegiate, erudite, learned, lettered, literary, scholastic, schooled; **TRADITIONAL:** conventional, conservative, established, formalistic; **THEORETICAL:** conjectural, speculative, suppositional

academician *n.* intellectual, egghead, scholar

academics *n.* courses, studies

academy *n.* college, conservatory, school

accede *v.* acquiesce, agree, allow, assent, comply, consent, permit, sanction

accelerate *v.* hasten, expedite, quicken, throttle

acceleration *n.* dispatch, hastening, quickening

accent *n.* **MODULATION:** beat, inflection, emphasis, rhythm; **SIGNIFICANCE:** importance, prominence

accent, accentuate *v.* emphasize, stress, underscore

accept *v.* **RECEIVE:** embrace, take, welcome; **ACQUIESCE:** accede, acknowledge, allow, assent, concede, concur, grant; **BELIEVE:** affirm, maintain, trust; **UNDERSTAND:** appreciate, conclude, construe

acceptable *adj.* adequate, agreeable, permissible, pleasant, pleasing, satisfactory, sufficient

acceptance *n.* concent, acknowledgement, agreement, assent, capitulation, concurrence, recognition

accepted *adj.* **ACCREDITED:** accustomed, acknowledged, allowed, recognized; **SETTLED:** admitted, affirmed, endorsed

accessible *adj.* approachable, attainable, available, convenient, obtainable, reachable

accessory *adj.* added, contributing, extra

accessory *n.* abettor, accomplice

accident *n.* **MISHAP:** casualty, misadventure, pileup, wreck; **CHANCE:** coincidence, fortune

accidental *adj.* **UNEXPECTED:** casual, chance, fortuitous, odd, random, unintentional, unplanned; **INCIDENTAL:** insignificant, minor, nonessential, secondary, subsidiary

acclaim *n.* applause, approval, enthusiasm, fame, plaudits, praise, recognition

acclaim *v.* applaud, celebrate, commend, laud, praise

acclamation *n.* acclaim, accolades, applause, approval, jubilation, plaudits, praise

acclimate *v.* accommodate, adapt, adjust, conform
acclimatize *v.* acclimate, adapt, adjust, conform
acclivity *n.* ascent, incline, slope, upgrade
accolade *n.* acknowledgement, esteem, praise, tribute
accommodate *v.* **AID:** abet, assist, oblige, provide, serve, supply; **ENTERTAIN:** board, house, lodge, quarter; **ADJUST:** adapt, conform, fit, harmonize, reconcile, temper; **RECEIVE:** contain, have, hold
accommodating *adj.* kind, gracious, helpful, obliging
accompaniment *n.* addition, accessory, adjunct, appendage, appurtenance
accompany *v.* **ATTEND:** chaperon, convey, escort, follow, join, see, show, usher; **APPEND:** augment, complement, complete, enhance, supplement
accomplice *n.* accessory, affiliate, associate, confederate, conspirator, partner
accomplish *v.* achieve, attain, complete, do, effect, execute, fulfill, make, manage, perform, realize
accomplished *adj.* skillful, able, cultivated, expert, proficient, talented
accomplishment *n.* achievement, attainment, exploit, feat, fulfillment, success
accord *n.* agreement, conformity, consent, harmony, peace, unanimity
accord *v.* **AGREE:** accommodate, adapt, affirm, coincide, concur, correspond; **BESTOW:** allow, deign, grant, concede, yield
accordance *n.* accord, agreement, coincidence, concordance, conformity, harmony
accost *v.* address, approach, confront, greet, meet, proposition, solicit, waylay

account *n.* **NARRATIVE:** anecdote, chronicle, description, exposé, journal, narration, recital, report, story, tale; **REASON:** excuse, grounds, motive; **WORTH:** advantage, benefit, estimation, importance, profit, reputation

account *v.* **EXPLAIN:** describe, justify; **REGARD:** consider, count,. credit, deem, estimate, hold, judge, reckon, think

accountable *adj.* answerable, culpable, liable, responsible

accredit *v.* certify, endorse, pass, ratify, recognize, sanction, support, uphold, validate, warrant

accrual, accruement *n.* accumulation, expansion, growth, increase, recovery, return, yield

accumulate *v.* accrue, amass, collect, cumulate, gather, heap, garner, increase, stockpile, store

accuracy *n.* exactness, precision, sureness

accurate *n.* careful, correct, exact, factual, faithful, flawless, precise, proper, right, true, unerring

accursed *adj.* doomed, bewitched, condemned, damned, haunted, ill–fated

accusation *n.* allegation, charge, complaint, denunciation, indictment, insinuation, slur, smear

accuse *v.* arraign, arrest, blame, charge, denounce, implicate, impute, incriminate, indict, involve

accustom *v.* familiarize, habituate, inure, season

ace *n.* champion, expert, genius, master, specialist, virtuoso

acerbate *n.* heighten, increase, intensify, worsen

acerbic *adj.* bitter, harsh, rough, sharp, sour

ache *n.* agony, pain, pang, spasm, twinge

ache *v.* hurt, pain, suffer, throb

achievable *adj.* attainable, feasible, obtainable

achieve *v.* accomplish, effect, fulfill, finish, reach, attain, gain, get, realize, secure

achy *adj.* aching, bruised, painful

acid *adj.* biting, cutting, sarcastic, sardonic, scornful, sharp, vitriolic

acknowledge *v.* admit, agree, allow, appreciate, approve, avow, concede, confess, confirm, declare, endorse, grant, ratify, recognize, reply, respond

acknowledgment *n.* ACCEPTANCE: affirmation, corroboration, recognition; RESPONSE: answer, call, greeting, letter, nod, note, reaction, reply, thanks

acme *n.* apex, peak, summit, top, zenith

acolyte *n.* aide, assistant, helper, subordinate

acquaint *v.* inform, accustom, advise, familiarize, reconnoiter, introduce, present

acquaintance *n.* friend, associate, colleague, companion, crony, pal

acquainted *adj.* conversant, familiar, introduced

acquiesce *v.* assent, accede, accept, agree, comply, concur, consent, submit, yield

acquire *v.* appropriate, attain, earn, obtain, gain, procure, secure

acquisitive *adj.* avaricious, grasping, greedy

acquisitiveness *n.* covetousness, greed

acquit *v.* absolve, exonerate, pardon, release

acquittal *n.* absolution, amnesty, deliverance, discharge, dismissal, exoneration, pardon, vindication

acreage *n.* grounds, land, property, spread, terrain

acrid *adj.* astringent, biting, bitter, caustic, harsh

acrimonious *adj.* acerbic, caustic, irascible, testy

acropolis *n.* bastion, citadel, blockhouse, fort, fortification, redoubt, stronghold

across *adv.* athwart, crosswise, over, transversely

act *n.* **EXPLOIT:** accomplishment, deed, feat, performance; **DECREE:** edict, law, order, resolution, statute, writ; **PERFORMANCE:** routine, sketch, stint, turn

act *v.* **DO:** accomplish, conduct, operate; **SUBSTITUTE:** represent, officiate, serve; **PERFORM:** appear, dramatize, impersonate, pretend, play, simulate

acting *adj.* deputy, officiating, surrogate, temporary

acting *n.* depiction, performance, role impersonation

action *n.* **MOTION:** activity, maneuver, movement; **FEAT:** accomplishment, exercise, transaction; **BEHAVIOR:** conduct, response; **MACHINE:** apparatus, contrivance, mechanism; **CONFLICT:** battle, contest, encounter, engagement, skirmish; **LAWSUIT:** case, claim, litigation, proceeding, process, suit

activate *v.* animate, begin, initiate, stimulate

active *adj.* animated, busy, dynamic, energetic, functioning, industrious, lively, living, mobile, moving, operative, spirited, tireless, working

actively *adv.* energetically, spryly, vigorously

activist *n.* agitator, firebrand, malcontent, radical, reformer, revolutionary

activity *n.* action, motion, movement, pastime

actor *n.* artist, entertainer, impersonator, mime, performer, player, thespian, trouper

actual *adj.* **FACTUAL:** certain, genuine, definite, true; **EXISTING:** concrete, material, real, tangible

actually *adv.* indeed, really, truly

actuate *v.* drive, impel, move, propel, push

acuity *n.* discernment, discrimination, insight, perception, perspicacity, sharpness, shrewdness

acumen *n.* cleverness, discernment, insight, intelligence, keenness, sagacity, shrewdness

acute *adj.* **POINTED:** keen, sharp; **IMPORTANT:** critical, crucial, intense, serious; **PERCEPTIVE:** astute, clever, discerning, intelligent, keen, penetrating

adage *n.* cliché, maxim, motto, proverb, saying, slogan

adamant *adj.* firm, fixed, insistent, obstinate, resolute, set, steadfast, stubborn, unbending, unyielding

adapt *v.* acclimatize, accustom, adjust, conform, fashion, fit, modify, reconcile, shape, tailor, temper

adaptable *adj.* docile, flexible, pliable, pliant, tractable, versatile

adaptation *n.* **ACCLIMATIZATION:** acculturation, conversion, revising; **DEVICE:** apparatus, appliance, contraption, contrivance, gadget, mechanism

add *v.* **AFFIX:** annex, append, attach, augment, connect, supplement, unite: **CALCULATE:** compute, figure, increase, sum, tally, total

addendum *n.* addition, adjunct, annexation, appendix, attachment, augmentation, codicil, rider

addict *n.* buff, devotee, fan, hound, junkie, lover

addicted *adj.* chronic, dependent, fanatical, fixated, habituated, hooked, inclined, obsessed

addictive *adj.* compelling, irresistible, overpowering

additional *adj.* added, auxiliary, collateral, extra

addle *v.* cloud, confound, confuse, obfuscate

addled *adj.* befuddled, bewildered, confounded, confused, dazed, disconcerted, flustered, muddled

add–on *n.* improvement, modernization, supplement

address *n.* **SPEECH:** discourse, lecture, oration, sermon; **LOCATION:** dwelling, house, lodging, residence

adept *adj.* able, capable, competent, expert, proficient, skilled

adequacy *n.* acceptability, plenty, sufficiency

adequate *adj.* ample, enough, satisfactory, suitable

adhere *v.* **STICK:** attach, cleave, cling, fasten, hold; **CONFORM:** comply, follow, heed, obey

adherent *n.* advocate, devotee, disciple, fan, follower

adhesive *n.* cement, epoxy, glue, mucilage

adjacent *adj.* abutting, adjoining, bordering, close, contiguous, near, nearby, neighboring, touching

adjoin *v.* abut, append, border, butt, meet, neighbor, touch, verge

adjourn *v.* defer, discontinue, dissolve, recess, interrupt, postpone, suspend

adjournment *n.* break, continuance, deferment, intermission, pause, postponement, recess

adjudicate *v.* arbitrate, decide, mediate, settle

adjudication *n.* determination, judgment, finding, ruling, verdict, sentence
adjudicator *n.* arbiter, judge, mediator, referee
adjunct *n.* accessory, addition, attachment
adjure *v.* ask, appeal, beg, beseech, entreat, implore, petition, plead, request, supplicate, urge
adjust *v.* adapt, alter, calibrate, correct, modify, regulate, tune, temper, true
adjustable *adj.* flexible, malleable, tractable, variable
adjustment *n.* **ALTERATION:** modification, setting; **COMPENSATION:** allotment, compromise, reconciliation, redress, remuneration, settlement
adjutant *n.* aide, assistant, attaché, deputy, helper
ad-lib *adj.* improvised, spontaneous, unrehearsed
administer *v.* **MANAGE:** control, direct, execute, oversee, supervise; **DISPENSE:** distribute, give, parcel
administrative *adj.* bureaucratic, executive, governmental, official, managerial
admirable *adj.* commendable, excellent, meritorious, noble, praiseworthy, splendid, superb, worthy
admiration *n.* approbation, awe, esteem, fondness, regard, respect, veneration
admire *v.* esteem, honor, regard, respect, revere, venerate
admirer *n.* **FAN:** devotee, enthusiast, follower, supporter; **BEAU:** adorer, suitor, sweetheart, wooer
admissible *adj.* allowable, lawful, legal, legitimate
admission *n.* **ACCESS:** admittance, entrée, entrance, entry; **AFFIRMATION:** acknowledgment, confirmation, disclosure

admit *v.* **ACCOMMODATE:** allow, grant, permit; **AFFIRM:** concede, disclose, divulge, expose, reveal

admittance *n.* access, admission, entrance

admonish *v.* caution, counsel, exhort, reprove, warn

admonition *n.* **COUNSEL:** advice, caution, warning; **REBUKE:** censure, reprimand, reproach, scolding

ado *n.* bother, bustle, commotion, fuss, stir

adolescence *n.* puberty, pubescence, teens, youth

adolescent *adj.* childish, immature, juvenile, youthful

adolescent *n.* minor, teen, teenager, youth

adopt *v.* **APPROPRIATE:** assume, borrow, espouse, utilize; **RATIFY:** approve, confirm, endorse, sanction

adorable *adj.* charming, cute, darling, delightful, enchanting, lovable, precious

adoration *n.* devotion, idolatry, veneration, worship

adore *v.* cherish, esteem, idolize, love, revere, venerate, worship

adorer *n.* admirer, beau, suitor, sweetheart, wooer

adorn *v.* beautify, bedeck, decorate, embellish, garnish, festoon, ornament, trim

adroit *adj.* adept, dexterous, expert, handy, quick, resourceful, skillful

adulation *n.* adoration, glorification, laudation, praise, worship

adult *adj.* developed, grown, mature, ripe

adulteration *n.* contamination, pollution, taint

adulterer *n.* debaucher, lecher, libertine, philanderer, rake, reprobate

adulterous *adj.* dissolute, immoral, licentious, lustful

adultery *n.* cuckoldry, fornication, infidelity

adulthood *n.* majority, maturity

advance *v.* **PROGRESS:** go, move, proceed, update; **BROACH:** introduce, propose, present, suggest; **PROMOTE:** encourage, foster, propound; **OFFER:** lend

advanced *adj.* aged, elderly, futuristic, precocious, radical, seasoned, unconventional

advancement *n.* betterment, elevation, preference, progression, promotion

advantage *n.* benefit, edge, gain, leverage, profit

adventure *n.* undertaking, experience, exploit

advantageous *adj.* beneficial, expedient, favorable, lucrative, profitable, worthwhile

advent *n.* appearance, arrival, coming

adventure *n.* escapade, exploit, feat, happening, quest, undertaking, venture

adventuresome, adventurous *adj.* bold, courageous, daring, enterprising, gallant

adversarial *adj.* antagonistic, hostile, unfriendly

adversary *n.* antagonist, enemy, foe, opponent

adverse *adj.* antagonistic, conflicting, contrary, hostile, negative, unfavorable

adversity *n.* affliction, distress, hardship, misery, misfortune, sorrow, trouble

advertise *v.* broadcast, exhibit, expose, proclaim, promote, publicize, show

advertisement, advertising *n.* blurb, broadside, endorsement, handbill, pitch, poster, plug

advice *n.* counsel, guidance, lesson, suggestion

advisable *adj.* advantageous, desirable, expedient, politic, prudent, sensible, sound

advise *v.* admonish, caution, counsel, consult, forewarn, inform, notify, recommend

advised *adj.* cautious, circumspect, deliberate

adviser, advisor *n.* attorney, consultant, counsel, counselor, elder, expert, guide, instructor, lawyer, mentor, patriarch, teacher, tutor

advocacy *n.* adoption, belief, espousal, promotion

advocate *v.* advance, bolster, champion, further, promote, recommend, support

aesthete *n.* collector, connoisseur, dilettante

aesthetic, aesthetical *adj.* artistic, discriminating, elegant, pleasing, polished, refined, tasteful

affable *adj.* agreeable, amiable, civil, cordial, courteous, friendly, gracious, obliging, pleasant, sociable

affair *n.* CONCERN: business, pursuit; ROMANCE: liaison, relationship, tryst, rendezvous; GATHERING: event, function, party

affect *v.* INFLUENCE: alter, change, modify, sway, stir, transform; PRETEND: assume, dissemble, fake, feign

affectation *n.* artificiality, pose, pretense

affection *n.* devotion, fondness, friendship, liking, love, regard, respect, tenderness, warmth

affectionate *adj.* attentive, devoted, loving, tender

affianced *adj.* betrothed, pledged, plighted

affidavit *n.* affirmation, deposition, oath, testimony

affiliate *n.* agent, associate, colleague, partner

affiliation *n.* alliance, association, coalition, confederation, connection, federation, pact, union

affinity *n.* **ATTRACTION:** affection, closeness, fondness; **SIMILARITY:** correspondence, likeness, resemblance

affirm *v.* **DECLARE:** assert, claim, maintain, state, swear, testify; **CONFIRM:** approve, endorse, ratify

affirmative *adj.* concurring, confirming, endorsing, supporting

affix *v.* add, append, attach, bind, connect, fasten

afflict *v.* ail, beset, distress, torment

affliction *n.* distress, hardship, misfortune, suffering

affluence *n.* abundance, prosperity, wealth

afford *v.* allow, grant, permit, provide, sustain

affront *v.* insult, abuse, offend, provoke, slight

aficionado *n.* buff, devotee, fan, hound, lover

afield *adv.* amiss, astray, awry

afoot *adj.* **WALKING:** hiking, marching; **FORTHCOMING:** brewing, happening, hatching, progressing

aforementioned *adj.* earlier, former, preceding, prior

afraid *adj.* anxious, apprehensive, disquieted, fearful, frightened, scared, shocked, terrified

after *adj., adv.* afterward, following, later, subsequent

aftereffect *n.* consequence, outcome, result

afterthought *n.* addendum, addition, appendix

agape *adj.* **ASTONISHED:** aghast appalled confounded dismayed horrified shocked; **AJAR:** open

age *n.* **PERIOD:** eon, epoch, era, generation, time; **STAGE:** adolescence, adulthood, childhood, infancy

age *v.* decline, deteriorate, develop, mature, mellow, ripen, season

ageless *adj.* classic, timeless, traditional

agenda *n.* aims, goals, program, calendar, list, plan

agent *n.* **MEDIUM:** agency, cause, instrument, means, method, vehicle; **REPRESENTATIVE:** ambassador, attorney, broker, factor, intermediary, proxy

agglomerate *v.* amass, concentrate, consolidate

aggrandize *v.* **ENLARGE:** amplify, expand, extend, increase; **ACCLAIM:** boast, exaggerate, extol, praise

aggravate *v.* **WORSEN:** deepen, exacerbate, heighten, increase, intensify; **PROVOKE:** anger, annoy, exasperate, irritate

aggravating *adj.* bothersome, disquieting, disturbing

aggravation *n.* **AFFLICTION:** annoyance, irritation; **WORSENING:** deepening, heightening

aggregate *adj.* combined, complete, entire, total

aggressive *adj.* **HOSTILE:** belligerent, combative, contentious, pugnacious; **ASSERTIVE:** determined, dynamic, energetic, enterprising, forward, pushy

aggressor *n.* attacker, intruder, invader, trespasser

aggrieve *v.* disturb, harass, irritate, trouble, worry

aggrieved *adj.* harmed, hurt, injured

aghast *adj.* appalled, horrified, shocked

agile *adj.* **QUICK:** brisk, deft, lithe, lively, nimble, sprightly, vigorous; **BRIGHT:** clever, keen, smart

agility *n.* dexterity, liveliness, nimbleness

agitate *v.* **STIR:** churn, mix, toss, tumble; **DISTURB:** discomfit, disquiet, fluster, perturb, trouble, unsettle, upset; **DEBATE:** argue, dispute

agitator *n.* activist, firebrand, rabble–rouser, radical

agnostic *n.* doubter, non–believer, skeptic, unbeliever

agonize *v.* struggle, suffer, writhe, toss

agony *n.* anguish, distress, misery, pain, suffering, torment

agree *v.* **COINCIDE:** correspond, equal, harmonize, match, suit; **COMPROMISE:** contract, resolve, settle; **CONSENT:** accede, acquiesce, allow, assent, concede

agreeable *adj.* **PLEASING:** amiable, congenial, gracious, pleasant, polite; **SUITABLE:** acceptable, satisfactory

agreement *n.* **COVENANT:** bargain, compact, contract, deal, pact, settlement, understanding; **ACCORD:** compromise, harmony, peace, unity

ahead *adj., adv.* before, earlier, preceding

aid *n.* **ASSISTANCE:** backing, charity, help, relief, support; **HELPER:** aide, assistant, colleague, supporter

aid *v.* assist, facilitate, help, serve, support, sustain

ailment *n.* illness, affliction, infirmity, sickness

air *n.* atmosphere, breeze; tune; affectation, manner

air *v.* ventilate; announce

alarm *v.* warn; frighten

alert *adj.* ready, aware, attentive, intelligent, wary

alert *v.* caution, inform, warn

alien *adj.* foreign, strange, unfamiliar

alienation *n.* animosity, disaffection

allay *v.* calm, alleviate

allegation *n.* accusation, assertion, claim

allege *v.* assert, attest, declare

alleviate *v.* abate, ease, relieve, lessen, soften

alliance *n.* union, treaty, marriage
allocate *v.* allot, designate
allow *v.* approve, grant, let, permit, sanction
allure *v.* tempt, attract
ally *n.* associate, backer, confederate
alms *n.* charity, dole, donation
aloof *adj.* cool, detached, distant, reserved
alter *v.* change, modify, adjust
altercate *v.* contend, oppose, quarrel, bicker
alternate *n.* replacement, substitute
alternative *n.* choice, option
altruism *n.* benevolence, charity, kindness
amateur *n.* beginner, neophyte, novice
amaze *v.* astonish, dumfound, stupefy
amazement *n.* awe, shock, surprise
ambassador *n.* diplomat, emissary, envoy, minister
ambiguous *adj.* indistinct, puzzling, unclear, vague
ambitious *adj.* determined, industrious
ambivalent *adj.* uncertain, wavering
ameliorate *v.* alleviate, improve, rectify
amenable *adj.* agreeable, docile, pliable, responsive
amend *v.* improve, change, correct
amenity *n.* courtesy, consideration, pleasantness
amiable, amicable *adj.* friendly, affable, agreeable, congenial, kindly, genial
amiss *adj.* wrong, faulty, erroneous, imperfect, awry
amity *n.* goodwill, regard, friendliness, affection
amnesty *n.* pardon, liberation, reprieve
among *prep.* amid, amongst, amidst
amount *n.* **TOTAL:** sum; **PRICE:** expense, output, outlay; **QUANTITY:** bulk, mass, number

ample *adj.* sufficient, plenty, adequate, enough

amplify *v.* increase, augment, magnify

amulet *n.* charm, talisman

amuse *v.* entertain, divert, cheer, enliven

amusement *n.* entertainment, recreation, pastime

analyze *v.* dissect, examine, investigate

anarchy *n.* disorder, turmoil, chaos

ancestor *n.* forebear, progenitor, forefather

ancestry *n.* lineage, heritage, parentage

ancient *adj.* old, antiquated, antique, aged

anecdote *n.* story, tale, incident, episode

anger *n.* ire, wrath, rage, fury, exasperation, irritation

anger *v.* infuriate, annoy, irritate enrage

angle *n.* **PLAN:** plot, scheme, maneuver; **VIEWPOINT:** outlook, standpoint, perspective; **INTERSECTION:** crotch, elbow, fork

angry *adj.* enraged, furious, infuriated, irate, raging, cross, annoyed, displeased, riled, hostile

anguish *n.* pain, wretchedness, agony

angular *adj.* intersecting, crossing, crotched, forked

animate *v.* activate, vitalize, arouse, energize

animosity *n.* hatred, dislike, enmity, displeasure

annex *v.* add, incorporate, append, attach, affix.

annihilate *v.* destroy, demolish, exterminate

annotate *v.* comment, explain, interpret

announcement *n.* declaration, publication, statement, bulletin, notice, communiqué, release

annoy *v.* bother, irritate, pester, trouble

annoyance *n.* irritation, pique, displeasure, nuisance, discontent, dissatisfaction, impatience,

annul *v.* invalidate, repeal, revoke, cancel
anoint *v.* sprinkle, consecrate
anonymous *adj.* unsigned, nameless, unknown
answer *v.* **REPLY:** respond, retort, acknowledge, refute, rebut; **EXPLAIN:** solve, elucidate, clarify
answerable *adj.* responsible, liable
antagonism *n.* hatred, enmity, hostility, opposition
antic *n.* prank, joke, trick, frolic, caper
anticipate *v.* expect, forecast, predict, assume, await
antipathy *n.* aversion, dislike, hatred, repulsion
antiquated, antique *adj.* old, outmoded, out–of–date
antiseptic *adj.* clean, germ–free, sterilized, pure
antithesis *n.* contrasting, reverse
antitoxin *n.* vaccine, antibody, serum
anxiety, anxiousness *n.* concern, trouble, misgiving
anxious *adj.* **EAGER:** desirous, zealous, fervent; **APPREHENSIVE:** concerned, troubled
apathetic *adj.* unemotional, unconcerned, indifferent.
ape *v.* imitate, mimic, copy, impersonate.
aperture *n.* opening, hole, slot
aphorism *n.* motto, proverb, saying
apologetic *adj.* regretful, contrite, remorseful, sorry
appall *v.* horrify, amaze, dismay, shock
apparel *n.* clothes, attire, suit, dress
apparent *adj.* open, visible, clear, manifest, obvious
apparition *n.* ghost, manifestation, phantom, spirit
appeal *n.* **PLEA:** request, petition, entreaty, prayer, supplication; **ATTRACTIVENESS:** charm, glamour

appeal *v.* **REQUEST:** beg, urge, petition; **FASCINATE:** attract, interest, engage
appear *v.* **EMERGE:** rise, loom, arrive, recur, materialize, show; **SEEM:** resemble
appearance *n.* bearing, demeanor, features
appease *v.* satisfy
append *v.* add, affix, attach, supplement
appendix *n.* supplement, attachment
appetite *n.* hunger, thirst, craving, longing, desire
appetizing *adj.* savory, tasty, delectable, delicious
applaud *v.* approve, cheer, clap, acclaim
applicable *adj.* suitable, appropriate, usable, fit
applicant *n.* petitioner, claimant, candidate.
application *n.* **USE:** employment, utilization; **ATTENTION:** devotion, zeal, diligence; **PETITION:** entreaty, appeal; **INSTRUMENT:** form, requisition
apply *v.* **REQUEST:** petition, beg; **UTILIZE:** employ, practice, exploit; **PERTAIN:** involve, affect
appoint *v.* name, select, designate
appointment *n.* **DESIGNATION:** selection, nomination, choice; **ENGAGEMENT:** meeting, rendezvous, date
appraise *v.* assess, price, assay, rate
appreciable *adj.* considerable, sizable, tangible, large
appreciate *v.* **THANK:** acknowledge; **ESTEEM:** honor, praise, admire
appreciative *adj.* grateful, obliged, satisfied, thankful
apprehend *v.* **ARREST:** detain, seize; **COMPREHEND:** understand, perceive, grasp
apprehension *n.* **FOREBODING:** trepidation, dread, misgiving, fear; **UNDERSTANDING:** comprehension; **ARREST:** capture, seizure, detention

apprentice *n.* beginner, student, learner

apprise *v.* notify, teach, warn

approach *n.* **ACCESS:** avenue, path, entrance, gate, way; **PLAN:** method, program, procedure

approbation *n.* approval, regard

appropriate *adj.* suitable proper, suited, fitting, fit

appropriate *v.* **SEIZE:** secure, usurp, take; **SET APART:** allocate, assign, reserve, apportion, budget, allot

appropriation *n.* stipend, grant, fund, allotment, allowance, allocation, contribution, support

approval *n.* **REGARD:** esteem, favor, admiration; **SANCTION:** endorsement, consent, permission

approve *v.* authorize, endorse, ratify, confirm, sanction, accredit, allow, advocate

approximate *adj.* inexact, imprecise, close

appurtenance *n.* adjunct, accessory

apropos *adj.* applicable, appropriate, befitting

apt *adj.* **APPROPRIATE:** apropos, suitable, fitting; **INCLINED:** probable, prone, liable, likely; **QUICK:** adept, clever, bright, intelligent, talented

aptitude *n.* ability, capability, competence, capacity

arbitrary *adj.* **OPTIONAL:** discretionary, unscientific; **WHIMSICAL:** capricious, fanciful, inconsistent; **AUTOCRATIC:** willful, tyrannical,

arbitrate *v.* settle, adjust, reconcile, negotiate

arch *n.* arc, curve, vault, bend, arching, archway

archaic *adj.* antiquated, old, obsolete

architect *n.* planner, designer, draftsman, artist

archive *n.* repository, vault, museum

ardent *adj.* fervent, impassioned, zealous, enthusiastic

arduous *adj.* hard, laborious, difficult, strenuous

argue *v.* dispute, contend, wrangle, bicker, debate

argumentative *adj.* hostile, contentious, factious

arid *adj.* parched, desert, dried, dry, barren

arise *v.* **GET UP:** rise, stand; **ASCEND:** mount, climb, rise

aristocracy *n.* nobility, elite, gentry

aristocratic *adj.* noble, refined, well–bred

arm *n.* limb, member, appendage, projection, branch

armistice *n.* treaty, cease–fire, truce

aroma *n.* smell, fragrance, perfume, odor

arouse *v.* awaken, stir, excite, stimulate

arraign *v.* accuse, summon

arrange *v.* order, regulate, systematize, organize

arrest *v.* apprehend, capture, imprison, incarcerate

arrival *n.* **ENTRANCE:** appearance, landing, debarkation; **NEWCOMER:** visitor

arrive *v.* land, disembark, reach, appear, attain

arrogance *n.* insolence, audacity, haughtiness, pride

art *n.* representation, illustration, abstraction, creation

artery *n.* **BLOOD VESSEL:** aorta, capillary, vein; **MAIN CHANNEL:** highway, line, route, canal, roadway

artful *adj.* crafty, cunning, clever, adroit, ingenious

article *n.* **WRITING:** essay, editorial, commentary; **ITEM:** object, substance, commodity, thing

articulate *v.* **SPEAK:** enunciate, pronounce, verbalize; **JOIN:** combine, connect, link

artifact *n.* antique, heirloom, relic
artifice *n.* ruse, scheme, trick
artificial *adj.* synthetic, counterfeit, false, imitation
artistic *adj.* imaginative, creative, cultured, sensitive, elegant, harmonious
artistry *n.* workmanship, skill, proficiency
artless *adj.* innocent, rough, unskilled
arty *adj.* affected, ostentatious
ascend *v.* soar, rise
askance *adv.* suspiciously, disapprovingly
aspect *n.* **APPEARANCE:** looks, countenance, face, features; **VIEW:** perspective, regard, slant, viewpoint
asperity *n.* roughness, harshness
aspiration *n.* desire, yearning, inclination, ambition
assail *v.* assault, attack
assailant *n.* antagonist, foe, enemy
assassin *n.* murderer, slayer, butcher, killer
assassinate *v.* **MURDER:** kill, slay, slaughter; **SLANDER:** defame, denigrate, libel
assault *n.* **ATTACK:** charge, advance, onslaught
assay *v.* test, analyze
assemble *v.* **CONVOKE:** convene, mobilize, gather; **CONSTRUCT:** erect, join, unite
assent *n.* approval, consent, permission, agreement
assert *v.* state, say, affirm, declare
assertion *n.* affirmation, statement, declaration
assess *v.* **TAX:** charge, exact; **ESTIMATE:** judge, reckon, guess
asset *n.* property, holdings, possessions, capital
assiduous *adj.* painstaking, diligent
assign *v.* **ALLOCATE:** allot, earmark; **APPOINT:** commission, name, select, deputize, charge, elect

assimilate *v.* **ABSORB:** digest, osmose; **UNDERSTAND:** grasp, learn, sense

assistance *n.* comfort, support, compensation, help

assistant *n.* aid, deputy, helper, flunky

associate *n.* comrade, peer, henchman, colleague, friend, ally, confederate, collaborator, teammate

associate *v.* relate, link, connect, join, compare

association *n.* **RELATIONSHIP:** friendship, community, camaraderie, membership; **RECOLLECTION:** impression, remembrance; **ORGANIZATION:** union, club

assortment *n.* variety, combination, group, collection

assume *v.* suppose, theorize, postulate, hypothesize, conjecture, imagine, surmise, opine, estimate, speculate, infer

assurance *n.* **GUARANTY:** support, pledge, promise; **CONFIDENCE:** trust, certainty, faith

assure *v.* **GUARANTEE:** aver, attest; **CONVINCE:** prove, persuade, induce

astonish *v.* shock, amaze, astound, surprise, stun

astonishment *n.* amazement, bewilderment, wonder

astute *adj.* perceptive, shrewd

asunder *adv.* apart, divided, separated, disjoined

atmosphere *n.* sense, impression, taste, character

atone *v.* compensate, pay

atrocious *adj.* cruel, offensive

atrocity *n.* **BRUTALITY:** wickedness, barbarity, cruelty; **OFFENSE:** outrage, horror, crime

attach *v.* **ADHERE:** join, connect, append, add; **ATTRIBUTE:** associate, impute, ascribe, give

attachment *n.* **AFFECTION:** fondness, liking, devotion; **ACCESSORY:** adjunct, annex, addition

attack *n.* **ASSAULT:** raid, onslaught, siege, invasion, incursion; **LIBEL:** slander, denunciation; **ILLNESS:** seizure, breakdown

attacker *n.* aggressor, assailant, antagonist, invader

attain *v.* achieve, accomplish, reach, gain

attempt *v.* endeavor, strike, venture, try

attend *v.* heed; minister; frequent, visit, revisit, haunt

attention *n.* regard, vigilance, heed, alertness, diligence, thoroughness, recognition

attentive *adj.* considerate, thoughtful

attest *v.* testify, certify

attitude *n.* **BEARING:** air, demeanor; **DISPOSITION:** inclination, nature, temperament, mood

attorney *n.* lawyer, barrister, counsel

attract *v.* **DRAW:** pull, drag, bring; **ALLURE:** entice, lure, charm, fascinate

attraction *n.* **EVENT:** spectacle, display, demonstration; **ALLUREMENT:** enticement, appeal

attractive *adj.* engaging, beautiful, handsome

attribute *n.* peculiarity, quality, characteristic, trait

attribute *v.* ascribe, impute, give

audacious *adj.* bold, daring, shameless

audible *adj.* perceptible, discernible

audience *n.* interview; spectators, patrons

audit *n.* checking, scrutiny, inspection, examination

auditorium *n.* hall, theater, playhouse, amphitheater

augment *v.* increase, enlarge, expand, magnify

auspices *n. pl.* protection, aegis, patronage, omen

austere *adj.* stern, harsh, hard, ascetic, severe, plain

authentic *adj.* genuine, real, true, actual

authenticate *v.* verify, confirm, validate, prove

author *n.* writer, journalist, columnist, playwright, poet, novelist, essayist

authority *n.* **COMMAND:** jurisdiction, power; **SPECIALIST:** expert, veteran, professional

authorization *n.* sanction, signature, permission

authorize *v.* **ALLOW:** permit, tolerate, suffer; **APPROVE:** sanction, ratify, affirm, endorse

autocratic *adj.* domineering, aggressive, absolute

autograph *n.* signature, handwriting

automatic *adj.* **MECHANIZED:** computerized, self–regulating, automated; **INVOLUNTARY:** instinctive, spontaneous

autonomous *adj.* self–governing, independent, free

auxiliary *adj.* **SUBSIDIARY:** secondary, subordinate; **SUPPLEMENTARY:** reserve, supplemental, spare, extra

available *adj.* accessible, convenient, feasible, handy, obtainable, possible

avarice *n.* acquisitiveness, greed

aver *v.* assert, claim, declare, swear

average *adj.* ordinary, medium, mediocre, common

averse *adj.* disinclined, opposed

aversion *n.* abhorrence, disgust, dislike, loathing

avocation *n.* hobby, sideline

avoid *v.* evade, shun, elude, dodge, withdraw,

avow *v.* affirm, assert, declare, swear

awake *adj.* alert, attentive, vigilant; conscious

awake, awaken *v.* stir, arise, waken, arouse
award *n.* citation, honor, scholarship, prize, judgment
award *v.* grant, confer, bestow, give
aware *adj.* conscious, knowledgeable, cognizant
awareness *n.* alertness, keenness, attentiveness, perception, apprehension
awe *n.* fright, wonder, reverence
awesome *adj.* striking, moving, exalted, grand
awkward *adj.* clumsy, bungling, gawky, floundering, ungainly, unwieldy, inept
axiom *n.* adage, maxim, proverb

babble *n.* chatter jabber, twaddle, nonsense.
babel *n.* bedlam, clamor, commotion
baby *adj.* juvenile, childish, small
backlash *n.* repercussion, reaction, recoil
badge *n.* marker, emblem, pin, medal, insignia, shield, symbol, medallion, crest
baffle *v.* perplex, confuse, puzzle, bewilder
baggage *n.* luggage, gear, trunk, valise, suitcase,
bail *v.* dip, scoop, empty, drain
bait *v.* **LURE:** entice, attract, draw; **TEASE:** provoke, torment, anger, nag, bother
balance *n.* **REMAINS:** excess, surplus, residue, remainder; **EQUILIBRIUM:** symmetry, equivalence, parity
balance *v.* equalize, even, compensate, adjust, coordinate, equate, match, harmonize
balcony *n.* gallery, verandah, terrace
baleful *adj.* noxious, harmful
balk *v.* refuse, demur, desist
balky *adj.* contrary, obstinate, perverse, stubborn

ball *n.* **SPHERE:** globe, spheroid, orb, globule, pellet, pill; **DANCE:** promenade, reception

ballad *n.* carol, chant, song

ballot *n.* tally, ticket, poll, vote

balm *n.* **OINTMENT:** salve, lotion, dressing, medicine; **SOLACE:** comfort, relief, refreshment, remedy

ban *n.* taboo, prohibition, limitation, refusal

ban *v.* forbid, prohibit, outlaw, prevent

banal *adj.* dull, trite, hackneyed, prosaic, trite

bandage *n.* compress, cast, gauze, dressing

bandage *v.* tie, swathe, truss, bind, fasten.

bandit *n.* highwayman, thief, brigand, robber

bang *n.* **REPORT:** blast, detonation; **BLOW:** hit, cuff, whack; **THRILL:** enjoyment, kick, excitement

banish *v.* exile, deport, expel, expatriate, ostracize, outlaw, isolate

bank *n.* shore, ledge, embankment, edge

bankrupt *adj.* failed, broke, insolvent

banner *n.* flag, colors, pennant, emblem; headline

banquet *n.* feast, repast, festivity, dinner

bar *n.* **STICK:** boom, crosspiece, rod; **OBSTRUCTION:** hindrance, hurdle, obstacle, barrier; **SALOON:** dive, tavern, lounge, cabaret, pub; **LAWYERS:** counselors, barristers, solicitors, jurists, attorneys, advocates; **STRIP:** stripe, ribbon, band

bar *v.* **OBSTRUCT:** barricade, blockade, impede; **BAN:** forbid, prevent, stop; **CLOSE:** shut, lock, seal

barbarian *n.* savage, brute, beast

barbaric *adj.* inhuman, brutal, fierce, cruel

bare *adj.* **UNCOVERED:** bald, naked; **PLAIN:** unadorned, simple, modest; **EMPTY:** barren, void, unfurnished

bare *v.* divulge, reveal, uncover, expose

bargain *n.* **DISCOUNT:** reduction, giveaway, steal **UNDERSTANDING:** agreement, compact, pact, contract, deal;

bargain *v.* barter, buy, sell, negotiate

barrel *n.* cask, keg, vat, receptacle, container

barren *adj.* childless, fallow, unproductive, fruitless

barricade *n.* obstacle, obstruction, barrier, blockade

barrier *n.* obstruction, hindrance, obstacle, hurdle, restriction, restraint, impediment, barricade

barter *v.* trade, bargain, swap, buy, sell

base *n.* **BOTTOM:** footing, foundation; **BASIS:** principle; **HEADQUARTERS:** terminal, harbor, station

bashful *adj.* retiring, reserved, timid, modest, shy

basic *adj.* fundamental, essential, central, primary

basin *n.* bowl, pan, tub, container

basis *n.* foundation, justification, reason, background, source, authority, principle, grounds

bask *v.* relax, enjoy, wallow

bathe *v.* soap, scour, scrub, wash.

battery *n.* beating, assault, mugging

bauble *n.* ornament, trifle, trinket

bazaar *n.* market, fair

beach *n.* shore, seaside, sand, coast

beached *v.* stranded, marooned, aground, abandoned

beacon *n.* signal, flare, beam

beam *n.* timber, brace, rafter, stringer, joist, girder, support, trestle, post

beam *v.* **TRANSMIT:** broadcast, send; **SHINE:** radiate, glitter, glare; **SMILE:** grin, laugh, smirk

bear *v.* **TOLERATE:** undergo, endure; **SUPPORT:** sustain

bearable *adj.* endurable, tolerable

beastly *adj.* brutal, savage, coarse, depraved, loathsome, vile, foul, base, disgusting, vulgar

beat *adj.* weary, fatigued, tired, exhausted

beat *v.* **HIT:** whip, flog, spank, scourge, buffet, bash; **PULSATE:** pound, thump, pulse, throb; **MIX:** whip, knead; **WORST:** overcome, conquer, defeat

beautiful *adj.* lovely, attractive, appealing, charming, enticing, elegant, gorgeous, exquisite, alluring

beckon *v.* summon, signal, motion

becoming *adj.* attractive, handsome, comely, fair

bedlam *n.* pandemonium, clamor, confusion, noise

befall *v.* occur, happen

beg *v.* entreat, implore, beseech, supplicate, solicit, plead, petition, request, ask

beggar *n.* panhandler, moocher, bum

begin *v.* initiate, start, inaugurate, launch, mount, create, institute, introduce, originate, found, establish, commence, arise

beguile *v.* charm, deceive

behavior *n.* conduct, performance

behold *v.* observe, regard, view

belief *n.* opinion, feeling, conviction

believable *adj.* trustworthy, creditable, convincing

believe *v.* trust, accept, think

believer *n.* convert, adherent, apostle, disciple, follower

bellicose *adj.* hostile, aggressive

belligerent *adj.* warlike, pugnacious, hostile

bellow *v.* howl, call, shout, cry, yell

beloved *adj.* cherished, loved, adored, worshipped, idolized, treasured, favored

beloved *n.* fiancé, sweetheart, lover

below *prep.* **BENEATH:** underneath, under; **INFERIOR:** subject, subordinate

bend *v.* turn, twist, contort, coil, curl, loop, curve

beneficial *adj.* advantageous, helpful, useful

benefit *v.* help, aid, serve, profit

benevolence *n.* altruism, charity, kindness

bent *adj.* curved, crooked, contorted, twisted

bent *n.* leaning, tendency, propensity, inclination

bequeath *v.* grant, give

beseech *v.* ask, implore

best *adj., adv.* first, greatest, finest, incomparable, unrivaled, unequaled, inimitable, foremost

best *v.* overcome, defeat, worst

bestow *v.* bequeath, present, offer, give, endow

betray *v.* **DOUBLE-CROSS:** delude, trick, deceive; **REVEAL:** divulge, disclose

betrayal *n.* treason, treachery, disloyalty

bewail *v.* complain, gripe, grumble, lament

bewilder *v.* confound, disconcert, puzzle, confuse.

bewildered *adj.* confused, muddled, dazed, puzzled, baffled, disconcerted, stupefied, befuddled, confounded

bewitch *v.* charm, enchant, fascinate, captivate

bias *n.* prejudice, partiality, preference, inclination

bicker *v.* squabble, argue, quarrel

bid *n.* proposal, proposition, declaration, suggestion

bigoted *adj.* biased, dogmatic, opinionated, prejudiced

billow *v.* surge, swell

bind *n.* dilemma, predicament

bind *v.* **SECURE:** attach, adhere, fasten; **JOIN:** unite, connect; **BANDAGE:** dress, treat; **CONTAIN:** shackle, fetter, leash, restrict, hitch, yoke, tether; **OBLIGATE:** oblige, compel, force

biography *n.* memoir, journal, autobiography, life

bit *n.* **FRAGMENT:** piece, crumb, particle, morsel, flake, scrap; **TRIFLE:** iota, mite

bite *n.* **MOUTHFUL:** taste, morsel, nibble; **WOUND:** sting, laceration

biting *adj.* **TANGY:** sharp, keen, sour; **SARCASTIC:** caustic, acrimonious, bitter

bitter *adj.* **ACRID:** astringent, acid; **INTENSE:** harsh, severe; **SARCASTIC:** acrimonious, caustic, biting

bizarre *adj.* unusual, unexpected, fantastic, grotesque

blackmail *n.* extortion, tribute, protection

blame *v.* charge, condemn, denounce, disparage

bland *adj.* insipid, flat, dull, tasteless

blanket *n.* quilt, robe, comforter, featherbed, throw, cloak, covering

blanket *v.* cover, envelop, conceal, bury

blast *v.* explode, dynamite, detonate; denounce

blatant *adj.* clear, obvious, plain

blaze *n.* conflagration, combustion, burning, fire

bleak *adj.* dreary, desolate, bare, cheerless, barren

bleary *adj.* blurred, fuzzy

bleed *v.* hemorrhage, gush, spurt, flow

blemish *n.* flaw, defect, stain, imperfection, dent

blemish *v.* damage, deface, mar

blend *n.* mixture, combination, compound, amalgam

blight *n.* disease, withering, mildew, decay

blind *adj.* **OBTUSE:** unseeing, unaware; **CLOSED:** obstructed, blocked; **RANDOM:** accidental, unplanned, aimless

blindly *adv.* wildly, frantically, heedlessly, carelessly, recklessly, aimlessly, indiscriminately

bliss *n.* joy, rapture, ecstasy, happiness

blithe *adj.* gay, lighthearted, vivacious

blizzard *n.* snowstorm, tempest, blast, gale

block *n.* **CHUNK:** slab, cake, clod, hunk; **BARRIER:** obstruction, hindrance, obstacle

block *v.* **IMPEDE:** prevent, hinder, restrict; **TACKLE:** check, stop

blockade *n.* barrier, barricade, bar, barrier

bloom *n.* **FLOWER:** blossom, floweret; **GLOW:** blush, flush

blossom *n.* flower, bloom, floweret, bud

blot *n.* flaw, stain, smudge, blemish

blotch *n.* stain, blemish

blow *n.* hit, wallop, rap, clout, buffet

blow *v.* **FLUTTER:** waft, whisk, flap, wave; **SPEND:** waste, squander

blue *adj., n.* despondent, depressed, melancholy, sad

bluff *n.* **BANK:** hill, cliff, precipice; **DECEPTION:** trick, ruse, delusion

bluff *v.* fool, mislead, trick, deceive

blunder *n.* mistake, lapse, oversight, error

blunt *adj.* **DULL:** unsharpened, round; **ABRUPT:** brusque, curt, bluff, rude

bluster *v.* brag, boast

board *n.* **PLANK:** lath, strip, lumber; **MEALS:** food, fare, provisions; **REGULATORS:** council, cabinet, committee

boast *n.* brag, pretension, self–satisfaction, bravado

boast *v.* gloat, swagger, swell, brag, strut, flaunt

boastful *adj.* bragging, pretentious, bombastic

body *n.* **CHASSIS:** fuselage, hull, skeleton; **GROUP:** society, organization; **ANATOMY:** physique, figure, trunk, build; **CORPSE:** cadaver, carcass, mummy, remains; **COLLECTION:** reservoir, supply, variety

bog *n.* marsh, swamp

boil *v.* cook, steep, seethe, stew, simmer

boisterous *adj.* rowdy, uproarious, noisy, loud, rude

bold *adj.* **DARING:** courageous, intrepid, fearless; **IMPERTINENT:** brazen, audacious, presumptuous, rude; **PROMINENT:** strong, clear, plain, definite

boldness *n.* audacity, self–reliance, courage

bombastic *adj.* high–sounding, pompous

bond *n.* **LINK:** attachment, connection, affiliation; **DEBENTURE:** security, warranty; **BAIL:** surety, guaranty

bonus *n.* reward, compensation, payment, incentive

boor *n.* yokel, lout, clown, bumpkin, churl, oaf, boob

boost *n.* **ASSISTANCE:** aid, help; **INCREASE:** addition, hike

boost *v.* **PUSH UPWARD:** raise, hoist; **INCREASE:** raise, heighten, expand; **SUPPORT:** promote, encourage

booth *n.* stall, counter, nook, corner, stand

border *n.* **EDGE:** hem, end, trim, fringe, margin; **BOUNDARY:** frontier, perimeter

bore *v.* **DRILL:** ream, perforate; **WEARY:** fatigue, tire

boredom *n.* apathy, doldrums, listlessness, monotony, tedium, indifference

botch *v.* bungle, blunder, mishandle

bottom *n.* base, foot; depths, bed, floor

bough *n.* limb, arm, fork, branch

boulder *n.* stone, slab, crag, rock

boulevard *n.* street, avenue, highway, road

bounce *v.* rebound, ricochet, recoil

bound *v.* **LEAP:** spring, vault, jump; **BOUNCE:** ricochet, recoil; **LIMIT:** restrict, confine, circumscribe

boundary *n.* border, rim, bounds, extremity, perimeter, extent, periphery, limit

bounteous *adj.* abundant, lavish, plentiful

bounty *n.* bonus, inducement, reward; profusion

bouquet *n.* fragrance, aroma, scent, smell

bow *v.* **CURTSEY:** stoop, dip; **YIELD:** submit, surrender, acquiesce, capitulate

bowl *n.* dish, vessel, tureen, pot, saucer, crock

boycott *v.* ostracize, avoid, strike

brace *v.* support, prop, bolster, steady

brackish *adj.* salty, disagreeable, tainted

brag *v.* boast, swagger, exult, gloat, boast

braggart *n.* blowhard, windbag, swaggerer

braid *v.* interweave, plait, twine

brain *n.* **INTELLECT:** genius, mentality; **SCHOLAR:** egghead, intellectual

brake *v.* check, dampen, slow, stop

branch *n.* **DIVISION:** office, bureau, extension; **SHOOT:** bough, limb, sprig, twig, arm, fork, growth

brand *n.* mark, scar, welt, earmark, trademark

brand *v.* blaze, stamp, imprint, mark

brandish *v.* wave, flourish, gesture, warn, threaten

brass *n.* boldness, impudence, effrontery, rudeness, impertinence, audacity

bravado *n.* pretense, bluster

brave *adj.* fearless, daring, dauntless, valiant, intrepid, bold, stout, stalwart

brawl *v.* fight, quarrel, squabble

brawn *n.* power, strength

brazen *adj.* bold, brassy, impudent

breach *n.* **BREAK:** opening, rupture; **VIOLATION:** infringement, transgression, crime

breadth *n.* extent, vastness, size, width

break *n.* **BREACH:** fracture, split, rupture; **PAUSE:** intermission, interim; **LUCK:** accident, opportunity

breakthrough *n.* finding, discovery, invention

breath *n.* inhalation, exhalation, gasp, sigh, wheeze

breathe *v.* respire, inhale, exhale, gasp, pant

breed *n.* strain, variety, kind, race, type

breeze *n.* zephyr, flurry, wind

brevity *n.* conciseness, shortness, terseness

brew *v.* make, concoct, ferment, mull, cook

bridge *n.* **STRUCTURE:** viaduct, pontoon, catwalk, trestle; **LINK:** connection, bond, tie

bridle *n.* halter, leash, restraint

brief *adj.* momentary, fleeting, concise, abrupt

brief *n.* abstract, outline, summary

bright *adj.* **QUICK-WITTED:** intelligent, clever, alert; **CLEAR:** sunny, fair; **LIVELY:** cheerful, vivacious; **SHINING:** luminous, lustrous, sparkling, illuminated

brighten *v.* lighten, glow; polish, intensify, shine

brightness *n.* shine, luster, illumination, light

brilliant *adj.* **SPARKLING:** shining, dazzling, gleaming, bright; **TALENTED:** profound, intelligent

bring *v.* transport, convey, bear, carry

brink *n.* edge, limit, brim, rim

brisk *adj.* invigorating, stimulating, active

briskly *adv.* energetically, brusquely, nimbly

bristle *n.* hair, fiber, quill, point
brittle *adj.* fragile, crisp, inelastic, weak
broad *adj.* wide, large, extensive, spacious, expansive, roomy
broadcast *v.* transmit, announce, air, send
broaden *v.* widen, expand, increase, grow
broad-minded *adj.* tolerant, progressive, unprejudiced, liberal
brochure *n.* handout, circular, pamphlet, folder
broil *v.* cook, sear, bake, roast
broken *adj.* **INOPERABLE:** busted, faulty; **FRACTURED:** shattered, smashed, damaged, cracked; **INCOHERENT:** muttered, mumbled
brood *v.* pine, grieve, fret, sulk, mope, muse, deliberate, worry
brook *n.* stream, creek, streamlet, river
broth *n.* soup, consommé, bouillon, stock
browbeat *v.* intimidate, bully, frighten, threaten
browse *v.* skim, peruse, scan, inspect, examine
bruise *v.* wound, damage, beat, injure, hurt
brush *n.* **THICKET:** undergrowth, shrubbery, grove, hedge, fern, scrub; **TOUCH:** rub, tap, stroke
brush *v.* **CLEAN:** sweep, whisk, wipe; **TOUCH LIGHTLY:** stroke, smooth, graze
brusque *adj.* abrupt, blunt, curt, terse
brutal *adj.* pitiless, harsh, unmerciful, cruel
brutalize *v.* degrade, demean
buckle *n.* clasp, clamp, harness, fastening, fastener
budge *v.* stir, move
budget *n.* projection, estimate, allocation, plan, funds
buffet *v.* batter, strike, whip
buffoon *n.* clown, jester, fool, jerk

bug *n.* **INSECT:** beetle, pest, spider, gnat; **MICROORGANISM:** bacillus, virus; **DEFECT:** flaw, fault, annoyance

bug *v.* **EAVESDROP:** spy, overhear, wiretap; **ANNOY:** irritate, pester, bother, disturb

build *v.* increase; construct, form, erect, make, manufacture, fabricate, fashion, produce, devise

bulb *n.* globe, globule, ball, knob

bulge *n.* swelling, protuberance, bump, prominence

bulk *n.* most, majority

bulk *v.* enlarge, expand

bull *n.* **NONSENSE:** balderdash, rubbish, trash; **ANIMAL:** steer, calf, ox, cow;

bulletin *n.* report, release, notice

bully *n.* ruffian, rowdy, tough, rascal

bully *v.* intimidate, tease, domineer, harass, threaten

bum *n.* derelict, loafer, hobo, tramp, vagrant, beggar

bump *n.* **COLLISION:** knock, jounce, jar, nudge; **BULGE:** swelling, projection, protuberance, lump

bump *v.* **COLLIDE:** strike, crash, hit; **SOUND:** thud, whack, sock

bun *n.* roll, muffin, scone, roll, pastry

bunch *n.* cluster, clump, group, sheaf, tuft, shock, bundle, knot, collection

bungle *v.* botch, blunder, fumble, mishandle, fail

bungler *n.* muddler, numskull, dolt, clod

burden *v.* hinder, encumber, hamper, strain, load, tax, try, trouble, oppress

burglar *n.* thief, housebreaker, robber, criminal

burglary *n.* stealing, robbery, theft

burial *n.* interment, funeral

burlesque *v.* imitate, mock, satirize

burly *adj.* strong, muscular

burn *v.* ignite, kindle, incinerate, blaze, scorch

burnish *v.* polish, shine, smooth

burnt *adj.* scorched, singed, charred, burned

burrow *n.* hole, shelter

burrow *v.* dig, hide

burst *v.* **EXPLODE:** erupt, rupture, disintegrate; **BREAK:** crack, split, fracture, destroy

bury *v.* **INTER:** entomb, enshrine, embalm; **HIDE:** cover, conceal, secrete; **DEFEAT:** overcome, conquer

bush *n.* bramble, thicket, hedge, shrubbery, plant

bushy *adj.* fuzzy, shaggy, tufted, woolly, bristly

bushed *adj.* tired, fatigued

busy *adj.* active, occupied, diligent, employed, working

butcher *v.* **MASSACRE:** slaughter, slay, kill; **RUIN:** mutilate, spoil, botch, destroy

button *n.* knob, catch, disk, fastener

buy *v.* obtain, purchase, get, procure, gain, shop

buzz *v.* hum, drone, whir

cabaret *n.* bar, café, nightclub

cabin *n.* house, cottage, hut, home, shelter

cabinet *n.* advisors, council, bureau, ministry

cable *n.* rope, cord, chain, wire

cacophony *n.* dissonance, noise

cadaver *n.* body, corpse, remains

cadaverous *adj.* pale, gaunt

cadence *n.* rhythm, meter, flow, beat, measure

cadge *v.* beg, freeload

café *n.* coffeehouse, restaurant, cafeteria, lunchroom

cage *n.* coop, jail, crate, enclosure, pen

cagey *adj.* cunning, shrewd, clever

calamity *n.* tragedy, cataclysm, catastrophe, disaster
calculate *v.* count, measure, reckon, enumerate, determine, forecast, weigh, gauge, compute, cipher
calculating *adj.* scheming, shrewd, crafty
calendar *n.* schedule, journal, diary, daybook, chronology, logbook, register, almanac, agenda, docket
calisthenics *n.* exercise, workout, gymnastics
callous *adj.* heartless, indifferent, unfeeling, hardened, insensitive
callow *adj.* inexperienced, immature
calm *adj.* tranquil, reserved, cool, composed, collected, impassive, aloof, serene, placid
calm *v.* tranquilize, soothe, pacify, quiet
calumniate *v.* defame, slander, sully, vilify
camouflage *v.* conceal, cover, veil, disguise, hide
campaign *v.* crusade, electioneer, contend, barnstorm, stump
canal *n.* waterway, trench, ditch, channel, duct
cancel *v.* invalidate, rescind, repeal, retract, void
cancerous *adj.* carcinogenic, virulent, mortal, harmful
candid *adj.* sincere, open, frank, honest
candidate *n.* nominee, aspirant, office–seeker
candor *n.* frankness, honesty
canny *adj.* cautious, watchful, shrewd
canon *n.* law, principle, standard, decree, rule
cantankerous *adj.* quarrelsome, disagreeable
canteen *n.* container, jug, flask, bottle
canvas *n.* SAILCLOTH: tarpaulin tenting, duck, tarp; PAINTING: portrait, oil, art

canyon *n.* gorge, gulch, gully, ravine, valley
capability *n.* capacity, skill, aptitude, ability
capable *adj.* proficient, competent, able
capacity *n.* limit, size, volume, scope, dimensions
cape *n.* **HEADLAND:** peninsula, point, jetty; **CLOAK:** mantilla, mantle, shawl, wrap, poncho;
caper *n.* **FROLIC:** play, romp; **PRANK:** trick, escapade
capital *n.* assets, cash, estate, property, wealth
capitalist *n.* entrepreneur, investor, financier
capitulate *v.* submit, surrender, yield
capsize *v.* upend, overturn, invert, tip over, upset
caption *n.* heading, title, inscription
captious *adj.* critical, fault-finding
captivate *v.* attract, charm, fascinate, bewitch
captive *adj.* restrained, incarcerated, jailed, bound
captive *n.* prisoner, hostage, convict
capture *v.* take, hold, seize, apprehend, arrest
care *n.* **CONCERN:** worry, anxiety, distress; **CAUTION:** concern, regard, precaution, vigilance; **CUSTODY:** keeping, watching
careen *v.* lean, swerve
career *n.* work, occupation, vocation, job, profession
careful *adj.* deliberate, meticulous, finicky, exacting, painstaking, conscientious, cautious, guarded, discreet, thrifty, wary
careless *adj.* loose, lax, incautious, reckless, indiscreet, imprudent, heedless, negligent, casual, rash
carelessness *n.* unconcern, nonchalance, neglect, negligence, disregard, imprudence, indifference

caress *v.* touch, love, embrace, cuddle, pat
cargo *n.* freight, baggage, lading, load
caricature *v.* mimic, ridicule, satirize
carnage *n.* bloodbath, massacre, slaughter
carnal *adj.* fleshly, worldly, sensuous, lewd
carnival *n.* merrymaking, festival, fair, entertainment
carouse *v.* drink, imbibe, party, revel
carriage *n.* **BEARING:** presence, look, demeanor, poise, air; **VEHICLE:** buggy, surrey, gig, sulky, hansom
carry *v.* **TRANSPORT:** convey, transfer, cart, take, bring, haul, tote; **TRANSMIT:** transfer, relay; **SUPPORT** bear, sustain, shoulder
cartel *n.* alliance, coalition, federation
carve *v.* fashion, shape, form, chisel, sculpture, cut
cascade *v.* cataract, flow, rapids
cast *n.* **REPRODUCTION:** facsimile, replica, copy; **ACTORS:** players, company, troupe; **APPEARANCE:** aspect, complexion; **TINGE:** hue, shade, tint, color
cast *v.* **THROW:** pitch, fling, hurl; **MOLD:** shape, form
caste *n.* position, status, birth
casual *adj.* **CHANCE:** unplanned, spontaneous; **BLASÉ:** apathetic, unconcerned, indifferent
catalog *n.* directory, index, classification
catalog *v.* list, organize
catastrophe *n.* disaster, calamity, misadventure, misery, affliction, devastation, tragedy, upheaval
categorize *v.* classify, type, arrange
caucus *n.* conference, faction
cause *n.* **AGENT:** condition, circumstances; **PURPOSE:** goal, motive, foundation, reason; **BELIEF:** principles, conviction, faith

cause *v.* originate, provoke, generate, occasion, begin
caution *n.* discretion, care, heed, prudence, warning
cautious *adj.* circumspect, watchful, wary, careful
cavil *v.* criticize, object
cavity *n.* pit, depression, basin, hole, hollow
cavort *v.* frolic, prance
cease *v.* stop, desist, terminate, discontinue, halt
cede *v.* relinquish, surrender, yield
celebrate *v.* **INDULGE:** feast, carouse, rejoice, revel; **COMMEMORATE:** observe, consecrate, honor
celebrity *n.* notable, dignitary, personage, luminary
celibate *adj.* unmarried, abstaining
cement *n.* adhesive, glue, tar, gum, mortar, paste
cement *v.* join, unite, mortar, plaster, connect, fasten
cemetery *n.* churchyard, necropolis, catacomb, tomb, vault, crypt, graveyard
censor *n.* restrict, suppress, expurgate
censor *v.* review; ban
censorship *n.* restriction, restraint
censure *v.* **BLAME:** criticize, judge, disapprove; **SCOLD:** rebuke, reprove, attack
census *n.* count, enumeration, tabulation, tally
center *n.* middle, nucleus, core, heart, essence, gist, kernel
center *v.* focus, concentrate, centralize
central *adj.* middle, midway, equidistant
cerebral *adj.* brainy, intelligent
ceremonial *adj.* ritualistic, stately, solemn, formal
ceremonious *adj.* formal, ritualistic
ceremony *n.* function, commemoration, rite, celebration, observance, ritual, formality, custom, tradition

certain *adj.* **BEYOND DOUBT:** conclusive, incontrovertible, irrefutable, true, unmistakable; **FIXED:** settled, concluded, definite, determined; **CONFIDENT:** assured, positive, untroubled, confident; **SPECIFIC:** definite, particular, singular, precise, express

certainly *adv.* positively, absolutely, unquestionably

certificate *n.* document, warrant, credentials, certification, document, warranty, guarantee

certify *v.* swear, attest, state, declare, testify

cessation *n.* ending, stopping

chagrin *n.* embarrassment, setback

chain *n.* **LINKS:** series, string, cable, manacle; **SEQUENCE:** succession, progression, continuity

chain *v.* connect, secure, fasten hold, bind, restrain

challenge *v.* **COMPETE:** defy, denounce, invite, dare, threaten; **QUESTION:** dispute, inquire, ask, doubt

challenging *adj.* difficult, intriguing

champion *n.* conqueror, victor, hero

chance *adj.* accidental, unplanned, unintentional, aimless, incidental, fortuitous

chance *v.* risk, venture, stake, hazard, wager, jeopardize, speculate

change *v.* **MAKE DIFFERENT:** vary, alter, transform, turn; **BECOME DIFFERENT:** evolve, transform, adapt, moderate, adjust; **EXCHANGE:** displace, supplant, transpose; **DRESS:** undress, disrobe

changeable *adj.* **FICKLE:** flighty, unreliable, unstable; **VARIABLE:** unsteady, unsettled, uncertain

channel *n.* conduit, duct, gutter, trough, artery

chant *n.* recitation, chorus, incantation

chaos *n.* confusion, disorder, turmoil, discord

character *n.* **SYMBOL:** mark, sign, figure, emblem; **QUALITY:** temperament, nature, attribute, characteristic; **ECCENTRIC:** crank, nut, oddball, weirdo

characteristic *n.* attribute, quality, faculty, peculiarity, aspect, distinction, nature, essence, component

charge *v.* **PRICE:** cost; **ACCUSE:** indict, censure, blame; **ATTACK:** assail, assault, invade

charitable *adj.* generous, philanthropic, forgiving

charlatan *n.* cheat, fake, fraud

charming *adj.* alluring, appealing, captivating, diverting, enchanting, fascinating, lovable, provocative

chart *n.* diagram, plan, map, graph

chase *v.* pursue, trail, track, seek, hunt

chastise *v.* scold, discipline, spank, punish

cheap *adj.* **INFERIOR:** shoddy, poor; **INEXPENSIVE:** competitive, reasonable, economical

cheapen *v.* depreciate, degrade, spoil, demean

cheat *n.* rogue, charlatan, fraud, swindler, chiseler, trickster

cheat *v.* defraud, swindle, beguile, deceive

check *v.* **CONTROL:** bridle, repress, inhibit, neutralize, restrain; **EXAMINE:** review, monitor, investigate

cheer *v.* **HEARTEN:** console, brighten, comfort, encourage, help; **APPLAUD:**, shout, salute, support, yell

cheerful *adj.* **HAPPY:** gay, merry, joyful; **BRIGHT:** sunny, sparkling, pleasant

cherish *v.* treasure, value, adore, love, protect

chest *n.* **BREAST:** thorax, bosom, peritoneum, ribs; **BOX:** case, coffer, strongbox, cabinet, crate

chew *v.* munch, masticate, nibble, gnaw, eat

chief *adj.* leading, first, foremost, main, principal

chilly *adj.* brisk, fresh, crisp, cold, cool

chivalrous *adj.* courteous, valiant, brave, noble, polite

choice *n.* selection, preference, election, favorite, pick

choke *v.* asphyxiate, strangle; gag, gasp

choose *v.* pick, prefer, appoint, favor, decide

chop *v.* cut, mince, fell, whack

chore *n.* task, routine, errand, job

chronic *adj.* deep–seated, persistent, lingering, protracted, prolonged, recurrent

chronologic, chronological *adj.* ordered, classified, sequential, consecutive

chunk *n.* lump, piece, mass, part

churlish *adj.* crude, vulgar, grouchy, surly

churn *v.* stir, beat, mix, agitate

circle *n.* disk, ring, loop, orbit, hoop

circle *v.* circumscribe, enclose, circulate, surround

circuitous *adj.* roundabout, devious

circular *adj.* spherical, globular, round

circulate *v.* send, report, distribute

circulation *n.* rotation, current, flow

circumference *n.* perimeter, periphery, boundary

circumspect *adj.* cautious, prudent

circumstance *n.* situation, condition, contingency, status, occurrence, episode

circumvent *v.* avoid, bypass, dodge, elude, evade

civic *adj.* civil, urban, municipal, public

civil *adj.* formal, polite, courteous, refined

claim *v.* **DEMAND:** request, own; **STATE:** assert, insist
clamor *n.* outcry, din, discord, noise, uproar
clan *n.* family, tribe, group, organization, race
clandestine *adj.* covert, furtive, secret, sly
clarify *v.* interpret, elucidate, explain
clash *v.* conflict, mismatch, contrast, differ
clasp *n.* fastener, buckle, pin, clamp
classic *n.* masterwork, masterpiece
classify *v.* arrange, order, organize, categorize, label, catalogue, tag, sort, index
clatter *n.* noise, racket, hubbub
clause *n.* provision, condition, codicil, requirement
clean *adj., adv.* **PURE:** unadulterated, undefiled, spotless, cleansed; **DISTINCT:** clear-cut, sharp, readable; **THOROUGH:** complete, entire, total, absolute
clean *v.* cleanse, wash, scrub, disinfect, polish, sterilize, scour
clear *adj., adv.* **OBVIOUS:** explicit, plain, manifest; **TRANSPARENT:** limpid, translucent; **UNCLOUDED:** sunny, bright, fair
clemency *n.* leniency, mercy
clench *v.* hold, grip, grasp
clever *adj.* **SKILLFUL:** apt, expert, adroit, able; **INTELLIGENT:** smart, bright, shrewd
cliché *n.* platitude, slogan, banality, triviality, motto
client *n.* customer, patient, patron, buyer
climax *n.* crisis, peak, culmination, zenith, summit,
climb *v.* scale, ascend, surmount, mount
cling *v.* hold, adhere, attach, clasp, stick
clip *v.* shorten, snip, crop; strike; cheat; fasten
cloak *v.* cover, conceal, camouflage

clog *v.* obstruct, impede, seal, close, hinder

cloister *v.* seclude, protect

close *adj.* nearby; like; confining; restrictive, limited,

close *n.* ending, conclusion

close *v.* **END:** conclude, finish, terminate; **SEAL:** shut, clog, block, bar, dam, cork; **CONNECT:** meet, unite, agree, join; **SHUT:** slam, fasten, bolt, bar, shutter, lock

cloth *n.* fabric, material, stuff, goods

clothe *v.* cover, attire, dress, costume

clothes, clothing *n.* apparel, raiment, garments, garb, vestments, attire, outfit, toggery, togs, duds

clown *n.* fool, buffoon, joker, harlequin

clumsy *adj.* ungainly, gawky, inexpert, awkward

cluster *n.* group, gathering, batch, clump, bunch

clutch *v.* grasp, grab, grip, hold, seize

clutter *n.* disarray, jumble, disorder, confusion

coach *v.* teach, train drill, instruct

coagulate *v.* clot, curdle, congeal, thicken

coalition *n.* union, group, association, faction

coarse *adj.* **ROUGH:** crude, unrefined; **VULGAR:** low, common, base, obscene

coast *n.* shore, shoreline, beach, seaboard

coast *v.* glide, float, drift, ride

coax *v.* cajole, wheedle, inveigle, urge

cocky *adj.* overconfident, flamboyant

codicil *n.* addendum, addition, appendix, rider

coerce *v.* force, compel, impel, constrain

cogent *adj.* forceful, compelling

cogitate *v.* consider, ponder, reflect

cognizance *n.* knowledge, awareness

coherent *adj.* comprehensible, intelligible, logical

coincide *v.* correspond, match, agree

coincidence *n.* chance, happening, accident

cold *adj.* **WINTRY:** crisp, cool, freezing, frosty, frigid, nippy, brisk, numbing, raw; **UNFEELING:** reserved, unfriendly, indifferent

collaborate *v.* cooperate, conspire

collapse *v.* drop, deflate, fall, fail

collateral *n.* security, guarantee, pledge, insurance

colleague *n.* associate, partner, collaborator

collect *v.* **CONSOLIDATE:** amass, accumulate, concentrate; **CONGREGATE:** assemble, flock, gather

collection *n.* assortment, accumulation, assemblage, concentration, mess, lot, heap, bunch

collector *n.* hobbyist, fancier, hoarder

collide *v.* hit, strike, crash; clash, disagree, oppose

collision *n.* impact, contact, encounter, crash

collusion *n.* conspiracy, plot

colorful *adj.* bright, vivid; picturesque, quaint

colossal *adj.* large, huge, enormous, immense

column *n.* **SUPPORT:** pillar, shaft, pylon, post; **COMMENTARY:** article, editorial

combat *n.* conflict, battle, struggle, warfare, fight

combine *v.* link, join, fuse, merge, blend, mix, unite

comedian *n.* comic, jester, entertainer, actor, clown

comedy *n.* farce, satire, burlesque, slapstick

comely *adj.* attractive, pleasing

comfort *n.* contentment, relaxation, repose, ease

comfort *v.* soothe, reassure, console
comfortable *adj.* **CONTENTED:** relaxed, untroubled, soothed, satisfied; **SNUG:** cozy, luxurious, rich
comic, comical *adj.* funny, silly, humorous, ironic
command *v.* **ORDER:** charge, tell, demand; **CONTROL:** rule, dominate, master
commemorate *v.* honor, memorialize
commence *v.* begin, start, originate
commend *v.* praise, laud, support, acclaim, approve
comment *v.* remark, criticize, mention, interject, say
commentary *n.* criticism, analysis, interpretation
commerce *n.* trading, marketing, business
commit *v.* **PERPETRATE:** complete, perform; **ENTRUST:** delegate, promise, charge, employ, dispatch
commitment *n.* responsibility, duty, promise
commotion *n.* disturbance, tumult, uproar
communicate *v.* inform, tell, confer, talk, converse, chat, write
communication *n.* utterance, writing, broadcasting, speaking, interchange
community *n.* public, people; village, hamlet
compact *adj.* small, light, dense
compact *n.* covenant
compact *v.* pack, compress
companion *n.* comrade, escort, chaperon, bodyguard
companionship *n.* brotherhood, fellowship, friendship
company *n.* **ASSEMBLY:** throng, band, gathering; **BUSINESS:** firm, corporation; **GUEST:** visitor, caller
comparable *adj.* **SIMILAR:** akin, relative, alike, like; **EQUAL:** equivalent, tantamount

compare *v.* LIKEN: relate, associate, link, contrast, correlate; EXAMINE: weigh, analyze

compassion *n.* concern, sympathy, pity

compatible *adj.* agreeable, congruous, harmonious

compel *v.* force, enforce, constrain, coerce

compelling *adj.* forceful, impressive

compensate *v.* offset, repay, recompense, remunerate

compete *v.* strive, struggle, oppose, clash, encounter

competent *adj.* qualified, suitable, fit, skilled, able

competition *n.* rivalry; contest, meet, game

compile *v.* gather, collect, assemble, accumulate, edit

complacent *adj.* self–satisfied, egotistic, happy, smug

complain *v.* grumble, remonstrate, fret, fuss, gripe

complaint *n.* OBJECTION: charge, criticism, reproach, accusation; ILLNESS: ailment, disease, infirmity

complete *v.* execute, consummate, perfect, accomplish, realize, perform, achieve, fulfill, conclude

complex *adj.* MULTIPLE: combined, compounded; CONVOLUTED: intricate, complicated, tortuous, knotty

complexion *n.* coloration, tinge, cast, pigmentation

compliance *n.* agreement, assent, conformity

complicate *v.* confound, jumble, tangle

complicated *adj.* intricate, tangled, complex

compliment *v.* congratulate, hail, toast, applaud, commend, acclaim, glorify

composure *n.* self–control, calmness, poise, aplomb

compound *v.* combine, mix

comprehend *v.* understand, grasp, discern, perceive

comprehensive *adj.* broad, extensive

comprise *v.* contain, embrace, embody

compromise *v.* settle, agree, conciliate

compulsive *adj.* driven, passionate

compulsory *adj.* obligatory, requisite, necessary

compunction *n.* apprehension, qualm, uneasiness,

conceal *v.* cover, screen, secrete, hide

concede *v.* acknowledge, grant, yield, admit, allow

conceit *n.* arrogance, narcissism, vanity

concept *n.* theory, idea, notion, thought

conceptual *adj.* theoretical, ideal

concern *v.* **PERTAIN:** relate, influence; **BOTHER:** worry

conciliate *v.* appease, placate

concise *adj.* succinct, brief, short

conclave *n.* gathering, meeting, parley

conclude *v.* **CLOSE:** terminate, finish, complete, achieve; **DEDUCE:** presume, reason, assume

concur *v.* correspond, coincide, agree, equal

concurrent *adj.* parallel, coexisting, simultaneous

condemn *v.* doom, sentence, damn, convict, punish

condescending *adj.* patronizing, disdainful, smug

condiment *n.* seasoning, relish

condition *n.* **REQUIREMENT:** stipulation, provision; **FITNESS:** tone, shape; **CIRCUMSTANCE:** situation, position, status; **MODIFIER:** limitation, restriction, qualification; **ILLNESS:** ailment, infirmity

condone *v.* forgive, disregard, excuse, overlook

conduct *n.* behavior, deportment, demeanor, manner
conduct *v.* LEAD: guide, escort, attend, accompany; MANAGE: administer, handle
confer *v.* converse, deliberate, discuss
conference *n.* meeting, discussion, gathering
confess *v.* acknowledge, own, concede, admit
confession *n.* disclosure, acknowledgment
confidant *n.* friend, adherent, companion
confident *adj.* assured, fearless, bold
confidential *adj.* secret, classified, intimate, private
confine *v.* restrain, restrict; imprison, incarcerate
confirm *v.* RATIFY: affirm, settle, approve, endorse; PROVE: validate, verify, authenticate, explain
confiscate *v.* seize, appropriate, impound, usurp
conflict *v.* clash, contrast, contend, fight
conform *v.* adapt, accommodate, reconcile, agree
conformity *n.* SIMILARITY: correspondence, resemblance; OBEDIENCE: submission, compliance
confound *v.* confuse, bewilder, puzzle, perplex
confront *v.* brave, defy, repel, dare, face
confrontation *n.* battle, strife, dispute
confuse *v.* bewilder, befuddle, puzzle, perplex, confound, fluster, disconcert, baffle, mystify
congeal *v.* thicken, solidify
congenial *adj.* friendly, compatible, harmonious
congregate *v.* gather, assemble, convene, meet
congruous *adj.* appropriate, suitable, fitting
conjecture *n.* guess, opinion, speculation

connect *v.* join, link, attach, associate
connoisseur *n.* critic, expert, judge
connotation *n.* implication, meaning
conquer *v.* overcome, subdue, crush, defeat
conquest *n.* triumph, success, conquering, victory
conscience *n.* duty, morals, shame
conscientious *adj.* thorough, fastidious, meticulous, complete, careful, reliable
conscious *adj.* awake, aware, sentient, cognizant, discerning, knowing, mindful, understanding
consecutive *adj.* ordered, chronological, sequential
consensus *n.* agreement, consent, unison, accord
consent *v.* acquiesce, agree, allow, approve
consequence *n.* **EFFECT:** outgrowth, end, outcome, result; **IMPORTANCE:** moment, value, weight
conservative *adj.* reserved, conventional
consider *v.* contemplate, regard, think, believe
considerable *adj.* **IMPORTANT:** noteworthy, significant; **SUBSTANTIAL:** abundant, lavish, bountiful, plentiful
considerate *adj.* kind, solicitous, polite, thoughtful
consideration *n.* **THOUGHTFULNESS:** attentiveness, kindness; **PAYMENT:** remuneration, salary, wage
consistent *adj.* constant, regular
console *v.* comfort, cheer, gladden, encourage
consolidate *v.* combine, mix, unify
consortium *n.* alliance, union
conspicuous *adj.* obvious, striking, prominent, flagrant, noticeable
conspiracy *n.* plan, intrigue, collusion, connivance, cabal

constant *adj.* unchanging, steadfast, steady, uniform, unvarying, unbroken
consternation *n.* confusion, distress
constituent *adj.* component, element, ingredient, part
constitute *v.* **FOUND:** create, establish, develop, frame; **MAKE UP:** compound, compose
constraint *n.* **FORCE:** coercion, compulsion, pressure; **SHYNESS:** restraint, humility, reserve; **CONFINEMENT:** captivity, detention, restriction, arrest
constrict *v.* squeeze, contract, tighten
construct *v.* build, erect, make, fabricate, create
constructive *adj.* helpful, useful, instructive, valuable, effective
consult *v.* confer, conspire, counsel, ask
consume *v.* **USE:** spend, deplete; **EAT:** absorb, devour
consummate *v.* complete, perfect
consumption *n.* use, spending, waste,
contact *v.* touch, reach, communicate
contagious *adj.* communicable, infectious, spreading, epidemic, endemic, catching
contain *v.* hold, keep, limit, stop, restrain
contaminate *v.* pollute, infect, defile, corrupt, dirty
contemplate *v.* study, ponder, consider, muse, think
contemporary *adj.* current, fashionable, modern
contempt *n.* disdain, disrespect, scorn, derision
contend *v.* compete, contest, dispute, fight, argue, claim
content, contented *adj.* satisfied, appeased, gratified
contention *n.* **ARGUMENT:** quarrel, struggle, competition, dispute; **ASSERTION:** charge, declaration

contest *n.* competition, trial, match, challenge, game
contest *v.* challenge, compete, oppose
contingency *n.* possibility, likelihood
continual *adj.* uninterrupted, unbroken
continue *v.* **PERSIST:** endure, persevere, progress; **RESUME:** renew, return, reinstate, reestablish
contort *v.* twist, deform, distort
contraband *n.* plunder, booty
contract *v.* **AGREE:** pledge, bargain, obligate; **REDUCE:** diminish, shrink, recede, condense, compress, decrease; **ACQUIRE:** catch, get, incur
contradiction *n.* incongruity, inconsistency, opposition, difference, opposite
contrary *adj.* **OPPOSED:** antagonistic, hostile; **DISAGREEABLE:** contradictory, unpropitious; **OBSTINATE:** headstrong, stubborn
contrast *v.* compare, differentiate, deviate, differ, vary
contribute *v.* give, endow, bestow, present, confer, bequest, grant, donate, bequeath, subsidize
contrive *v.* create, devise, scheme, improvise, invent
control *v.* **CHECK:** constrain, repress, restrain; **DIRECT:** lead, dominate, supervise, head, manage, govern
controversial *adj.* disputable, debatable, uncertain
controversy *n.* contention, debate, quarrel, difference
convene *v.* assemble, congregate, collect, gather
convenient *adj.* accessible, available, handy
convention *n.* **CUSTOM:** practice, habit, fashion; **GATHERING:** assembly, convocation
conventional *adj.* accepted, customary, typical, commonplace, traditional, formal

conversation *n.* talk, discussion, discourse, speech
converse *v.* speak, talk, visit
converse *n.* antithesis, reverse, opposite
conversion *n.* change, turn, regeneration
convert *v.* alter, transform, change
convey *v.* transport, transfer, send
convict *n.* felon, criminal, prisoner
convict *v.* condemn, sentence, doom
conviction *n.* persuasion, confidence, belief, faith
convince *v.* persuade, establish, satisfy
convincing *adj.* reasonable, plausible, likely
convivial *adj.* congenial, gregarious
cooperate *v.* conspire, participate, agree
copious *adj.* abundant, abounding
copy *v.* **REPRODUCE:** duplicate, counterfeit, forge, depict, portray; **IMITATE:** mimic, ape
cordial *adj.* friendly, genial, warm–hearted
core *n.* essence, gist, heart, center, hub
corporation *n.* enterprise, company, business
corporeal *adj.* material, tangible
corpse *n.* body, remains, cadaver
correct *adj.* **ACCURATE:** true, right; **PROPER:** suitable
correct *v.* remedy, rectify, amend, repair
correctness *n.* **ACCURACY:** precision, exactness; **PROPRIETY:** decency, decorum, fitness
correlation *n.* interdependence, equivalence
correspond *v.* **COMPARE:** match, resemble, conform; **COMMUNICATE:** write
correspondence *n.* **LIKENESS:** conformity, equivalence, similarity; **COMMUNICATION:** message, letter
corroborate *v.* confirm, prove, support

corrupt *adj.* immoral, underhanded, fraudulent, crooked, nefarious, unscrupulous, dishonest
corrupt *v.* debase, pervert, adulterate, taint
cost *n.* price, value, expense, charge
costly *adj.* expensive, splendid, precious
costume *n.* dress, clothing, attire, apparel, garb
couch *n.* sofa, lounge, davenport, chair
council *n.* group, cabinet, committee
counsel *n.* **ADVICE:** guidance, instruction, suggestion; **ADVISER:** lawyer, attorney, barrister
countenance *n.* appearance, aspect
countenance *v.* approve, endorse
counter *v.* react, respond
counter *n.* board, shelf, ledge
counteract *v.* mitigate, check, hinder
counterfeit *adj.* forged, fraudulent
countermand *v.* cancel, reverse
countless *adj.* innumerable, incalculable, infinite
coup *n.* feat, achievement
couple *n.* pair, two, set, brace,
couple *v.* join, unite, link, copulate
courage *n.* valor, boldness, audacity, mettle, stoutheartedness, gallantry, daring
course *n.* route, passage, pathway, road
courteous *adj.* well–mannered, courtly, affable, polite
courtesy *n.* affability, politeness, refinement
covenant *n.* agreement, contract
cover *v.* **WRAP:** envelop, enshroud, encase; **PROTECT:** shield, screen, shelter; **HIDE:** screen, mask, disguise; **INCLUDE:** embrace, incorporate; **TRAVEL:** traverse; **FLOOD:** drench, engulf; **REPORT:** recount, narrate, relate

covert *adj.* secret, hidden, disguised

cower *v.* cringe, shrink, quake, tremble, shake, snivel, flinch, quail, grovel

coy *adj.* shy, demur, evasive, bashful, humble

cozy *adj.* comfortable, secure, sheltered, snug, safe

crack *n.* **OPENING:** crevice, fissure, rift; **COMMENT:** retort, jest, joke, remark

crack *v.* **BREAK:** cleave, burst, split, sever; **DAMAGE:** injure, hurt, impair; **SOLVE:** answer, decode

craft *n.* **TRADE:** occupation, career, work, job; **SKILL:** proficiency, competence, aptitude, ability

craftsman *n.* artisan, journeyman, machinist, artist

craggy *adj.* rough, steep, irregular

cramp *n.* spasm, crick, pang, pain

cramped *adj.* confined, restraining, restricted

crank *n.* **DEVICE:** bracket, arm, handle; **PERSON:** eccentric, complainer, grouch

cranky *adj.* irritable, ill–tempered, disagreeable

crash *v.* **FALL:** plunge, tumble; **COLLIDE:** jostle, bump, jolt, hit; **MAKE NOISE:** clatter, bang, smash; **BREAK:** shatter, splinter; **GO UNINVITED:** invade, intrude

crate *n.* box, carton

crater *n.* depression, hollow, opening, abyss, hole

craving *n.* need, longing, yearning, desire

crawl *v.* creep, wriggle, squirm, slither, writhe, grovel

crazy *adj.* crazed, demented, mad, insane, foolish

cream *n.* lotion, cosmetic, jelly, salve, emulsion

creamy *adj.* smooth, buttery, rich, soft

create *v.* originate, build, fashion, shape, fabricate

creative *adj.* imaginative, inventive, artistic, original
credibility *n.* likelihood, probability
credible *adj.* plausible, believable, reliable
creed *n.* belief, doctrine, dogma, faith
creep *v.* slither, writhe, crawl
crestfallen *adj.* saddened, disheartened
crevice *n.* crack, chasm, cleft, slit, gap
crew *n.* company, troupe, squad, team
crime *n.* transgression, wrongdoing, offense, violation
criminal *adj.* illegal, felonious, bad
criminal *n.* lawbreaker, felon, crook, gangster, thief
cringe *v.* cower, shrink, flinch, quail, wince, crawl
crisis *n.* straits, plight, predicament, trauma
crisp *adj.* invigorating, brisk, bracing, stimulating; fresh, green
criterion *n.* basis, standard, principle
critic *n.* **REVIEWER:** commentator, analyst; **FAULTFINDER:** detractor, complainer
critical *adj.* **CRUCIAL:** decisive, significant; **DISAPPROVING:** condemning, disparaging; **ANALYTICAL:** perceptive, discerning, observant
criticize *v.* **EVALUATE:** study, analyze, examine; **FIND FAULT:** chastise, reprove, reprimand, blame
crook *n.* **CRIMINAL:** swindler, thief; **BEND:** notch, fork, angle
crooked *adj.* **CURVED:** bowed, twisted, bent; **DISHONEST:** iniquitous, devious, corrupt, nefarious
crop *v.* trim, cut, clip
cross *adj.* cranky, pettish, critical, irritable
cross *v.* **INTERSECT:** divide, traverse, span; **INTERBREED:** mingle, cross–pollinate, mix
crucial *adj.* **CRITICAL:** decisive, climatic, deciding; **SEVERE:** trying, taxing, hard, difficult

crude *adj.* unrefined, rough, unpolished, coarse

cruel *adj.* heartless, malevolent, vicious, savage

crumb *n.* piece, fragment, particle, scrap, pinch, bit

crumble *v.* decay, disintegrate, collapse

crumple *v.* collapse, rumple, crush, crease, wrinkle

crush *v.* **SUBDUE:** defeat, overwhelm, annihilate; **BREAK:** smash, pulverize, powder, grind

cry *v.* weep, sob, wail, sorrow, grieve

cuddle *v.* embrace, snuggle, nestle

cuddly *adj.* affectionate, lovable

cue *n.* signal, hint, prompt

cuff *n.* slap, blow, punch, hit

cultivate *v.* nurture, educate, refine, improve, teach

cultivation *n.* horticulture, agriculture, gardening

cultural *adj.* educational, enlightening, enriching

culture *n.* **FOLKWAYS:** convention,, custom, mores; **REFINEMENT:** breeding, gentility, manners, polish

cunning *adj.* sly, crafty, clever, skillful, ingenious

cure *v.* restore, heal, remedy

curious *adj.* **UNUSUAL:** strange, odd, queer, unique **INQUISITIVE:** interested, inquiring, questioning;

current *adj.* prevailing, contemporary, fashionable

current *n.* drift, flow, tide

curt *adj.* brusque, brief, concise, terse

curtain *n.* hanging, screen, drape, drapery, shutter

curve *n.* arc, bow, arch

curve *v.* deviate, vow, crook, twist, bend

custodian *n.* caretaker, attendant, gatekeeper

custody *n.* care, protection, guardianship

custom *n.* tradition, practice, convention, ritual

customary *adj.* usual, habitual, conventional

cut *v.* **REDUCE:** shorten, curtail, lessen, decrease; **SEVER:** separate, cleave; **CROSS:** intersect, pass

cynic *n.* skeptic, mocker, scoffer, detractor, critic

cynical *adj.* sardonic, unbelieving, sneering, sarcastic

dainty *adj.* delicate, fragile, petite, airy

dally *v.* dawdle, trifle with, putter, dabble

dam *v.* obstruct, check, restrict, restrain

damage *v.* injure, scratch, mar, deface, break

damages *n.* compensation, reparations, costs, reimbursement, expense

damp *adj.* moist, humid, sodden, wet

danger *n.* risk, peril, jeopardy, threat, menace

dangerous *adj.* perilous, serious, vital, hazardous, risky, deadly, precarious, treacherous, unsafe

dangle *v.* hang, droop, sway, suspend

dare *n.* challenge, defy

dare *v.* **VENTURE:** undertake, endeavor, hazard, risk, try; **DEFY:** confront, oppose, challenge, face

daring *adj.* bold, courageous, fearless, brave

dark *adj.* **SINISTER:** evil, bad, gloomy, dismal, immoral, corrupt; **UNLIT:** dim, shadowy, somber, indistinct, dusky, murky, gloomy, obscure, shady, hazy

darken *v.* cloud, shade, shadow, blacken, shade

darkness *n.* **GLOOM:** murkiness, nightfall, night; **EVIL:** wickedness, sin, corruption; **SECRECY:** concealment, obscurity,

dart *n.* missile, barb, arrow, weapon

dart *v.* shoot, speed, plunge, thrust, hurtle, fling, heave, pitch, dash, spurt, skim, fly
dash *n.* sprinkle, scattering, trace
dash *v.* DISCOURAGE: dampen, dismay, dispirit; RUSH: race, sprint, speed, hurry
dashing *adj.* adventurous, dapper
date *n.* APPOINTMENT: rendezvous, engagement, call, visit; COMPANION: partner, friend, lover
date *v.* ACCOMPANY: court, escort, accompany
dawn *n.* start, sunrise, daybreak, morning, beginning
daze *n.* stupor, bewilderment, distraction, confusion
daze *v.* stun, bewilder
dazzle *v.* blind, amaze,
dead *adj.* LIFELESS: deceased, perished, inanimate, defunct; EXHAUSTED: wearied, worn, spent, tired; NUMB: insensible, anesthetized
deaden *v.* anesthetize, dull, chloroform, numb
deal *n.* agreement, pledge, pact, contract
deal *v.* trade, barter, bargain, buy, sell, distribute
dealer *n.* vendor, businessman, merchant
debar *v.* exclude, prohibit, restrict
debate *v.* discuss, contend, contest, dispute, argue
debris *n.* remains, rubble, rubbish, wreckage, trash
debt *n.* obligation, liability, mortgage, note
decadent *adj.* immoral, wicked, degenerate, bad
deceit *n.* misrepresentation, trickery, fraud, duplicity, deception, dishonesty
deceitful *adj.* tricky, cunning, insincere, dishonest
deceive *v.* mislead, swindle, delude, defraud, victimize, betray, hoodwink, dupe, fleece, bilk

decent *adj.* seemly, respectable, proper, virtuous, ethical, trustworthy, upright, good
deception *n.* trickery, craftiness, treachery, betrayal, pretense, deceit, duplicity, dishonesty
decide *v.* settle, determine, judge, select, pick
decision *n.* judgment, resolution, opinion
decisive *adj.* conclusive, resolved, final, definitive, absolute, definite, determined
declaration *n.* statement, assertion, affirmation, proclamation, affidavit, testimony, announcement
declare *v.* state, assert, tell, affirm, maintain, testify, certify, contend, allege, profess, swear
decline *v.* **REFUSE:** reject; **DETERIORATE:** degenerate, backslide
decorate *v.* adorn, beautify, renovate, brighten, enhance, embellish, elaborate
decoration *n.* **EMBELLISHMENT:** adornment, ornamentation; **CITATION:** medal, ribbon
decorative *adj.* ornamental, embellishing, beautifying, ornate
decrease *v.* lessen, diminish, decline, subside, shrink, reduce, restrain, blunt, curtail
decree *n.* proclamation, edict, declaration, pronouncement, judgment
decrepit *adj.* worn, aged
dedicate *v.* devote, apportion, assign
dedication *n.* sanctification, devotion
deduce *v.* conclude, infer
deduction *n.* **SUBTRACTION:** reduction, decrease, discount; **REASONING:** inference, thought; **CONCLUSION:** answer, judgment
deed *n.* **ACTION:** act, commission, accomplishment; **DOCUMENT:** release, agreement, charter, title

deep *adj.* comprehensive, acute, penetrating, profound

default *n.* failure, neglect, shortcoming, insufficiency

defeat *v.* overcome, conquer, vanquish, subdue, overthrow, crush, overwhelm, repulse, decimate

defect *n.* imperfection, fault, deficiency, flaw

defect *v.* abandon, forsake, desert, leave

defective *adj.* imperfect, poor, inadequate, faulty

defend *v.* **PROTECT:** shield, shelter; **JUSTIFY:** alibi, endorse, support

defender *n.* champion, patron, guardian, protector

defense *n.* **RESISTANCE:** protection, security, backing; **PLEA:** denial, alibi, explanation, justification, proof

defer *v.* postpone, delay, suspend

deference *n.* regard, veneration, homage, reverence

deferent, deferential *adj.* respectful, obedient

defiant *adj.* resistant, obstinate, rebellious

deficient *adj.* lacking, defective, insufficient, skimpy, meager, inadequate,

deficit *n.* shortage, paucity, deficiency, lack

defile *v.* corrupt, debase, ravish, violate, molest

define *v.* **LIMIT:** bound, confine, circumscribe, edge; **DESCRIBE:** designate, characterize, represent, exemplify, explain, name

definite *adj.* **EXACT:** fixed, precise, positive, specific, categorical; **DISTINCT:** unmistakable, sharp, obvious; **POSITIVE:** sure, certain

definition *n.* meaning, terminology, signification, translation, explanation, description

definitive *adj.* conclusive, final, absolute

deform *v.* damage, disfigure, deface
defraud *v.* hoax, dupe, cheat, deceive
deft *adj.* skillful, dexterous
defy *v.* resist, oppose, insult, face, dare
degenerate *adj.* corrupted, depraved
degradation *n.* depravity, corruption, degeneration, evil
degrade *v.* disgrace, debase, discredit, diminish, humble
degree *n.* **MEASURE:** gradation, size, dimension; **RANGE:** extent, quality, potency, proportion, intensity, scope; **DIPLOMA:** baccalaureate, doctorate, sheepskin,
dehydrate *v.* dry, desiccate, parch, drain
deify *v.* exalt, idealize, worship
deity *n.* god, divinity
dejected *adj.* dispirited, depressed, sad
delay *v.* postpone, defer, impede, detain, check, curb, procrastinate, suspend
delectable *adj.* delicious, pleasing, tasty
delegate *n.* legate, emissary, proxy, deputy, consul, minister, ambassador, agent, representative
delegate *v.* authorize, appoint, commission, name, nominate, select, choose, assign, deputize
deliberate *adj.* intentional, conscious, willful, considered, planned, calculated, intended, purposeful, premeditated, designed, unhurried
deliberate *v.* confer, consider, ponder
delicacy *n.* **FINENESS:** daintiness, flimsiness, softness, lightness; **FOOD:** tidbit, morsel
delicate *adj.* **FINE:** dainty, fragile, frail; **SICKLY:** susceptible, feeble, weak
delicious *adj.* tasty, savory, appetizing, delectable
delight *n.* enjoyment, joy, pleasure, happiness

delight *v.* fascinate, amuse, entertain

delightful *adj.* charming, amusing, clever

delinquent *adj.* **LAX:** tardy, negligent, derelict; **OVERDUE:** owed, due, unpaid

deliver *v.* **BRING FORTH:** produce, provide; **FREE:** liberate, save; **TRANSFER:** pass, remit, give; **DISTRIBUTE:** allot, dispense

delude *v.* mislead, deceive

deluge *v.* flood, overwhelm

delusion *n.* phantasm, hallucination, illusion

demand *v.* request, charge, direct, command, ask

demanding *adj.* challenging, difficult, imperious, fussy, exacting, critical

demean *v.* debase, humble

demented *adj.* crazy, bemused, unbalanced, insane

demolish *v.* destroy, wreck, devastate, obliterate

demonstrate *v.* **PROVE:** show, confirm; **ILLUSTRATE:** exhibit, manifest, parade, display

demonstration *n.* **EXHIBITION:** showing, presentation, display; **RALLY:** march, sit–in, protest

demoralize *v.* dishearten, weaken, enfeeble, discourage

demure *adj.* modest, reserved

denial *n.* refusal, repudiation, rejection, refutation

denounce *v.* condemn, accuse, blame, revile, reproach, rebuke, scold, reprimand

dense *adj.* **COMPACT:** thick, solid, impenetrable; **SLOW–WITTED:** stupid, dull, ignorant

deny *v.* contradict, disagree, disavow, disclaim, repudiate, controvert, renounce

depart *v.* leave, go, quit, withdraw

departure *n.* embarkation, evacuation, exodus, exit

dependable *adj.* trustworthy, sure, reliable
depict *v.* represent, picture,
depletion *n.* exhaustion, consumption, deficiency
deport *v.* exile, expel, banish
depreciate *v.* deteriorate, lessen, worsen, decrease
depreciation *n.* harm, shrinkage, loss
depressed *adj.* discouraged, disheartened, sad
deprive *v.* strip, despoil, divest, seize
deputy *n.* assistant, lieutenant, aide, delegate
derelict *adj.* abandoned, negligent, delinquent
derivation *n.* source, beginning, origin
derive *v.* obtain, determine, conclude
derivative *adj.* borrowed, learned
derogatory *adj.* disparaging, belittling, faultfinding, detracting, critical, sarcastic
descend *v.* plunge, sink, dip, plummet, tumble
descent *n.* **INCLINE:** declivity, slide, inclination; **RELATIONSHIP:** extraction, lineage, family; **DROP:** sinking, tumble, decline, fall
describe *v.* recount, portray, depict, illustrate, define, explain
description *n.* portrayal, account, brief, summary, depiction, characterization
desert *v.* abandon, defect, leave
deserter *n.* runaway, fugitive, defector, traitor
deserve *v.* merit, earn, rate
deserved *adj.* justified, merited, rightful, fitting, just
deserving *adj.* needy; rightful, fitting, worthy
design *n.* plan, schematic, rendering, pattern, layout, diagram, drawing, sketch, blueprint, plan

design *v.* invent, devise, sketch, plan
designate *v.* specify, appoint, indicate, name, choose
desire *n.* aspiration, longing, craving, lust, wish, mania, hunger, yearning, hankering, itch, yen, passion
desire *v.* want, wish, covet, crave, need
desist *v.* cease, abstain
desolate *adj.* forsaken, dreary, deserted, uninhabited, abandoned, isolated, disconsolate, forlorn,
despair *n.* hopelessness, depression, discouragement, desperation, gloom
despicable *adj.* detestable, contemptible, abject, base
despise *v.* disdain, scorn, condemn, hate
despondent *adj.* dejected, discouraged, depressed
destiny *n.* fate, future, fortune, doom
destitute *adj.* lacking, impoverished, penniless, poor
destroy *v.* ruin, demolish, raze, eradicate, annihilate
detach *v.* disconnect, separate, divide
detached *adj.* **ALOOF:** disinterested, apathetic, uninvolved, unconcerned, indifferent; **CUT OFF:** separated, loosened, divided, disjoined
detail *n.* particular, aspect, minutia
detail *v.* itemize, catalogue, describe
detain *v.* delay, hold, keep, inhibit, restrain
detect *v.* distinguish, identify, discover
deter *v.* discourage, caution, dissuade, prevent, warn
deteriorate *v.* worsen, depreciate, lessen, degenerate
determine *v.* **DEFINE:** circumscribe, delimit, restrict; **ASCERTAIN:** learn, discover; **RESOLVE:** settle, conclude, decide
detest *v.* dislike, loathe, abhor, despise, hate

detestable *adj.* disgusting, abhorrent, despicable

detract *v.* diminish, lessen, depreciate, discredit

devastation *n.* destruction, waste

develop *v.* **IMPROVE:** enlarge, expand, extend, promote, intensify; **GROW:** mature, evolve; **REVEAL:** unfold, unravel, uncover

deviation *n.* change, alteration, difference, variation

device *n.* **APPARATUS:** contrivance, mechanism, appliance, contraption, implement, utensil; **METHOD:** artifice, scheme, design, dodge, trick, ruse, plan, technique

devious *adj.* deceptive, crafty, indirect, foxy, insidious, shrewd, dishonest

devote *v.* assign, apply, dedicate

devotion *n.* affection, allegiance, consecration, faithfulness, loyalty, worship

devour *v.* eat, gulp, swallow, gorge

devout *adj.* religious, devoted, pious, reverent, faithful, holy

diabolical *adj.* fiendish, wicked

diagnosis *n.* analysis, determination, investigation, summary

dialect *n.* idiom, jargon, cant, vernacular, patois

dialogue *n.* conversation, talk, exchange

diaphanous *adj.* fine, transparent, thin, airy

diary *n.* journal, chronicle, log, record

diatribe *n.* tirade, denunciation

dictator *n.* ruler, autocrat, despot, tyrant, oppressor

diction *n.* enunciation, articulation, vocabulary

die *v.* **EXPIRE:** perish, succumb, croak; **DECLINE:** fade, ebb, wither, weaken

diet *v.* reduce, fast, starve, abstain

differ *v.* vary, diverge, contrast, conflict

difference *n.* **VARIANCE:** deviation, departure, exception; **DISAGREEMENT:** divergence, diversity, departure, differentiation, contrast

different *adj.* **UNLIKE:** assorted, diverse; **UNUSUAL:** strange, unconventional

difficult *adj.* **LABORIOUS:** strenuous, exacting, arduous, demanding, onerous, formidable; **INTRICATE:** involved, perplexing, puzzling, mystifying, bewildering, complicated

difficulty *n.* **OBSTACLE:** obstruction, impediment, hindrance, barrier; **DISTURBANCE:** trouble, distress, frustration, anxiety

diffident *adj.* shy, insecure

diffuse *v.* spread, disperse

digest *v.* **CONDENSE:** summarize, recap; **EAT:** absorb, consume; **UNDERSTAND:** learn, study

dignify *v.* honor, exalt, elevate, praise

dignity *n.* bearing, poise, stateliness, majesty, class, pride

dilemma *n.* predicament, quandary, difficulty

dilettante *n.* dabbler, trifler

diligence *n.* perseverance, industry, vigor, carefulness, intensity, attention, care

diligent *adj.* industrious, painstaking

dilute *v.* thin, weaken, add, mix, reduce

diminish *v.* reduce, lessen, depreciate, decrease

dingy *adj.* drab, dirty, grimy, muddy, soiled

diplomacy *n.* finesse, tact, artfulness, skill, discretion

diplomat *n.* ambassador, consul, minister, legate, emissary, envoy, agent, representative, statesman

diplomatic *adj.* tactful, gracious, calculating, conciliatory, subtle, discreet, politic, polite

dire *adj.* serious, desperate, dreadful, terrible, frightful

direct *adj.* **IMMEDIATE:** prompt, succeeding, resultant; **SINCERE:** frank, straightforward, outspoken, candid; **STRAIGHT:** undeviating, unswerving

direct *v.* **POINT OUT:** guide, conduct, show, lead; **COMMAND:** instruct, order, govern, manage, charge; **AIM:** sight, train, level

direction *n.* **TENDENCY:** bias, bent, proclivity, inclination; **POSITION:** objective, bearing; **SUPERVISION:** management, superintendence, control, administration

directly *adv.* instantly, quickly, immediately

directory *n.* reference, list, register, record, roster

disability *n.* feebleness, incapacity, injury, weakness

disable *v.* incapacitate, cripple, impair

disadvantage *n.* obstacle, restraint, handicap, inconvenience, drawback, weakness

disagree *v.* **DIFFER:** dissent, object, oppose, quarrel; **EFFECT:** nauseate, bother

disagreeable *adj.* obnoxious, offensive, irritable, rude, bothersome, upsetting, disturbing, offensive

disagreement *n.* **DISCORD:** contention, strife, conflict, controversy, opposition, hostility, clash, quarrel; **INCONSISTENCY:** discrepancy, dissimilarity, disparity

disappear *v.* fade, evaporate, vanish

disappearance *n.* departure, desertion, escape, exodus, disintegration, evaporation

disappoint *v.* dissatisfy, disillusion, frustrate, miscarry, thwart, foil, baffle

disapprove *v.* condemn, chastise, reprove, denounce

disarray *n.* confusion, disorder
disaster *n.* calamity, mishap, debacle, misadventure, defeat, failure, tragedy, cataclysm, catastrophe
disburse *v.* pay, expend, use, contribute, spend
discard *v.* reject, expel, dispossess, relinquish
discerning *adj.* discriminating, perceptive, penetrating
discharge *v.* **UNLOAD:** remove, unpack, empty; **RELEASE:** liberate, free, fire
discipline *v.* **TRAIN:** control; **PUNISH:** chastise, correct
disclose *v.* reveal, confess, publish
disclosure *n.* exposé. confession, admission
discomfort *n.* annoyance, uneasiness, trouble, displeasure, embarrassment
disconcert *v.* confuse, embarrass
disconnect *v.* detach, separate, disengage, cut, divide
disconsolate *adj.* dejected, gloomy, inconsolable
discontinue *v.* stop, end, close, cease
discord *n.* conflict, strife, contention, disagreement
discount *v.* **REBATE:** allow, deduct, lower, reduce; **MINIMIZE:** reject, diminish, discredit, decrease
discourage *v.* dissuade, repress, scare, dampen, daunt, demoralize, depress
discourse *v.* converse, write, speak
discourteous *adj.* impolite, rude, boorish, crude
discourtesy *n.* impudence, vulgarity, rudeness
discover *v.* ascertain, detect, recognize, determine, observe, uncover, find, learn
discovery *n.* detection, disclosure, determination
discredit *v.* question, disbelieve, distrust, doubt

discreet *adj.* prudent, cautious, discerning, reserved, watchful, circumspect, politic, diplomatic
discrepancy *n.* variance, inconsistency
discrete *adj.* unconnected, distinctive
discretion *n.* caution, wariness, prudence, tact
discriminate *v.* differentiate, separate, distinguish
discrimination *n.* PERCEPTION: acuteness, judgment; PARTIALITY: bias, bigotry, prejudice
discuss *v.* talk, argue, debate, dispute, confer, reason
discussion *n.* conversation, exchange, contention, dialogue, dispute
disease *n.* sickness, malady, ailment, illness, infirmity
disfavor *n.* disapproval, displeasure, disappointment
disfigure *v.* damage, deface, mar, mutilate
disgrace *v.* dishonor, debase, shame, degrade, discredit, humble, stigmatize
disgraceful *adj.* dishonorable, disreputable, shocking, offensive, shameful
disguise *v.* alter, conceal, cloak, cover, obscure
disgust *v.* offend, repel, revolt, nauseate, sicken, shock, upset
disgusting *adj.* repugnant, revolting, sickening, offensive
disheveled *adj.* untidy, rumpled
dishonest *adj.* deceitful, treacherous, deceptive, sneaky, underhanded, unscrupulous, disreputable, contemptible, false
dishonor *n.* shame, ignominy, abasement, disgrace
disillusion *v.* disenchant, disappoint
disinclined *adj.* hesitant, reluctant
disinfect *v.* sanitize, sterilize, purify, fumigate, clean

disintegrate *v.* crumble, disperse, dissolve
disinterested *adj.* impartial, indifferent, unconcerned
disjointed *adj.* disconnected, unattached, separated; incoherent, rambling
dislike *v.* detest, deplore, abhor, hate, abominate, loathe, despise, scorn
dislodge *v.* eject, evict, uproot, oust, remove
disloyalty *n.* treason, betrayal, dishonesty
dismal *adj.* dreary, bleak, gloomy, melancholy, desolate, morbid, ghastly, gruesome, dusky, cheerless, dingy, murky, bleak, somber
dismantle *v.* disassemble, undo, demolish, level, ruin, raze, fell, destroy
dismay *n.* terror, dread, anxiety, fear
dismiss *v.* reject, repudiate, disperse, expel, abolish, dispossess, exile, expatriate, banish, deport
dismissal *n.* expulsion, removal
disobedience *n.* insubordination, defiance, insurgence, mutiny, revolt, noncompliance, rebellion
disobedient *adj.* insubordinate, refractory, defiant, rebellious, unruly
disobey *v.* balk, decline, refuse, disregard, defy
disorder *n.* confusion, disarray, rebellion, anarchy, turmoil, chaos
disorderly *adj.* **UNRULY:** intemperate, drunk, rowdy; **CONFUSED:** jumbled, scattered, messy, untidy, cluttered, unkempt, disorganized
disorganize *v.* disperse, scatter, disrupt
disorient *v.* confuse, bewilder
disown *v.* disinherit, repudiate, deny
disparage *v.* discredit, belittle
disparate *adj.* dissimilar, diversified

dispatch *v.* **SEND:** transmit, forward; **END:** conclude, kill

dispel *v.* disperse, dissipate, distribute, scatter

dispense *v.* distribute, apportion, assign, allocate

disperse *v.* scatter, separate, disband

displace *v.* **REMOVE:** transpose, dislodge; **MISLAY:** misplace, disarrange, lose

display *n.* exhibition, exhibit, presentation, performance, parade, pageant

display *v.* show, exhibit, uncover, present, unveil

displease *v.* dissatisfy, annoy, vex, provoke

displeasure *n.* disapproval, annoyance, resentment, anger

disposed *adj.* prone, inclined, apt, likely

disposition *n.* **ARRANGEMENT:** distribution, organization, plan; **TEMPERAMENT:** character, temper, mood

disproportionate *adj.* uneven, irregular

disprove *v.* refute, invalidate, deny

disputable *adj.* doubtful, dubious, questionable

dispute *n.* conflict, squabble, disturbance, feud

dispute *v.* argue, debate, contradict, quarrel, discuss

disqualify *v.* preclude, disentitle, disbar

disregard *v.* ignore, neglect

disreputable *adj.* offensive, shameful

disrespect *n.* discourtesy, insolence, irreverence

disrupt *v.* intrude, obstruct, break, interrupt

disruption *n.* disturbance, agitation, confusion

dissatisfaction *n.* displeasure, disapproval, objection

disseminate *v.* scatter, spread, sow, propagate, broadcast, distribute

dissension *n.* disagreement, difference, dispute

dissent *v.* disagree, contradict, differ

disservice *n.* wrong, injury, injustice, insult

dissident *adj.* hostile, opposed

dissipated *adj.* scattered, dispersed, disseminated, strewn, wasted, squandered, spent, depleted

dissolution *n.* dissolving, termination

dissolve *v.* liquefy, evaporate, disintegrate: disappear

distant *adj.* **RESERVED:** aloof; **AFAR:** abroad, removed

distasteful *adj.* unpleasant, disagreeable, repugnant

distend *v.* distort, inflate, stretch, enlarge

distinct *adj.* **PERCEPTIBLE:** clear, sharp, enunciated, audible lucid, plain, obvious, clear, definite; **DISCRETE:** separate, disunited

distinction *n.* **DEFINITION:** separation, difference; **ACHIEVEMENT:** repute, renown, prominence, fame

distinctive *adj.* characteristic unique, peculiar, distinguishing,

distinguish *v.* **DISCERN:** detect, notice, discover; **HONOR:** celebrate, acknowledge, admire, praise

distinguished *n.* **MARKED:** characterized, labeled, identified, unique, conspicuous, separated; **NOTABLE:** celebrated, eminent, illustrious, venerable, renowned, prominent, reputable, famous

distort *v.* alter, pervert, misinterpret, misconstrue

distortion *n.* **DEFORMITY:** malformation, twist, mutilation, contortion; **MISREPRESENTATION:** perversion, lie

distract *v.* detract, amuse, mislead

distracted *adj.* distraught, frenzied, troubled
distraction *n.* CONFUSION: perplexity, abstraction, complication, confusion; DIVERSION: amusement, pastime, preoccupation, entertainment, game
distraught *adj.* troubled, distressed
distress *n.* pain, anxiety, worry, sorrow, wretchedness, suffering, ordeal, anguish, grief, trouble
distress *v.* irritate, disturb, upset, bother
distribute *v.* disburse, dispense, issue, allocate
distributor *n.* wholesaler, jobber, merchant
district *n.* area, neighborhood, community, vicinity
distrust *v.* mistrust, suspect, disbelieve, doubt
distrustful *adj.* doubting, fearful, suspicious
disturb *v.* trouble, worry, perplex, startle, alarm, arouse, depress, distress, provoke, irritate, harass
diverge *v.* radiate, veer, swerve, deviate
divers *adj.* several, varied
diverse *adj.* dissimilar, assorted, different, distinct
diversify *v.* vary, expand, alter, change, increase
diversion *n.* entertainment, recreation, amusement, play, sport
divert *v.* deflect, redirect, avert, turn; distract, disturb
dividend *n.* bonus, profit, share
divine *adj.* godlike, sacred, hallowed, consecrated, anointed, sanctified, ordained, revered, venerated
division *n.* PARTITION: section, compartment, parcel, branch; RIFT: disagreement, difficulty, dispute

divulge *v.* reveal, disclose, impart, confess, expose

do *v.* EXECUTE: complete, fulfill, obey, perform, act, work, labor, produce, create, accomplish, succeed, perform; SUFFICE: serve, satisfy

docile *adj.* submissive, meek, mild, tractable, pliant, willing, obliging, manageable, tame, obedient

doctor *n.* physician, surgeon, intern, veterinarian, chiropractor, homeopath, osteopath, anesthetist, dentist, pediatrician, gynecologist, oculist, obstetrician, psychiatrist, psychoanalyst, orthopedist, neurologist, cardiologist, pathologist, dermatologist, endocrinologist, urologist, hematologist

doctor *v.* treat, attend, administer

doctrine *n.* policy, conviction, tradition, canon

document *n.* record, paper, diary, report

documentary *n.* book, movie, report

dogmatic *adj.* dictatorial, authoritarian, stubborn, intolerant, opinionated, domineering, tyrannical

dolt *n.* simpleton, nitwit, blockhead, fool

domain *n.* territory, dominion, field, specialty, area

domestic *adj.* indigenous, native, homemade

domesticate *v.* control, adapt, tame, breed, teach, train

domicile *n.* residence, home

dominant *adj.* commanding, authoritative, assertive, aggressive, powerful

dominate *v.* control, rule, manage, subjugate, govern

domineering *adj.* overbearing, despotic, imperious, oppressive

dominion *n.* sovereignty, region, district, state, nation

donate *v.* contribute, grant, bestow, bequeath, distribute, give, provide
donation *n.* contribution, offering, present, gift
donor *n.* benefactor, contributor, patron, philanthropist, giver
dote *v.* adore, pet, admire, love
doubt *n.* uncertainty, skepticism, mistrust, suspicion, misgiving, apprehension
doubt *v.* wonder, question
doubtful *adj.* **UNCERTAIN:** dubious, questioning, unsure, wavering, hesitating, unresolved, suspicious; **IMPROBABLE:** questionable, unconvincing
doubtless *adj.* positively, certainly, unquestionably, surely
douse *v.* immerse, wet, submerge, soak
dowdy *adj.* shabby, untidy, slovenly, plain
doze *v.* sleep, nap, drowse, slumber
drab *adj.* dismal, dingy, colorless, dreary, dull
draft *n.* **SKETCH:** layout, plans, blueprint, design; **CURRENT:** breeze, gust, puff, wind; **CONSCRIPTION:** induction
drag *n.* **IMPEDANCE:** restraint, hindrance, burden, impediment, barrier; **TIRESOME:** bother, annoyance, hang–up, nuisance
drag *v.* **PULL:** haul, move, transport, draw; **LAG:** straggle, dawdle, loiter, pause; **SLOW:** crawl, delay
drain *n.* duct, channel, sewer, conduit, pipe
drain *v.* **EXHAUST:** weary, tire, spend, weaken; **EMPTY:** exude, trickle, ooze, flow
drama *n.* play, production, dramatization, show, melodrama, tragicomedy, opera, operetta, mystery
dramatic *adj.* tense, climactic, moving, exciting

dramatist *n.* playwright, author, writer

dramatize *v.* enact, perform, exaggerate

drastic *adj.* extreme, extravagant, exorbitant, radical

draw *v.* **PULL:** drag, attract, lug, tow, haul; **PORTRAY:** sketch, outline, trace, depict

drawback *n.* disadvantage, shortcoming, hindrance

dread *n.* awe, horror, terror, fear

dreadful *adj.* unpleasant, hideous, fearful, shameful, frightful

dreary *adj.* bleak, dismal, dull. damp, raw

dribble *v.* trickle, spout, squirt, drop

drift *n.* tendency, bent, trend, inclination, impulse, bias, leaning, disposition

drift *v.* wander, stray, gravitate, flow

drink *v.* swallow, gulp, sip, guzzle, imbibe

drive *n.* **RIDE:** trip, outing, airing, tour, excursion, jaunt, spin, journey; **PATH:** driveway, approach, boulevard, avenue, road; **FORCE:** energy, effort, enthusiasm, vigor, impulse

drive *v.* urge, impel, propel, compel, coerce, induce, force, press, stimulate, provoke, push

drop *n.* **SMALL AMOUNT:** speck, dash, dab, bit; **DECLINE:** fall, tumble, reduction, decrease, slump, lowering

drowsy *adj.* sleepy, sluggish, languid, indolent, lazy

drug *n.* pills, medicine, sedative, potion, essence, salts, powder, tonic, opiate, downers

drug *v.* anesthetize, desensitize, deaden

drunk *adj.* intoxicated, inebriated, befuddled, tipsy, tanked, soused, pickled, stewed, tight

dry *adj.* **ARID:** parched, desiccated, barren, dehydrated, drained; **BORING:** uninteresting, tedious, dull; **HUMOROUS:** sarcastic, cynical, biting, funny

dry *v.* evaporate, dehydrate, blot, sponge, scorch

dubious *adj.* VAGUE: ambiguous, indefinite, unclear, obscure; DOUBTFUL: indecisive, perplexed, hesitant, uncertain, questionable

due *adj.* SCHEDULED: expected; FITTING: deserved; COLLECTABLE: unsatisfied, unpaid, outstanding

dull *adj.* COLORLESS: gloomy, somber, drab, dismal, dark, dingy, dusky, plain, gray, flat; UNINTELLIGENT: slow, retarded, witless, stupid; UNINTERESTING: prosaic, hackneyed, monotonous, humdrum, tedious, dreary, dismal, insipid, boring, ordinary, uninspiring, tame, routine, repetitious

duly *adv.* properly, rightfully, decorously, justly

dumb *adj.* simple–minded, dull, stupid

dumfound *v.* astonish, shock

dungeon *n.* cell, vault

duplicity *n.* artifice, deceit, deception

durability *n.* stamina, persistence, endurance

durable *adj.* strong, form, enduring, permanent

duration *n.* interval, span, term

duress *n.* threat, coercion, compulsion, control, pressure, restraint

dusk *n.* gloom, twilight, dawn, night

dutiful *adj.* obedient, devoted, respectful, conscientious, faithful

duty *n.* obligation, liability, burden, responsibility

dwell *v.* reside, live, inhabit, stay, lodge, settle, remain, continue, occupy

dweller *n.* inhabitant, tenant, occupant, resident

dwelling *n.* house, establishment, lodging, home

dynamic *adj.* forceful, intense, energetic, compelling, vigorous, electric, effective, influential, charismatic, active, powerful

dynasty *n.* succession, sovereignty

eager *adj.* impatient, anxious, keen, fervent, zealous

early *adj., adv.* primitive; premature, preceding, unexpected

earn *v.* **DESERVE:** win, merit, gain; **PAYMENT:** obtain, attain, get, procure, realize, acquire, secure

earnest *adj.* serious, intense, important, ardent, zealous, warm, enthusiastic

earthly *adj.* human, mortal, mundane

earthy *adj.* coarse, dull, crude, unrefined, natural

ease *n.* **COMFORT:** rest, peace, prosperity, leisure, calm, tranquillity; **EFFORTLESSNESS:** snap, breeze, cinch, pushover

ease *v.* relieve, alleviate, allay, comfort, soothe, unburden, release, soften, calm, pacify

easily *adv.* readily, effortlessly, smoothly

easy *adj.* **UNTROUBLED:** secure, prosperous, leisurely, peaceful, calm, tranquil, contented, carefree, unhurried, relaxing; **MANAGEABLE:** simple, pushover; **LAX:** lenient, indulgent, kind

eat *v.* **DEVOUR:** chew, swallow, feast, dine, gorge, feed; **REDUCE:** erode, corrode, waste, rust, spill

ebb *v.* decline, recede, subside, decrease

ebullient *adj.* exuberant enthusiastic

eccentric *adj.* unconventional, odd, queer, strange, unusual

eccentricity *n.* peculiarity, abnormality, idiosyncrasy

eclipse *v.* darken, diminish, obscure

economic *adj.* financial, commercial

economical *adj.* CAREFUL: thrifty, prudent, frugal, watchful, tight; INEXPENSIVE: cheap, reasonable, fair, moderate; EFFICIENT: practical, methodical

economist *n.* statistician, analyst, expert

economize *v.* husband, manage, stint, conserve, scrimp

ecstasy *n.* joy, rapture, delight, happiness

ecumenical *adj.* general, universal,

edible *adj.* palatable, good, delicious, satisfying, savory, tasty, nutritious, digestible

edict *n.* decree, order

educate *v.* teach, train, inform, tutor, instruct

education *n.* LEARNING: schooling, study, instruction, guidance, apprenticeship, tutelage, indoctrination; KNOWLEDGE: learning, wisdom, scholarship

educational *adj.* enlightening, instructive, enriching, cultural

educator *n.* pedagogue, instructor, tutor, teacher

effect *n.* conclusion, consequence, outcome, result

effect *v.* produce, cause, make, begin

effective *adj.* efficient, serviceable, useful, adequate, productive, competent, practical

effectual *adj.* adequate, efficient, qualified, effective

effervescent *adj.* bubbly, lively, vivacious

efficiency *n.* productivity, capability, ability

efficient *adj.* competent, fitted, able, capable, qualified, skilled, adept, experienced, practical, productive, economical, effective, expedient, streamlined

effort *n.* attempt, undertaking, struggle, try, venture

effortless *adj.* simple, offhand, smooth, easy

effrontery *n.* boldness, insolence

egotism *n.* conceit, vanity, pride, self–love, overconfidence, haughtiness, arrogance

egotistical *adj.* conceited, vain, boastful, pompous, arrogant, insolent, affected, self–centered, blustering, proud, pretentious, overbearing

egregious *adj.* bad, outrageous

eject *v.* discard, reject, oust, evict

elaborate *adj.* **DETAILED:** intricate, complicated, involved, complex; **ORNAMENTED:** gaudy, decorated, showy, fussy, dressy, flowery, flashy, ornate;

elect *v.* choose, name, select

elective *adj.* optional, voluntary, selective

elegance *n.* taste, cultivation, beauty, gracefulness, magnificence, courtliness, charm, polish, sophistication, splendor, style

elegant *adj.* ornate, polished, perfected, elaborate, adorned, embellished, artistic, rich

element *n.* substance, component, portion, particle, detail, part

elementary *adj.* primary, introductory, rudimentary, easy, fundamental, essential, basic

elevate *v.* **RAISE:** lift, hoist, heave, tilt; **PROMOTE:** advance, appoint, further

elevated *adj.* towering, tall, high, raised

eligibility *n.* fitness, acceptability, capability, ability

eligible *adj.* qualified, suitable, fit, usable

eliminate *v.* remove, reject, exclude, disqualify, oust, discard, dismiss, drop

elongate *v.* prolong, lengthen, extend, stretch

eloquence *n.* fluency, wit, wittiness, expressiveness, diction, articulation, delivery

eloquent *adj.* vocal, articulate, outspoken, fluent

else *adj.* different, other, more

elude *v.* evade, escape, dodge, shun, avoid

elusive *adj.* evasive, fleeting, fugitive, intangible, temporary

embargo *n.* restriction, prohibition, impediment, restraint

embarrass *v.* distress, disconcert, chagrin, confound, trouble, disturb, fluster, shame

embarrassment *n.* chagrin, mortification, discomfiture, humiliation, awkwardness

embezzle *v.* thieve, forge, pilfer, steal

embezzlement *n.* fraud, misappropriation, theft

embezzler *n.* fraud, thief, robber, defaulter, criminal

embrace *v.* hug, enfold, squeeze, grip

emerge *v.* rise, arrive, appear, form, evolve

emergency *n.* crisis, predicament, difficulty

emigrant *n.* exile, expatriate, colonist, migrant, pilgrim, refugee

emigrate *v.* migrate, immigrate, quit, leave

emigration *n.* departure, leaving, displacement, exodus, movement, migration, settling

eminence *n.* standing, prominence, distinction, fame

eminent *adj.* renowned, exalted, celebrated, prominent, dignified, distinguished

emissary *n.* intermediary, ambassador, consul, agent

emotion *n.* excitement, sentiment, passion

emotional *adj.* hysterical, demonstrative, ardent, enthusiastic, passionate, excitable, impulsive, impetuous, temperamental, irrational, sentimental, affectionate, neurotic, high–strung

emphatic *adj.* definite, assured, strong, determined, forceful, earnest, positive, dynamic

employ *v.* **USE:** operate, manipulate, apply; **ENGAGE:** contract, procure, hire

employer *n.* owner, manager, proprietor, executive, superintendent, supervisor, businessman

employment *n.* job, profession, vocation, business, trade, work

emulate *v.* imitate, equal, compete, follow

encompass *v.* include, encircle, gird, surround

encounter *n.* **MEETING:** interview, rendezvous, appointment; **VIOLENCE:** conflict, clash, collision, fight

encourage *v.* support, inspire, cheer, praise, fortify, help, aid, reassure, reinforce, back, strengthen

encouraging *adj.* bright, good, promising, hopeful

endeavor *n.* attempt, effort, enterprise, undertaking

endeavor *v.* attempt, aim, try

endorse *v.* **SUPPORT:** approve, sanction, acknowledge; **SIGN:** countersign, underwrite, subscribe, notarize

endorsement *n.* support, sanction, permission

endurable *adj.* tolerable, supportable, bearable

endurance *n.* sufferance, fortitude, tolerance, perseverance, stamina

endure *v.* **CONTINUE:** sustain, prevail, stay, persist; **BEAR UP:** suffer, tolerate, allow, permit, withstand

engross *v.* absorb, busy, fill, occupy

enhance *v.* embellish, magnify, amplify, increase

enigma *n.* problem, riddle, parable, puzzle

enjoy *v.* relish, luxuriate, delight, like

enjoyable *adj.* agreeable, welcome, genial, pleasant
enjoyment *n.* satisfaction, gratification, diversion, entertainment, indulgence
enlighten *v.* inform, divulge, acquaint, teach, tell
enormous *adj.* monstrous, immense, huge, large
enterprise *n.* undertaking, endeavor, affair, business
entertain *v.* **AMUSE:** cheer, delight, beguile, charm, captivate, stimulate, satisfy, distract, indulge; **HOST:** receive, invite, welcome
entertainer *n.* performer, player, artist, actor
entertaining *adj.* diverting, amusing, engaging, enchanting, witty, clever, interesting, stimulating, captivating, absorbing
entertainment *n.* amusement, enjoyment, diversion
enthusiasm *n.* excitement, interest, fervor, ardor, eagerness, zeal
enthusiast *n.* **ZEALOT:** fanatic, fan, believer; **FOLLOWER:** partisan, supporter, participant
enthusiastic *adj.* interested, excited, exhilarated, eager, ardent, spirited, zestful, fervent
entrance *n.* access, entry, passage, approach, admittance, introduction, debut, enrollment
entrance *v.* delight, enchant
envelop *v.* encompass, contain, hide, surround, wrap
envelope *n.* pouch, pocket, wrapper
enviable *adj.* good, superior, excellent
envious *adj.* covetous, resentful, desiring, wishful, greedy, jealous
envy *v.* begrudge, covet, crave
episode *n.* event, happening, occurrence, event

equilibrium *n.* balance, stability
equip *v.* outfit, train, furnish, implement, provide
equipment *n.* tools, implements, utensils, apparatus, devices, tackle, machinery, fittings
equitable *adj.* fair, impartial, just, moral
equity *n.* **FAIRNESS:** impartiality; **ASSETS:** investment, money, property
equivalent *adj.* equal, corresponding, commensurate, comparable, similar
eradicate *v.* destroy, eliminate, exterminate
erase *v.* remove, delete, obliterate, eradicate
erect *adj.* vertical, upright, perpendicular, straight
erect *v.* construct, fabricate, build
erection *n.* building, construction
erratic *adj.* **STRANGE:** eccentric, queer, unusual; **WANDERING:** rambling, roving; **VARIABLE:** deviating, inconsistent, unpredictable, irregular
erroneous *adj.* inaccurate, incorrect, untrue, false
erudite *adj.* scholarly, learned
erupt *v.* eruct, eject, emit, explode
eruption *n.* burst, outburst, flow, upheaval, explosion
escape *n.* flight, retreat, evasion, avoidance
escape *v.* elude, avoid, flee, evade, disappear, vanish
escort *n.* guide, attendant, guard, companion
escort *v.* accompany, attend, date, guard, guide
espouse *v.* marry, advocate, adopt, uphold, support
essay *n.* article, dissertation, thesis, tract, treatise, writing
essence *n.* pith, core, kernel, gist, nature, basis, substance, nucleus, germ

essential *adj.* **BASIC:** fundamental, primary; **NECESSARY:** imperative, required, indispensable

establish *v.* **FOUND:** institute, organize, erect, build; **PROVE:** verify, authenticate, confirm; **SECURE:** fix, stabilize, fasten

establishment *n.* business, organization, company, corporation, enterprise

ethical *adj.* moral, humane, respectable, decent, honest, noble

ethics *n.* morality, mores, decency, integrity, honor

etiquette *n.* conduct, manners, behavior, convention

euphoria *n.* relaxation, health, well-being, happiness

evade *v.* avoid, dodge, shun, elude, baffle, shift, conceal, deceive, veil, hide

evasion *n.* subterfuge, equivocation, trickery

evasive *adj.* vague, fugitive, shifty, sly

event *n.* occasion, incident, happening, occurrence, function, situation, affair, experience

eventful *adj.* momentous, memorable, important

eventual *adj.* inevitable, ultimate, consequent

eventually *adv.* ultimately, finally

evolve *v.* unfold, develop, emerge, grow

exact *adj.* **ACCURATE:** precise, correct, perfect, definite; **CLEAR:** sharp, distinct

exacting *adj.* precise, careful, critical, difficult

exactness *n.* precision, scrupulousness, accuracy

exaggerate *v.* overstate, misrepresent, falsify, magnify, amplify, heighten, distort, stretch, elaborate, color, fabricate

exaggerated *adj.* overwrought, extravagant, melodramatic, distorted, pronounced

exaggeration *n.* misrepresentation, elaboration

examination *n.* **TEST:** review, questionnaire, quiz, exam, midterm; **SCRUTINY:** inspection, analysis, study

examine *v.* **INSPECT:** analyze, scrutinize, explore, probe; **TEST:** question, interrogate

exasperate *v.* annoy, irritate

exceed *v.* excel, outdo

exceedingly *adv.* remarkable, greatly

excel *v.* surpass, transcend, exceed

excellence *n.* superiority, distinction, perfection

excellent *adj.* outstanding, exceptional, first–class, exquisite, choice, select

excess *n.* **ABUNDANCE:** profusion, surplus; **OVERINDULGENCE:** prodigality, dissipation, intemperance, greed, waste

excessive *adj.* immoderate, extravagant, exorbitant, extreme

excitable *adj.* sensitive, high–strung, nervous

excite *v.* provoke, stimulate, inflame, arouse, stir, provoke, incite

excitement *n.* disturbance, tumult, turmoil, stir, agitation, stimulation, commotion, fuss

exclaim *v.* shout, call, yell

exclamation *n.* yell, clamor, cry

exclude *v.* except, reject, ban, bar

exclusion *n.* prohibition, repudiation, expulsion, separation, eviction

execute *v.* perform, act, do, effect

exemplify *v.* illustrate, represent

exempt *adj.* privileged, excused, unrestricted, immune

exemption *n.* exception, immunity, privilege

exhaust *v.* debilitate, tire, weaken, weary; deplete, use

exhaustion *n.* weariness, fatigue, depletion

exhilaration *n.* elation, excitement

exhort *v.* entreat, beg

exist *v.* live, survive, be, endure

existence *n.* being, actuality, presence, reality

exorbitant *adj.* excessive, extravagant, wasteful

exotic *adj.* **FOREIGN:** imported, extrinsic; **PECULIAR:** strange, different, fascinating, unusual

expand *v.* extend, augment, dilate, grow

expanse *n.* extent, reach, space, span, spread, scope, range

expansion *n.* enlargement, augmentation, extension, increase

expect *v.* **ANTICIPATE:** await, hope; **ASSUME:** presume, suppose, suspect; **REQUIRE:** demand, exact

expectancy *n.* hope, prospect, likelihood, anticipation

expectant *adj.* hopeful, awaiting, anticipating, eager

expedient *adj.* convenient, profitable, useful, practical

expedite *v.* speed, quicken

expel *v.* **EJECT:** dislodge, evict; **DISMISS:** suspend, discharge, oust

expenditure *n.* outgo, payment, expense

experience *n.* background, skill, knowledge, practice, maturity, judgment, know–how

experience *v.* undergo, feel, endure

expert *adj.* skillful, practiced, proficient, able

expert *n.* graduate, master, specialist

explain *v.* interpret, elucidate, illustrate, clarify, illuminate, expound, teach, demonstrate, define

explainable *adj.* explicable, accountable, intelligible, understandable

explanation *n.* account, justification, analysis, commentary, brief, breakdown, proof

expletive *n.* exclamation

explicit *adj.* clear, express, sure, plain, definite, understandable

exploit *n.* deed, venture, achievement, escapade

exploit *v.* utilize, employ, use

exploration *n.* investigation, research, search

explore *v.* examine, search, hunt, seek

explorer *n.* adventurer, traveler, pioneer, voyager, mountaineer, seafarer, navigator

explosion *n.* detonation, blast, discharge

explosive *adj.* stormy, fiery, forceful, raging, violent, uncontrollable, frenzied, savage

expose *v.* **UNCOVER:** disclose, reveal, unmask, unfold; **ENDANGER:** imperil

exposition *n.* **MAKING CLEAR:** elucidation, delineation, explication, explanation; **EXHIBITION:** exhibit, showing, performance, display

exposure *n.* disclosure, betrayal, display, publication, unveiling

express *v.* declare, tell, signify, utter

expression *n.* appearance, cast, character, looks, grimace, smile, smirk, mug, sneer, pout, grin

expressive *adj.* eloquent, demonstrative, dramatic, stirring, articulate, stimulating, spirited, lively

expulsion *n.* ejection, suspension, purge, removal

exquisite *adj.* fine, scrupulous, precise, dainty

extemporaneous *adj.* spontaneous, impromptu

extend *v.* enlarge, lengthen, increase, reach, spread, continue

extension *n.* section, branch, addition
extensive *adj.* wide, broad, great
extent *n.* SIZE: span, space, area, expanse, bulk; DEGREE: scope, reach, range, magnitude, intensity
exterior *adj.* outer, outlying, outermost, outside
exterminate *v.* annihilate, eradicate, destroy, abolish
extinction *n.* extermination, destruction
extinguish *v.* smother, choke, quench, stifle, douse
extort *v.* extract, wrench, force, steal
extortion *n.* fraud, blackmail, theft
extra *adj.* additional, other, spare, reserve, supplemental, auxiliary, added, more
extract *v.* evoke, derive, secure, obtain
extract *n.* distillation, infusion, concentration, essence
extraneous *adj.* foreign; incidental
extraordinary *adj.* unusual, remarkable, curious, amazing
extravagance *n.* excess, lavishness, improvidence, waste
extravagant *adj.* lavish, prodigal, immoderate, wasteful
extreme *adj.* outermost, utmost, immoderate, excessive, outrageous, preposterous, exaggerated
extremist *n.* zealot, fanatic, die–hard, radical
exuberance *n.* fervor, eagerness, exhilaration, zeal
exuberant *adj.* ardent, vivacious, passionate, zealous
eye *n.* APPRECIATION: perception, taste, discrimination; CENTER: focus, core, heart, kernel, nub
eyesore *n.* distortion, deformity, ugliness
eyewitness *n.* onlooker, observer

fable *n.* story, allegory, tale, parable

fabric *n.* cloth, textile, stuff, material, goods

fabricate *v.* **PRODUCE:** build, construct, erect, make, form, manufacture, devise; **LIE:** misrepresent, contrive, prevaricate

fabulous *adj.* fictitious, remarkable, amazing, immense, unusual

façade *n.* face, appearance, look, front

face *n.* **VISAGE:**, countenance, appearance, features, profile; **SURFACE:** finish, front; **PRESTIGE:** status, reputation, standing

face *v.* **CONFRONT:** defy, meet, challenge, encounter, endure, suffer, bear; **REFINISH:** front, cover, redecorate, paint

facet *n.* surface, aspect, face, side, plane

facetious *adj.* humorous, whimsical, ridiculous, funny

facile *adj.* easy, simple, obvious, apparent, fluent

facilitate *v.* promote, aid, simplify, help

facility *n.* **EQUIPMENT:** material, tools, plant, buildings; **AGENCY:** department, bureau, company, office

facsimile *n.* copy, duplicate, reproduction, mirror

fact *n.* **CERTAINTY:** truth, actuality, reality, evidence, **EVENT:** action, deed, happening, occurrence, manifestation, experience, act, episode, incident

faction *n.* party, clique, gang, crew, wing, block, lobby, sect, cell

factious *adj.* turbulent, contentious, hostile, opposing

factor *n.* **AGENT:** proxy, representative; **CONSTITUENT:** cause, part, portion, determinant

factory *n.* manufactory, plant, shop, industry, mill, foundry, forge

factual *adj.* exact, specific, descriptive, accurate

faculty *n.* **ABILITY:** aptitude, peculiarity, strength, forte; **TEACHERS:** instructors, mentors, professors, tutors, lecturers, advisers, scholars, fellows

fad *n.* fancy, style, craze, fashion, eccentricity, innovation, vogue, fashion

fade *v.* **PALE:** bleach, blanch, dim, vanish; **DIMINISH:** hush, quiet, sink, decrease

fail *v.* miss, falter, flounder, fizzle, flop, lessen, worsen, sink, decrease

failure *n.* **DEFAULT:** fiasco, bankruptcy, miscarriage, breakdown, stoppage, collapse, downfall, flop, washout; **FLOP:** incompetent, underachiever, dropout, dud

faint *adj.* **FALTERING:** shaky, dizzy, weak, **VAGUE:** thin, hazy, indistinct, dull; **SUBDUED:** low, soft, quiet, muffled, hushed

faint *v.* swoon, drop, collapse, succumb

fair *adj.* **JUST:** forthright, impartial, scrupulous, honest, decent, honorable, reasonable, righteous, evenhanded, principled, trustworthy; **AVERAGE:** ordinary, mediocre, commonplace; **PLEASANT:** clear, sunny, bright, calm, placid, tranquil, favorable, balmy, mild

fair *n.* exposition, carnival, bazaar, festival, market

fairly *adv.* **HONESTLY:** reasonably, honorably, justly; **SOMEWHAT:** moderately, reasonably, adequately

fairy *n.* spirit, sprite, elf, enchantress, nymph, pixy

faith *n.* **TRUST:** confidence, credence, assurance, acceptance, conviction, sureness, reliance; **FORMAL BELIEF:** creed, doctrine, dogma, tenet, revelation, credo, gospel, canon, theology

faithful *adj.* reliable, dependable, incorruptible, scrupulous, firm, sure, unswerving, conscientious, steadfast

fake *adj.* pretended, fraudulent, bogus, false

fake *n.* counterfeit, copy, imitation, fraud, fabrication, forgery; cheat, charlatan

fake *v.* feign, simulate, disguise, pretend

fall *v.* **DROP:** decline, sink, topple, settle, droop, stumble, trip, plunge, descend, totter, recede, ebb, diminish, flop; **SUBMIT:** yield, surrender, succumb, resign, capitulate

fallacy *n.* inconsistency, mistake, ambiguity, paradox, miscalculation, quirk, flaw, heresy, error

fallibility *n.* imperfection, frailty

fallible *adj.* frail, imperfect, erring, unreliable, questionable, wrong

fallow *adj.* dormant, idle, unplowed, unplanted, unproductive, uncultivated

false *adj.* **UNFAITHFUL:** treacherous, disloyal, underhanded, deceitful, unscrupulous, untrustworthy; **SPURIOUS:** fanciful, untruthful, deceptive, fallacious, misleading, erroneous, inaccurate, fraudulent; **COUNTERFEIT:** fabricated, bogus, forged, faked, contrived, phony

falsehood *n.* deception, distortion, prevarication, story, lie, fabrication

falsify *v.* misrepresent, adulterate, counterfeit, deceive, lie, forge

falter *v.* waver, fluctuate, hesitate, vacillate, stumble

fame *n.* renown, glory, distinction, eminence, esteem, name, note, greatness, rank, position, standing, pre–eminence, regard, popularity

familiar *adj.* everyday, customary, accustomed, common, ordinary, informal, commonplace

familiarity *n.* friendliness, acquaintanceship, fellowship, friendship; comprehension, awareness

familiarize *v.* acquaint, accustom

family *n.* household, relatives, clan, relations, tribe, dynasty, descendants, forbears, heirs, genealogy, descent, parentage, extraction, kinship, lineage

famine *n.* starvation, want, misery, hunger

famished *a.* starving, hungering, starved, hungry

famous *adj.* known, renowned, eminent, foremost, famed, celebrated, noted, prominent, reputable, renowned, notable, notorious

fan *n.* supporter, follower, amateur, devotee

fanatical *adj.* enthusiastic, obsessed, passionate, devoted, zealous

fanciful *adj.* unreal, incredible, whimsical, fantastic

fancy *adj.* elaborate, ornamental, intricate, elegant, embellished, rich, adorned, ostentatious, gaudy, showy, baroque, lavish, ornate

fancy *n.* **WHIMSY:** imagination, caprice, levity, humor; **WHIM:** notion, impulse, idea; **INCLINATION:** wishes, will, preference, desire

fantastic *adj.* fanciful, whimsical, capricious, strange, odd, queer, quaint, peculiar, outlandish, wonderful, exotic, ludicrous, ridiculous, preposterous, grotesque, absurd

fantasy *n.* illusion, flight, figment, fiction

far *adj.* distant, faraway, remote

farce *n.* satire, travesty, burlesque

fare *n.* FOOD: menu, rations, meals; FEE: charge, passage, passage, tariff, expense

fare *v.* experience, prosper, happen

farewell *n.* good–bye, valediction, parting, departure

farfetched *adj.* unbelievable, strained, fantastic

farm *v.* cultivate, till, garden, ranch, homestead

farmer *n.* planter, grower, stockman, agriculturist, rancher, homesteader, peasant, peon, herdsman, plowman, sharecropper, gardener, horticulturist

farsighted *adj.* aware, perceptive, sagacious

farthest *adj.* remotest, ultimate, last, furthest

fascinate *v.* charm, captivate, entrance, enchant, bewitch, enrapture, delight, please, attract, lure, seduce, entice, intoxicate, tantalize

fascination *n.* charm, enchantment, attraction

fashion *n.* manner, custom, convention, vogue, mode, usage, observance, style, craze

fashion *v.* make, model, shape, form, create, mold, adapt

fashionable *adj.* smart, stylish, chic

fast *adj.* RAPID: swift, fleet, quick, speedy, brisk, accelerated, hasty, nimble; FIXED: attached, immovable, firm

fasten *v.* lock, fix, tie, lace, close, bind, tighten, attach, secure, anchor, grip, clasp, clamp, pin, nail, tack, bolt, rivet, set, weld, cement, glue

fat *adj.* portly, stout, obese, corpulent, fleshy, plump, bulky, heavy

fatal *adj.* mortal, lethal, deadly

fatality *n.* casualty, death

fate *n.* destiny, fortune, luck, doom

fated *adj.* lost, destined, elected, doomed

fateful *adj.* **FATAL:** deadly, destructive, ruinous, lethal; **MOMENTOUS:** portentous, critical, decisive, crucial

father *n.* **PARENT:** sire, progenitor, procreator, forebear, ancestor; **ORIGINATOR:** founder, inventor, promoter, author; **PRIEST:** pastor, ecclesiastic, parson

fatigue *n.* weariness, exhaustion, lassitude

fatten *v.* feed, stuff, plump, cram, fill

fault *n.* **DELINQUENCY:** wrongdoing, transgression, crime, impropriety, misconduct, failing; **ERROR:** defect, blunder, mistake, misdeed; **RESPONSIBILITY:** liability, accountability, blame

favor *v.* indulge, prefer, pick, choose, value, prize, esteem

favorable *adj.* well–disposed, kind, well–intentioned, propitious, beneficial

favorite *adj.* beloved, favored, preferred, adored

favorite *n.* darling, pet

favoritism *n.* bias, partiality, inequity, inclination

faze *v.* discourage, bother, intimidate, worry, disturb

fear *n.* dread, fright, dismay, awe, anxiety, foreboding, concern, alarm

fearful *adj.* timid, shy, apprehensive, cowardly

fearless *adj.* bold, daring, courageous, dashing, brave

feasible *adj.* expedient, worthwhile, convenient, practicable, possible, attainable

feast *n.* banquet, entertainment, festival, fiesta, barbecue, picnic, dinner

feast *v.* eat, entertain

feat *n.* deed, act, effort, achievement

feature *n.* **ATTRACTION:** highlight, specialty; **CHARACTERISTIC:** quality, peculiarity, property; **ARTICLE:** column, commentary, editorial, story

federation *n.* confederacy, affiliation, alliance

fee *n.* price, remuneration, salary, charge, honorarium

feeble *adj.* weak, faint, fragile, puny

feeble-minded *adj.* foolish, retarded, senile, dull

feed *n.* fodder, provisions, pasture, forage

feed *v.* feast, nourish, dine, fatten, cater, serve

feel *v.* **TOUCH:** caress, fondle, paw, grasp; **EXPERIENCE:** sense, perceive; **BELIEVE:** consider, hold, think

feeling *n.* **SENSATION:** sensibility, sensitiveness, perception, receptivity, responsiveness, awareness, enjoyment, sensuality, pain, pleasure, reflex; **REACTION:** opinion, thought, outlook, attitude; **SENSITIVITY:** taste, tenderness, discernment, refinement, culture, faculty, judgment

feign *v.* pretend, dissemble, imagine, fabricate

fellow *n.* **YOUTH:** chap, lad, boy, stripling, apprentice, adolescent, juvenile, youngster, kid; **ASSOCIATE:** member, peer, colleague, friend

fellowship *n.* **COMRADESHIP:** conviviality, sociability, intimacy, friendliness, affability, camaraderie; **PAYMENT:** stipend, scholarship, honorarium, subsidy

felon *n.* criminal, outlaw, delinquent, convict

felony *n.* crime, misconduct, offense, transgression

feminine *adj.* soft, delicate, gentle, ladylike, matronly, maidenly, tender, womanly

fence *n.* hedge, divider, barrier, backstop, railing, barricade, barrier

ferment *v.* effervesce, foam, froth, bubble, seethe, fizz, work, ripen, rise

ferocious *adj.* savage, fierce, wild

ferocity *n.* fierceness, brutality, barbarity, cruelty

ferry *n.* ferryboat, barge, packet

ferry *v.* carry, convey

fertile *adj.* productive, inventive, fruitful, rich, productive, fat, teeming, yielding, arable, flowering

fertility *n.* fruitfulness, virility, productiveness

fertilization *n.* impregnation, pollination, breeding, propagation, procreation

fervent *adj.* zealous, eager, ardent, enthusiastic

fervor *n.* ardor, enthusiasm, zeal

festival *n.* celebration, festivity, feast

festive *adj.* gay, merry, joyful, happy

festivity *n.* revelry, amusement, entertainment

fetch *v.* get, retrieve, carry

fetish *n.* fixation, craze, mania, obsession

fetter *n.* shackle, restraint

fetus *n.* embryo, organism, child

feud *n.* quarrel, strife, bickering, fight

feverish *adj.* burning, hot

few *adj.* sparse, scanty, scattering, inconsiderable

fib *n.* prevarication, fabrication, misrepresentation, lie

fiber *n.* thread, filament, cord, string, strand

fibrous *adj.* veined, hairy, coarse, stringy

fickle *adj.* inconstant, capricious, whimsical, mercurial, changing

fiction *n.* novel, tale, romance, story, fabrication, myth

fictitious *adj.* imaginary, made-up, untrue, false

fidelity *n.* faithfulness, fealty, loyalty, devotion

fidget *v.* stir, twitch, worry, wiggle

field *n.* pasture, meadow, acreage, plot, patch, garden, grassland, tract

fiend *n.* **MONSTER:** barbarian, brute, beast, devil; **ADDICT:** fan, aficionado, monomaniac

fierce *n.* ferocious, savage, wild, untamed, brutal, monstrous, vicious, dangerous, violent, threatening

fiery *adj.* impetuous, hotheaded

fight *n.* **CONFLICT:** struggle, battle, strife, contention, quarrel, dispute, confrontation, brawl, fracas, altercation, bickering, wrangling, argument, conflict, clash, scuffle, engagement; **METTLE:** hardihood, boldness, courage

fight *v.* conflict, battle, oppose, grapple

figurative *adj.* metaphorical, allegorical, illustrative

figure *n.* **FORM:** design, statue, shape, structure; **TORSO:** body, frame, development, build, posture, attitude, pose, carriage; **SUM:** total, number; **PRICE:** value, worth

figure *v.* **COMPUTE:** calculate, reckon, number, count; **CONCLUDE:** suppose, think, opine, decide

file *v.* **SMOOTH:** abrade, rasp, scrape, finish; **ARRANGE:** classify, index, categorize, catalogue, register, list

fill *v.* pack, stuff, charge, inflate

filter *v.* strain, purify, sieve, refine, clarify, separate

filth *n.* dirt, contamination, pollution, muck, slop, squalor, grime, garbage, sludge

filthy *adj.* dirty, foul, squalid, corrupt

final *adj.* last, terminal, concluding, ultimate, decisive

finance *n.* business, commerce, economics

finances *n.* resources, money, capital, funds, wealth

financial *adj.* economic, business, monetary, commercial

financier *n.* capitalist, banker, merchant, executive

find *v.* discover, detect, notice, perceive, discern, uncover, expose

finding *n.* verdict, decision, sentence, judgment

fine *adj.* **EXACT:** precise, accurate, definite; **SMALL:** thin, subtle; **LIGHT:** powdery, granular

fine *n.* punishment, penalty, damage, forfeit

fine *v.* penalize, exact, tax, levy, punish

finish *v.* **END:** perfect, achieve; **POLISH:** wax, stain, cover, paint; **COMPLETE:** cease, close, end, stop

fire *n.* burning, flame, blaze, embers, sparks, glow, warmth, combustion, conflagration

fire *v.* **INFLAME:** kindle, enkindle, ignite, light, burn, rekindle, relight, animate; **DISCHARGE:** shoot, set, off, hurl; **DISMISS:** discharge, eject

firm *adj.* **FIXED:** stable, solid, rooted, immovable, fastened, motionless, secured; **HARD:** solid, dense, compact, impenetrable, impervious, rigid, hardened, inflexible, unyielding; **SETTLED:** determined, steadfast, resolute, constant

firmament *n.* sky, heavens

first *adj.* beginning, original, primary, prime, initial, earliest, introductory

first-rate *adj.* prime, choice, excellent, superior, select, exceptional, best

fishy *adj.* improbable, dubious, implausible, unlikely

fit *adj.* **APPROPRIATE:** advantageous, suitable, proper, practicable, beneficial, desirable; **HEALTHY:** trim, competent, robust

fit *n.* **ADJUSTMENT:** adaptation; **CONVULSION:** attack, rage, spasm, seizure, stroke, paroxysm; **TANTRUM:** burst, rush, outburst, huff, rage, spell

fit *v.* **ADAPT:** arrange, alter, adjust; **CONFORM:** qualify, relate, belong, match, correspond

fitting *n.* connection, component, constituent

fixture *n.* equipment, convenience, appliance, machine, device

fizzle *n.* disappointment, fiasco, defeat, failure

flabby *adj.* soft, yielding, limp, tender, fat

flag *n.* banner, standard, colors, emblem

flagrant *adj.* obvious, notorious, disgraceful, infamous, outrageous

flair *n.* talent, aptitude, gift, ability

flamboyant *adj.* bombastic, ostentatious, ornate

flame *n.* blaze, flare, flash, fire

flame *v.* burn, blaze, oxidize

flange *n.* edge, rim, projection

flap *n.* fold, tab, cover, appendage, tag

flap *v.* flutter, flash, swing, wave

flare *v.* blaze, glow, burn, flash

flash *v.* gleam, glimmer, sparkle, glitter, glisten, glare, shine, glow, twinkle, reflect, radiate, flicker

flashy *adj.* gaudy, showy, ostentatious, ornate

flask *n.* bottle, decanter, jug, canteen

flat *adj.* **LEVEL:** even, smooth, extended, prostrate, horizontal, prone; **TASTELESS:** unseasoned, insipid, flavorless

flatter *v.* adulate, glorify, praise

flattery *adj.* adulation, compliments, praise, tribute, fawning, blarney
flaunt *v.* display, vaunt, brandish, boast
flavor *n.* taste, tang, relish
flavor *v.* season, salt, pepper, spice
flavoring *n.* essence, extract, seasoning, additive
flaw *n.* defect, imperfection, stain, blemish, break, breach
flaw *v.* mar, crack
fleck *n.* spot, mite, dot, bit
flee *v.* run, desert, depart, abscond, escape, retreat
fleet *adj.* swift, transient
flexibility *n.* pliancy, suppleness, elasticity, litheness
flexible *adj.* limber, lithe, supple, elastic, malleable, pliable, tractable
flicker *v.* sparkle, twinkle, glitter, flash, shine
flight *n.* **ESCAPE:** fleeing, retreat; **STEPS:** stairs, staircase, ascent; **SOARING:** flying, aviation, aeronautics, gliding
flighty *adj.* capricious, fickle, whimsical, changing
flimsy *adj.* thin; weak; slight, infirm, frail, insubstantial, fragile, decrepit
flinch *v.* wince, start, cringe
fling *n.* escapade, indulgence, party, celebration
fling *v.* hurl, toss, sling, throw
flippant *adj.* pert, frivolous, impudent, saucy, rude
flirt *n.* coquette, tease, siren
flirt *v.* trifle, tease, seduce
float *v.* waft, drift
flock *n.* congregation, group, pack, litter, herd, gaggle, company, crowd
flock *v.* gather, throng, congregate, crowd
flog *v.* beat, lash

flood *v.* inundate, swamp, overflow, deluge, submerge, immerse

floor *n.* **DECK:** tiles, planking, carpet, rug, linoleum; **LEVEL:** story, landing, basement, mezzanine, downstairs, upstairs, loft, attic, garret, penthouse

flop *v.* **FALL:** tumble, slump, drop; **FAIL:** miscarry, founder, bomb

flounder *v.* struggle, wallow, blunder

flourish *v.* **THRIVE:** increase, wax, succeed, adorn; **BRANDISH:** wave

flout *v.* sneer, disregard

flow *n.* current, tide, movement, progress

flow *v.* stream, course, move, run, rush, whirl, surge, spurt, squirt, gush, trickle, spew

flower *n.* spray, cluster, shoot, posy, herb, vine, annual, perennial, plant

flower *v.* bloom, open, blossom, blow

flowery *adj.* elaborate, ornamented, rococo, ornate

fluctuate *v.* waver, vacillate, falter, hesitate

fluctuation, *n.* variation, inconstancy, change

fluent *adj.* eloquent, glib, smooth, verbose, chatty, articulate, persuasive, silver–tongued

fluid *adj.* flowing, liquid, watery, molten, liquefied

fluid *n.* liquid, liquor, solution

flunk *v.* fail, miss, drop

fluster *v.* disconcert, confuse

flutter *v.* flap, ripple, wiggle, wave

flutter *n.* agitation, motion

fly *v.* **FLEE:** escape, retreat, withdraw; **SOAR:** float, glide, hover, swoop, drift, circle; **RUSH:** dart, speed

foam *n.* froth, fluff, bubbles, lather

focus *v.* **ATTRACT:** converge, convene, center; **CLEAR:** adjust, detail, sharpen
foe *n.* enemy, opponent, antagonist, adversary
fog *n.* mist, haze, cloud, film, steam, wisp, smoke, soup, smog
foggy *adj.* dull, misty, gray, hazy
foible *n.* failing, weakness
fold *v.* **DOUBLE:** crease, crimp, ruffle, pucker, gather, lap, overlap, overlay; **FAIL:** bankrupt, close
folder *n.* circular, pamphlet, paper, bulletin, advertisement, brochure, throwaway
foliage *n.* leaves, greenery
folk *n.* people, race, nation, community, tribe, society, population, clan
folklore *n.* custom, superstition, tradition, tales, legend, folkways, myth
folks *n.* family, kin, relatives, relations
follow *v.* **COME AFTER:** ensue, postdate, succeed; **IMITATE:** conform, copy, mirror, reflect, mimic; **OBSERVE:** heed, regard, watch, comply; **UNDERSTAND:** comprehend, catch, realize; **RESULT:** happen, ensue
follower *n.* disciple, pupil, protégé, supporter, backer, devotee, believer, admirer
following *adj.* subsequent, succeeding, next, ensuing
following *n.* clientele, audience, adherents, supporters, patrons
foment *v.* encourage, incite
fond *adj.* loving, enamored, attached, affectionate
food *n.* victuals, foodstuffs, nutriment, refreshment, edibles, comestibles, provisions, sustenance, rations, board, cuisine, nourishment

fool *n.* nitwit, simpleton, dunce, oaf, ninny, nincompoop, dolt, buffoon, blockhead, clown

fool *v.* deceive, trick, dupe, mislead

foolish *adj.* silly, simple, frivolous

foothold *n.* ledge, footing, niche, step

forbear *v.* abstain, stop

forbearance *n.* patience, clemency

forbid *v.* prohibit, debar, restrain, inhibit, preclude, oppose, obstruct, bar, prevent, outlaw, disallow, ban

forbidding *adj.* unpleasant, offensive, repulsive, grim

force *n.* **STRENGTH:** energy, power, might; **DOMINANCE:** competency, energy, willpower, drive, determination, authority; **ORGANIZATION:** group, band, unit

force *v.* compel, coerce, press, drive, make, impel, oblige, require, demand, command, impose, exact

forceful *adj.* commanding, dominant, powerful, dynamic, intense

forebode *v.* apprehend, foretell

foreboding *n.* premonition, dread, presentiment, anticipation, apprehension

forecast *n.* prognosis, divination, foresight, prophecy

forecast *v.* predict, predetermine, foretell, foresee, anticipate

forefather *n.* ancestor, progenitor, forebear, father, parent, sire, forerunner, predecessor, originator, precursor, procreator, patriarch, founder, kinsman

foregoing *n.* prior, former, previous, preceding

foreign *adj.* alien, remote, exotic, strange, distant, different, alien, imported, borrowed, abroad

foreigner *n.* stranger, immigrant, newcomer, alien

foreman *n.* overseer, manager, supervisor, superintendent, boss
foremost *adj.* original, primary, first
forerunner *n.* herald, harbinger, precursor, sign
foresee *v.* prophesy, predict, foretell
foresight *n.* carefulness, husbandry, prudence
forestall *v.* thwart, prevent, preclude, hinder
foretell *v.* prophesy, predict, divine, foresee, forebode, augur, portend, foreshadow
forethought *n.* provision, planning, foresight
forever *adv.* always, everlastingly, perpetually, eternally, endlessly, forevermore
forewarn *v.* admonish, alarm, warm
forfeit *v.* lose, sacrifice, relinquish, abandon
forge *v.* counterfeit, falsify, fabricate, feign, imitate, copy, duplicate, reproduce
forgery *n.* imitation, copy, counterfeit, fake
forget *v.* neglect, overlook, ignore, slight, disregard, skip, exclude
forgetful *adj.* inattentive, neglectful, heedless, careless, distracted
forgive *v.* absolve, acquit, pardon, overlook, excuse, exonerate
forgiveness *n.* absolution, pardon, acquittal, exoneration, dispensation, reprieve, amnesty, respite
forgo *v.* quit, relinquish, waive, abandon
fork *v.* branch, divide
form *n.* **SHAPE:** figure, appearance, configuration, arrangement, formation, structure, contour, profile, silhouette; **CEREMONY:** manner, mode, custom, method; **PATTERN:** model, die, mold; **DOCUMENT:** chart, questionnaire, application

form *v.* SHAPE: mold, model, make, fashion, construct, devise, design, produce, build, create; INSTRUCT: rear, breed, teach; DEVELOP: accumulate, harden, set, rise, appear, grow, mature, materialize

formal *adj.* REGULAR: orderly, precise, set; POLITE: reserved, conventional, stiff

formality *n.* decorum, etiquette, correctness, behavior

format *n.* arrangement, construction, form

formation *n.* form, structure, arrangement, composition, development, fabrication, generation, creation, genesis, constitution

former *adj.* earlier, previous, foregoing, preceding

formerly *adj.* before, once, previously, earlier

formula *n.* equation, recipe, directions

formulate *v.* systematize, express, form

forsake *v.* desert, abandon, leave, quit

fort *n.* fortress, stronghold, citadel, acropolis, redoubt

fortification *n.* stronghold, fort, fortress, defense, barricade, battlement, stockade, bastion, bulwark

fortify *v.* strengthen, barricade, entrench, buttress

fortitude *n.* strength, firmness, valor, fearlessness, determination

fortress *n.* stronghold, fort

fortune *n.* CHANCE: luck, fate, uncertainty; WEALTH: riches, possessions, inheritance, estate

fortunate *adj.* lucky, favorable

forward *adj.* bold, presumptuous, impertinent, fresh

fossil *n.* remains, specimen, skeleton, relic

foster *v.* nurse, raise, cherish, nourish, encourage

foul *adj.* **FILTHY:** impure, disgusting, nasty, vulgar, coarse, offensive; **UNFAIR:** inequitable, unjust

found *v.* institute, establish, endow

foundation *n.* **BASIS:** reason, justification, authority; **BASE:** footing, pier, groundwork, bed, substructure, underpinning; **INSTITUTION:** organization, endowment, institute, society, charity

founder *n.* originator, patron

foxy *adj.* sly, crafty, cunning, artful

fraction *n.* fragment, section, portion, part, division

fractious *adj.* cross, irritable

fracture *n.* rupture, shattering, breach, dislocation, shearing, separating

fracture *v.* break, crack

fragile *adj.* frail, brittle, delicate, dainty, weak

fragment *n.* piece, scrap, remnant, bit

fragrance *n.* perfume, aroma, smell

fragrant *adj.* aromatic, sweet, perfumed

frail *adj.* fragile, feeble, breakable, tender, dainty

frame *n.* **SKELETON:** framework, scaffolding, support; **BORDER:** margin, fringe, hem, trim, outline

frame *v.* **MAKE:** construct, erect, raise, build; **SURROUND:** encircle, confine, enclose

franchise *n.* right, privilege

frank *adj.* candid, open, sincere, direct, ingenuous, forthright, outspoken, straightforward, blunt

frantic *adj.* excited, distracted, frenetic, frenzied

fraternity *n.* society, brotherhood, fellowship

fraud *n.* **DECEIT:** trickery, duplicity, guile, deception; **TRICKSTER:** impostor, pretender, charlatan, cheat

fraudulent *adj.* dishonest, deceitful, tricky

freak *n.* monstrosity, rarity, malformation, oddity, aberration, curiosity

free *adj.* **SOVEREIGN:** independent, autonomous, democratic, liberated; **UNIMPEDED:** unobstructed, unconstrained, loose, unhampered; **GRATIS:** gratuitous, complimentary

free *v.* release, discharge, rescue, extricate, undo, acquit, dismiss, pardon, redeem, disentangle

freedom *n.* **LIBERTY:** independence, sovereignty, autonomy; **EXEMPTION:** privilege, immunity, license, indulgence, latitude

freeway *n.* turnpike, highway, road, thoroughfare

freeze *v.* **SOLIDIFY:** congeal, harden; **CONTROL:** seal, terminate, immobilize

freight *n.* **CARGO:** load, encumbrance, consignment, goods, tonnage

frenzy *n.* excitement, rage, craze, furor, insanity

frequency *n.* repetition, recurrence, reiteration, regularity

frequent *adj.* **OFTEN:** habitual, customary, intermittent, periodic, commonplace; **REGULAR:** repeated, recurrent, incessant, continual

frequent *v.* visit, attend

fresh *adj.* **NEW:** green, recent, current, late, untried; **UNSPOILED:** uncontaminated, preserved; **COLORFUL:** vivid, bright; **POTABLE:** drinkable, cool, clear, pure, clean, sweet, safe; **REFRESHED:** rested, restored, relaxed, reinvigorated, revived;

INEXPERIENCED: untrained, untried, unskilled

fret *v.* worry, irritate, agitate, vex, bother

friction *n.* **RUBBING:** attrition, abrasion, erosion, grinding; **ANTAGONISM:** trouble, animosity, quarrel, discontent, hatred

friend *n.* schoolmate, playmate, roommate, companion, intimate, confidant, comrade, fellow, pal, chum, crony, buddy

friendly *adj.* kindly, amiable, neighborly, sociable, civil, affectionate, attentive, agreeable, accommodating, pleasant, cordial, congenial

fright *n.* fear, panic, terror, dread, horror

frighten *v.* terrify, scare, intimidate, threaten, badger, petrify, terrorize

frightful *adj.* **FEARFUL:** awful, dreadful, terrible; **UNPLEASANT:** calamitous, shocking, offensive

frill *n.* ruffle, frivolity, ornamentation

frisky *adj.* spirited, dashing, playful, active

frivolous *adj.* unimportant, slight, trifling, superficial, petty, trivial

frock *n.* dress, garment

frontier *n.* boundary, wilderness, hinterland

frosting *n.* covering, coating, icing

frosty *adj.* frigid, freezing, chilly, cold

froth *n.* foam, bubbles, fizz, effervescence, lather

frown *v.* scowl, grimace, pout, glare, sulk, glower

frugal *adj.* thrifty, economical, sparing, saving, parsimonious, careful

fruitful *adj.* prolific, productive, fecund, fertile

fruitless *adj.* vain, unprofitable, empty, futile

frustrate *v.* defeat, thwart, foil, balk, prevent

frustration *n.* disappointment, impediment, failure

fry *v.* sauté, sear, singe, brown, pan–fry

fuel *n.* coal, gas, oil, charcoal, propane, peat, firewood, kindling, gasoline, kerosene

fugitive *adj.* fleeting, passing

fugitive *n.* outlaw, runaway, exile, outcast

fulfill *v.* complete, accomplish, achieve, effect

full *adj.* **SATURATED:** crammed, packed, jammed, stuffed, glutted, gorged, loaded; **ABUNDANT:** copious, ample, plentiful, sufficient, adequate, lavish, extravagant, profuse

fumble *v.* mishandle, bungle, mismanage, botch

fun *n.* amusement, relaxation, diversion, entertainment, pleasure, celebration, holiday, enjoyment

function *n.* duty, employment, capacity, use; action, event, party

function *v.* perform, run, work, operate

functional *adj.* utilitarian, practical

fund *n.* money, capital, endowment, gift

fundamental *adj.* basic, underlying, primary, rudimentary, elemental, structural, original

funds *n.* capital, wealth, cash, collateral, money, assets, currency, savings, revenue, stocks, property, bonds, means, affluence, belongings, resources, securities, profits

funeral *n.* interment, burial, entombment, requiem

funny *adj.* **COMIC:** laughable, comical, whimsical, amusing, entertaining, diverting, humorous, witty, jocular, droll; **SUSPICIOUS:** curious, unusual, odd

fur *n.* pelt, hide, hair, coat, brush
furbish *v.* polish, spruce, renovate
furious *adj.* raging, enraged, fierce, angry
furnace *n.* heater, boiler, kiln, forge
furnish *v.* supply, equip, stock, provide
furor *n.* tumult, excitement, stir, disturbance
further *adj.* additional, more, distant
further *v.* promote, advance
fury *n.* rage, anger, wrath
fuse *v.* meld, blend
fuss *n.* quarrel, complaint, bother, disturbance, stir
fuss *v.* wrangle, whine, whimper, object, complain
fussy *adj.* fastidious, particular, meticulous, careful
futile *adj.* useless, vain, fruitless, hopeless, purposeless, ineffective, ineffectual, unproductive, empty, hollow
future *adj.* impending, imminent, destined, fated, prospective, expected, approaching, ultimate
fuzz *n.* nap, fluff, fur, hair

gab *vi.* talk, chatter, gossip, jabber, babble
gabble *v.* jabber, cackle
gadget *n.* device, contrivance, object, contraption
gag *v.* **RETCH:** sicken, choke, vomit; **MUZZLE:** muffle, silence, stifle, throttle
gaiety *n.* merriment, jollity, mirth, exhilaration
gain *n.* profit, increase, accrual, accumulation
gain *v.* **INCREASE:** augment, expand, enlarge, grow; **ADVANCE:** progress, overtake; **ACHIEVE:** attain, realize, reach, succeed
gait *n.* walk, step, stride, pace, carriage, movement
gale *n.* wind, hurricane, blow, typhoon, storm

gallant *adj.* noble, brave, courageous, courteous, intrepid

gallantry *n.* heroism, valor, bravery, courage

gallery *n.* **ONLOOKERS:** spectators, audience, public; **MUSEUM:** salon, studio, hall, showroom

gallop *v.* leap, run, spring, bound, hurdle, swing, stride, lope, amble, trot

gamble *v.* bet, wager, plunge, speculate, risk, chance

gambol *v.* leap, play

game *adj.* spirited, hardy, resolute, brave

game *n.* **MEAT:** fish, fowl, quarry, wildlife; **ENTERTAINMENT:** play, sport, recreation;

gang *n.* band, group, horde, troop

gangster *n.* criminal, gunman, racketeer

gap *n.* **BREACH:** cleft, rift, hole; **BREAK:** hiatus, recess, lull, pause; **PASS:** chasm, hollow, ravine, gorge, canyon, gully, gulch

garbage *n.* refuse, trash, waste

garden *n.* patch, field, plot, bed, terrace, oasis

garish *adj.* showy, gaudy, ostentatious, ornate

garment *n.* dress, attire, apparel, clothes

garnish *v.* adorn, decorate, embellish, beautify, deck

gaseous *adj.* vaporous, effervescent, aeriform, light

gash *n.* wound, slash, slice, cut

gasp *v.* gulp, pant, puff, wheeze, blow, snort

gate *n.* entrance, ingress, passage, barrier, doorway

gather *v.* **COLLECT:** aggregate, amass, accumulate, assemble, garner; **INFER:** conclude, deduce, assume, learn, understand; **ASSEMBLE:** meet, congregate, flock, convene, collect, reunite, converge, concentrate

gathering *n.* assembly, meeting, conclave, caucus, parley, council, conference, congregation, convention, rally, throng, huddle, turnout, meet

gaudy *a.* showy, flashy, tawdry, ornate

gauge *v.* measure, check, weigh, calibrate, calculate

gaunt *adj.* thin, lean, haggard, emaciated, scraggy

gauze *n.* fabric, veil, bandage, dressing

gawk *v.* stare, ogle, gaze, look

gay *adj.* lively, showy, merry, cheerful, vivacious

gaze *v.* stare, watch, gape, look

gazette *n.* journal, newspaper

gear *n.* **COG:** pinion, sprocket; **BELONGINGS:** equipment, material, tackle

gem *n.* stone, jewel, bauble, ornament

genealogy *n.* derivation, lineage, extraction, family

general *adj.* **COMMON:** usual, customary, prevailing; **INDEFINITE:** uncertain, imprecise; **COMPREHENSIVE:** extensive, broad, universal, ecumenical, ubiquitous

generality *n.* abstraction, principle

generalize *v.* theorize, speculate, postulate

generally *adj.* commonly, ordinarily, regularly

generate *v.* produce, form, make, create

generosity *n.* hospitality, benevolence, charity, philanthropy, altruism, unselfishness, kindness

generous *adj.* bountiful, lavish, profuse, prodigal, unstinting, magnanimous

genesis *n.* generation, creation

genial *adj.* cordial, kind, warmhearted, friendly

genius *n.* talent, intellect, intelligence, gift, aptitude, astuteness, acumen, capability

gentility *n.* decorum, propriety, refinement, behavior

gentle *adj.* **SOFT:** tender, smooth; **KIND:** tender, considerate, benign; **TAMED:** domesticated, trained;

genuine *adj.* **AUTHENTIC:** actual, original, authenticated; **SINCERE:** unaffected, trustworthy, reliable, staunch, certain, valid, positive, frank

germ *n.* microbe, bacterium, virus, parasite, bug

germinate *v.* sprout, begin, generate

gesture *n.* movement, indication, intimation, sign

get *v.* **OBTAIN:** procure, capture, take, grab, attain, gain, secure, collect, purchase, receive, possess, acquire; **BECOME:** grow, develop; **RECEIVE:** take, accept; **BEAT;** vanquish, overpower, defeat; **PREPARE:** make, arrange; **CONTRACT:** succumb, catch; **UNDERSTAND:** comprehend, perceive, know; **IRRITATE:** annoy, provoke, vex, bother

ghastly *adj.* terrifying, hideous, horrible, frightening, frightful, repulsive, disgusting, abhorrent, offensive

ghost *n.* spirit, apparition, vision, specter, phantom, spook, devil

giant *adj.* monstrous, colossal, enormous, large

giant *n.* colossus, behemoth, leviathan

gibberish *n.* jargon, chatter, claptrap, nonsense

gibe *v.* sneer, mock, taunt

giddy, *adj.* high, towering, lofty, steep

gift *n.* **PRESENT:** donation, grant, endowment, bequest, legacy, reward, remembrance, bonus, subsidy, contribution; **TALENT:** aptitude, faculty, capacity, capability, ability

gigantic *adj.* massive, huge, immense, large

giggle *v.* laugh, titter, chuckle, snicker

gimmick *n.* device, stratagem, catch, method, trick

girdle *n.* belt, cinch, sash, underwear

girdle *v.* bind, enclose, encircle, clasp, surround

girl *n.* schoolgirl, lass, woman, coed, lassie, damsel, maid, maiden

girth *n.* circumference, size

gist *n.* substance, essence, basis

give *v.* **BESTOW:** donate, grant, confer, impart, present, endow, bequeath, award, contribute, convey; **YIELD:** retreat, collapse, fall, contract, shrink, recede

glacial *adj.* icy, frozen, polar, cold

glad *adj.* exhilarated, animated, jovial, happy

glamour *n.* allurement, charm, attraction, beauty

glance *v.* **LOOK:** see, peep, glimpse; **RICOCHET:** skip, rebound, bounce

glare *v.* **SHINE:** light, beam, glow, radiate; **STARE:** pierce, glower, scowl, frown

glaring *adj.* **SHINING:** blinding, dazzling, blazing, bright; **OBVIOUS:** conspicuous, evident, obtrusive

glass *n.* tumbler, goblet, beaker, chalice, cup

gleam *v.* glow, flash

glee *n.* joy, gaiety, joviality, merriment, mirth

glib *adj.* fluent, pat

glide *v.* float, drift, waft, skim, fly, flit, soar

glimmer *n.* gleam, flash, flicker, light

glimpse *n.* view, flash, impression, sight

glisten *v.* sparkle, glitter, shimmer, flicker, shine

glitter *n.* luster, brilliancy, sparkle, shimmer, gleam

glitter *v.* glare, shimmer, sparkle, shine

globule *n.* drop, particle

gloom *n.* **DARKNESS:** cloudiness; **SADNESS:** depression, dejection, melancholia, despondency, morbidity, pessimism, foreboding, misgiving, mourning

gloomy *adj.* dreary, depressing, discouraging, dismal

glorify *v.* laud, commend, acclaim, honor, exalt, praise

glorious *adj.* splendid, excellent, exalted, celebrated, grand, illustrious, remarkable

glory *n.* **SPLENDOR:** grandeur, majesty, brilliance, richness, beauty, fineness; **HONOR:** renown, distinction, reputation, fame

glory *v.* triumph, exult, boast

gloss *n.* brightness, sheen

glossy, *adj.* shining, reflecting, lustrous, bright

glow *v.* shine, gleam, redden, radiate, burn

glower *v.* stare, scowl

glue *n.* adhesive, paste, gum, cement, repair

glue *v.* paste, join

glum *adj.* sullen, moody, morose, sad

glut *v.* **OVEREAT:** stuff, cram, gorge, feast, devour; **OVERSUPPLY:** overwhelm, overstock, fill, flood

gluttony *n.* voracity, edacity, intemperance, greed

gnarled *adj.* knotted, twisted, contorted, bent

gnaw *v.* tear, crunch, champ, masticate, bite, chew

go *v.* **LEAVE:** withdraw, depart, vacate, flee, fly, run, escape; **PROCEED:** advance, progress, move; **FUNCTION:** run, perform, operate; **SUIT:** conform, accord, harmonize, agree, fit; **EXTEND:** stretch, cover, reach; **ELAPSE:** transpire, pass; **DIE:** depart, succumb

goad *v.* prod, urge, prompt, spur, drive, press, push, impel, force, stimulate, provoke, encourage

goal *n.* aim, ambition, objective, intent, end

go–between *n.* middleman, referee, mediator, agent

god *n.* deity, divinity

godly *adj.* righteous, devout, pious, holy

gone *adj.* moved, withdrawn, retired, departed, dissolved, decayed, extinct

good *adj.* **MORAL:** upright, honest, respectable, noble, ethical, fair, pure, decent, honorable; **KIND:** considerate, tolerant, generous; **RELIABLE:** trustworthy, dependable, loyal; **SOUND:** safe, solid, stable, reliable; **PLEASANT:** agreeable, satisfying, enjoyable; **HEALTHY:** sound, normal, vigorous; **OBEDIENT:** dutiful, tractable, well–behaved; **GENUINE:** valid, real, sound; **DELICIOUS:** tasty, flavorful, tasteful

good–for–nothing *n.* loafer, vagabond, bum, vagrant

good–looking *adj.* clean–cut, attractive, impressive, beautiful, handsome

good–natured *adj.* cordial, kindly, amiable, friendly

goodness *n.* decency, morality, honesty, virtue

goof *v.* err, flub, fail

gorge *n.* chasm, abyss, crevasse, ravine

gorge *v.* glut, surfeit, stuff, eat, fill

gorgeous *adj.* beautiful, dazzling, superb, sumptuous, impressive, grand

gory *adj.* blood–soaked, bloodstained, offensive

gossip *n.* **RUMOR:** scandal, meddling, hearsay, slander, defamation; **TALEBEARER:** snoop, meddler, tattler, scandalmonger, muckraker, backbiter

gossip *v.* tattle, chat, report, blab, babble, repeat

govern *v.* rule, administer, oversee, supervise, dictate, tyrannize

governmental *adj.* political, administrative, executive, regulatory, bureaucratic, supervisory

gown *n.* dress, garment, garb, clothes, dress

grab *v.* seize, clutch, grasp, take

grace *n.* **CHARM:** nimbleness, agility, poise, dexterity, symmetry, balance, style, harmony; **MERCY:** forgiveness, love, charity

graceful *adj.* **SUPPLE:** agile, lithe, nimble, dexterous, sprightly; **ELEGANT:** neat, trim, dainty, comely, slender, exquisite, statuesque; cultured, seemly, becoming, polite

gracious *adj.* **GENIAL:** amiable, courteous, condescending, polite; **MERCIFUL:** tender, loving, charitable, kind

grade *n.* **RANK;** class, category, classification; **SLOPE:** incline, gradient, slant, inclination, pitch, ascent, descent, ramp, climb, elevation, height, hill; **EMBANKMENT:** fill, causeway, dike, dam

grade *v.* arrange, rate, assort, rank

gradual *adj.* creeping, regular, continuous, regulated, piecemeal, gentle

grand *adj.* splendid, stately, dignified, regal, noble, illustrious, august, majestic, overwhelming

grandeur *n.* splendor, magnificence, pomp, glory, luxury, stateliness, beauty, ceremony, majesty

grandstand, *n.* seats, spectators

grant *n.* gift, boon, reward, present, allowance, stipend, donation, endowment, bequest

grant *v.* **BESTOW:** impart, allow; **ADMIT:** concede, accede, acquiesce, acknowledge

graph *n.* diagram, chart, design, plan

graphic *adj.* **PICTORIAL:** illustrated, visual, sketched, pictured; **VIVID:** clear, picturesque, comprehensible, striking, expressive, eloquent, poetic

grasp *n.* grip, hold, clutch, cinch

grasp *v.* **SEIZE:** clutch, enclose, clasp, grip, hold; **UNDERSTAND:** comprehend, perceive, apprehend, follow

grassland *n.* plains, meadow, prairie, field

grate *v.* rub, rasp, grind, abrade

grateful *adj.* thankful, appreciative, pleased, obliged

gratify *v.* please, satisfy

gratitude *n.* appreciation, acknowledgment, thanks

gratuitous *adj.* free, voluntary

gratuity *n.* present, tip, largess

grave *adj.* **WEIGHTY:** important, momentous, serious, consequential, critical; **SOMBER:** solemn, serious, sober

grave *n.* vault, sepulcher, tomb, crypt, mausoleum, catacomb

gravity *n.* importance, seriousness, significance

gravy *n.* juices, sauce, dressing

graze *v.* **FEED:** browse, nibble, forage, eat, munch, ruminate; **PASS LIGHTLY:** brush, scrape, rub, touch

greasy *adj.* creamy, fatty, oily

great *adj.* **LARGE:** numerous, big, commanding, vast; **EXCELLENT:** exceptional, surpassing, transcendent; **EMINENT:** grand, majestic, exalted, famous, renowned, celebrated, distinguished, noted

greedy *adj.* avid, grasping, rapacious, selfish, miserly, intemperate, mercenary, covetous

green *adj.* **VERDANT:** growing, leafy, flourishing, grassy, sprouting, lush; **IMMATURE:** young, unripe, maturing, developing; **INEXPERIENCED:** youthful, callow

greet *v.* hail, welcome, address, recognize, embrace, nod, acknowledge, bow

greeting *n.* salutation, welcome, regards

gregarious *adj.* companionable, friendly

grief *n.* sorrow, sadness, melancholy, mourning, misery, anguish, despondency, heartache, gloom

grievance *n.* hardship, injury, complaint, objection

grieve *v.* lament, bewail, regret, sorrow, mourn

grill *v.* broil, roast, sauté, barbecue, cook

grim *adj.* **SULLEN:** gloomy, sulky, morose, glum; **STERN:** austere, strict, harsh, severe; **RELENTLESS:** implacable, inexorable, uncompromising

grimace *n.* smirk, smile, sneer

grime *n.* dirt, soil, smudge, filth

grin *n.* smile, simper, smirk, wry

grin *v.* smirk, simper, beam, smile

grind *v.* crush, powder, mill, granulate, crumble

grip *n.* **GRASP:** hold, clutch, clasp, catch, clench, embrace, handshake; **SUITCASE:** valise, satchel, bag

grip *v.* grasp, clutch, clasp, seize

gripe *n.* complaint, grievance, beef, objection

gripe *v.* grumble, mutter, complain

grit *n.* pluck, courage; sand, dust

gritty *adj.* rough, abrasive, sandy, granular, scratchy

groan *n.* moan, sob, grunt, cry
groan *v.* moan, murmur, keen, cry
groceries *n.* food, edibles, comestibles, foodstuffs
groggy *adj.* sleepy, dizzy, reeling, tired
groom *v.* tend, rub, down, comb, brush
groove *n.* furrow, rut, channel, trench, depression, furrow, gutter, ditch
grope *v.* feel, search, fumble, touch, feel
gross *adj.* **WHOLE:** total, entire; **FAT:** corpulent, obese, huge; **OBSCENE:** indecent, shameful, lewd, coarse
grotesque *adj.* ludicrous, odd, bizarre, malformed, ugly, distorted, deformed
grotto *n.* cave, cavern, hollow
grouch *n.* complainer, grumbler, growler, sourpuss, sorehead, crank, bellyacher
grouch *v.* mutter, grumble, gripe, complain
grouchy *adv.* surly, ill-tempered, crusty, irritable
group *n.* **GATHERING:** assemblage, cluster, crowd; **COLLECTION:** accumulation, assortment, combination; **ORGANIZATION:** association, club, society
group *v.* assemble, file, assort, arrange, classify
grovel *v.* crawl, wallow, beg, kneel, crouch, kowtow, cower, snivel
grow *v.* **INCREASE:** expand, swell, wax, thrive, enlarge, multiply, flourish; **CHANGE:** become, develop, evolve, progress, age, ripen, blossom, mature; **CULTIVATE:** raise, tend, foster, produce, plant, breed
growl *v.* snarl, grumble, bark, grunt, cry
grown *adj.* aged, adult, mature
grub *v.* dig, root
grudge *n.* enmity, spite, rancor, animosity, hatred

grudge *v.* envy, begrudge, covet
gruel *n.* porridge, cereal
gruesome *adj.* horrible, ghastly, grim, grisly, frightful
gruff *adj.* bluff, churlish, harsh, grating, hoarse
grumble *v.* complain, growl, whine, protest, fuss
grumpy *adj.* sullen, grouchy, cantankerous, irritable
grunt *v.* snort, groan, mutter, grumble
guarantee *n.* surety, promise, bond
guarantee *v.* pledge, endorse, warrant, insure
guaranty *n.* warranty, contract, certificate
guard *n.* sentry, sentinel, watchman
guard *v.* protect, watch, patrol, picket, tend
guarded *adj.* PROTECTED: safe, secured, defended; CAUTIOUS: circumspect, careful
guardian *n.* protector, overseer, trustee, custodian, keeper, defender, supervisor, baby–sitter
guess *v.* estimate, presume, infer, speculate, imagine, surmise, theorize, venture, suppose, presume
guest *n.* visitor, caller
guidance *n.* direction, leadership, supervision
guide *n.* leader, pilot, pathfinder, scout, escort, director, conductor, pioneer
guide *v.* lead, direct, conduct, escort
guilt *n.* responsibility, culpability, blame, error, fault, liability, weakness, failing
guilty *adj.* condemned, censured, incriminated, indicted, judged, damned, reproachable, chargeable
guise *n.* appearance, disguise
gulch *n.* ravine, gully, ditch, gorge

gulf *n.* **CHASM:** abyss, abysm, depth, ravine, **BAY:** inlet, sound, cove
gull, *v.* deceive, trick, cheat
gullible *adj.* innocent, trustful, simple, naïve
gully *n.* channel, ditch, chasm, crevasse, ravine
gurgle *v.* babble, ripple, murmur
guru *n.* teacher, instructor, mentor
gush *v.* **FLOW:** pour, well, spew
gust *n.* blast, burst, blow, breeze, wind
gusto, *n.* enjoyment, zest, zeal, fervor, ardor
gutter *n.* channel, gully, sewer, drain, trough
guttural *adj.* throaty, gruff, deep, hoarse
guy *n.* **MAN:** chap, lad, fellow; **GUIDE:** rope, chain, cable
guzzle *v.* swill, quaff, swig, drink
gymnasium *n.* arena, coliseum, ring, rink, pit, gym
gymnast *n.* acrobat, tumbler, jumper, athlete
gypsy *n.* wanderer; tramp, vagrant, traveler

habiliments *n.* dress, garments
habit *n.* **CUSTOM:** mode, practice, fashion, manner; **DRESS:** costume; **OBSESSION:** addiction, fixation
habitat *n.* environment, territory, surroundings
habitual *adj.* customary, frequent, periodic, continual, routine, rooted, systematic, recurrent, repeated, accustomed, established, repetitious, stereotyped
hack *adj.* routine, trite
hack *v.* chop, whack, mangle, cut
hackneyed *adj.* commonplace, trite
hag *n.* crone, shrew, ogress, hellcat, fishwife, harridan, witch
haggard *adj.* gaunt, worn, tired

haggle *v.* bargain, wrangle, deal, argue, buy, sell

hail *v.* call, greet, salute, cheer, welcome, honor

halfhearted *adj.* indecisive, irresolute, indifferent

halfway *adj.* partial, midway, incomplete, partially, imperfectly, insufficiently, moderately, middling

halfway *adv.* half, partly

hall *n.* **PUBLIC ROOM:** chamber, assembly, arena, ballroom, church, clubhouse, salon, lounge, amphitheater, gallery; **ENTRANCE:** foyer, corridor, hallway

hallmark *n.* label, endorsement, seal, emblem

hallow *v.* bless, consecrate, enshrine, sanctify

hallucination *n.* delusion, vision

hallway *n.* foyer, entrance, way, corridor, entrance

halt *n.* stop, cessation, termination

halt *v.* check, terminate, suspend, interrupt, block, stem, deter, stall, curb, restrict, arrest, suppress, intercept, obstruct, hinder, impede, squelch

halve *v.* divide, split, bisect

hamlet *n.* town, village

hamper *v.* hinder, slow, thwart, embarrass

hand *n.* **WORKMAN:** helper, worker, laborer; **PENMANSHIP:** calligraphy, script; **APPLAUSE:** ovation, reception, handclapping; **CARDS:** deal, round, game

handbag *n.* pocketbook, bag, purse

handbook *n.* textbook, directory, guidebook

handcuff *v.* restrain, shackle

handicap *n.* disadvantage, obstacle, impediment, affliction, hindrance, disorder, injury

handicap *v.* encumber, hinder

handily *adv.* easily, skillfully, smoothly, cleverly

handle *v.* **HOLD:** touch, finger, check, examine, feel; **MANAGE:** manipulate, operate, use, work; **DEAL:** retail, market, sell

handsome *adj.* attractive, impressive, stately, robust, well-dressed, slick, beautiful

hand-to-mouth *adj.* marginal, minimal, borderline

handwriting *n.* penmanship, hand, writing, script, scrawl, scribble, calligraphy, scratching

handy *adj.* **USEFUL:** beneficial, advantageous, gainful, helpful, profitable, usable; **CONVENIENT:** near, nearby; **DEXTEROUS:** able

hang *v.* **SUSPEND:** dangle, droop, drape; **WAVE:** flap, swing; **KILL:** execute, lynch

hanging *adj.* **DANGLING:** swaying, swinging, overhanging, pendulous, drooping; **TENTATIVE:** uncertain, pending, indeterminate

hang-out *n.* bar, joint, hole, headquarters, room

hang-up *n.* problem, predicament, difficulty

haphazard *adj.* accidental, random, offhand, casual, slipshod, reckless, irregular, unplanned, aimless

happen *v.* befall, occur, ensue, arise, transpire

happening *n.* incident, affair, accident, event

happily *adv.* joyously, gladly, cheerily, gaily, merrily, brightly, blissfully, cheerfully, gleefully

happiness *n.* mirth, merrymaking, cheer, merriment, delight, gladness, hilarity, gaiety, cheerfulness, rejoicing, exhilaration

happy *adj.* joyous, merry, mirthful, gay, laughing, contented, genial, cheery, jolly, sparkling, blissful, exhilarated, pleased, gratified, ecstatic, overjoyed, radiant, smiling, elated

happy–go–lucky *adj.* easygoing, unconcerned, thoughtless, irresponsible

harangue *n.* speech, tirade

harass *v.* annoy, attack, tease, vex, irritate, bother

harbor *n.* refuge, port, pier, inlet, wharf, dock

harbor *v.* **CONSIDER:** entertain, cherish, regard; **PROTECT:** shelter, secure, defend, lodge

hard *adj.* **COMPACT:** unyielding, solid, impermeable, tough, dense, firm; **DIFFICULT:** arduous, tricky, trying, tedious, complex, abstract, puzzling, troublesome, laborious; **CRUEL:** perverse, unrelenting, vengeful; **SEVERE:** harsh, exacting, grim

harden *v.* steel, temper, solidify, crystallize, clot, petrify, compact, concentrate, fossilize, toughen

hardheaded *adj.* willful, stubborn, headstrong

hardhearted *adj.* cold, unfeeling, heartless, cruel

hardly *adv.* scarcely, barely, imperceptibly, infrequently, somewhat, rarely, slightly, sparsely

hardship *n.* trial, sorrow, worry, difficulty, grief

hardware *n.* appliance, fixture, casting, metalware, implement, tool, fitting, utensil, equipment

hardy *adj.* tough, resistant, staunch, seasoned, solid, rugged, robust, hearty, hale, vigorous, sturdy, solid, substantial, strong

hark, harken *v.* listen, heed, attend, observe

harm *n.* INJURY: infliction, damage; impairment, EVIL: wickedness, abuse, outrage

harm *v.* injure, wreck, cripple, hurt

harmful *adj.* injurious, detrimental, hurtful, noxious, evil, adverse, sinister, virulent, corroding, toxic, painful, malicious, malignant, unwholesome, corrupting, menacing, damaging, disastrous, catastrophic, destructive, unhealthy

harmless *adj.* pure, innocent, powerless, controllable, manageable, safe, trustworthy, sanitary

harmonious *adj.* HARMONIC: tuneful, musical, melodic; CONGRUOUS: agreeable, corresponding, suitable, adapted, similar, like, cooperative, friendly, conforming, balanced, symmetrical

harp *v.* carp, nag, repeat, pester, complain

harridan *n.* witch, hag, nag

harrow *v.* torment, distress

harry *v.* plunder, harass

harsh *adj.* rough, severe, discordant, jangling, cacophonous, grating, dissonant, creaking, clashing, jarring, clamorous, hoarse, rasping, screeching, earsplitting, tuneless, shrill

harvest *n.* crops, yield, fruit, grain, produce, vegetable

harvest *v.* glean, gather, accumulate, collect, garner, cut, pluck, pick, cull, hoard, mow

hasp *n.* fastener, latch

hassle *n.* dispute, squabble

haste *n.* speed, dispatch, precipitation, rashness, impetuousness, foolhardiness, recklessness, hastiness, carelessness, heedlessness

hasten *v.* **HURRY:** rush, fly, sprint; **EXPEDITE:** accelerate, quicken, push, urge, goad, press

hasty *adj.* **HURRIED:** quick, speedy, swift, fast; **CARELESS:** precipitate, foolhardy, careless, rash

hat *n.* headgear, headpiece, helmet, chapeau, bonnet, cap, derby, sombrero, topper, bowler, Panama, fedora, beret, turban, hood, cowl, beret

hate *n.* dislike, animosity, enmity, hatred

hate *v.* **DETEST:** abhor, abominate, loathe, resent, despise, dislike

hateful *adj.* odious, detestable, repugnant, offensive

hatred *n.* abhorrence, loathing, rancor, repugnance, repulsion, disgust, displeasure, contempt, bitterness, antagonism, animosity, malice, malevolence, spleen, hostility, alienation

haughty *adj.* disdainful, arrogant, proud, egotistic

haul *n.* **PULL:** tug, lift, wrench; **DISTANCE:** voyage, trip; **SPOILS:** take, find, booty

haul *v.* drag, pull, bring, draw

haunt *v.* **FREQUENT:** habituate, visit; **OBSESS:** torment, possess, trouble, hound, terrify, plague, vex, worry, frighten, harass, annoy, bother, disturb

haunting *adj.* eerie, unforgettable, seductive, frightful

have *v.* **OWN:** keep, retain, use, maintain, control, possess, treasure, hold; **BEAR:** beget, produce

haven *n.* harbor, port, refuge, shelter

havoc *n.* destruction, confusion, devastation, plunder

hazard *n.* chance, risk, peril, jeopardy, danger

hazard *v.* chance, try, guess, gamble, risk

haze *n.* fog, mist, smog, cloudiness

hazy *adj.* vague, cloudy, foggy, murky, misty, unclear, overcast, gauzy, vaporous, smoky, dim, indistinct, dusky, obscure, veiled, blurred, faint

head *n.* **SKULL:** brainpan, scalp, crown; **LEADER:** chief, commander, officer, ruler; **TOP:** summit, peak, crest; **BEGINNING:** front, start, source, origin; **INTELLIGENCE:** brains, foresight, ingenuity, judgment

head *v.* lead, direct, supervise, manage

headache *n.* **PAIN:** migraine, neuralgia; **PROBLEM:** vexation, difficulty, trouble

headway *n.* progress, advance, increase, promotion

heal *v.* cure, restore, renew, regenerate, remedy, rejuvenate, medicate, revive, rehabilitate, resuscitate, salve, help, ameliorate, doctor

health *n.* vigor, wholeness, healthfulness, fitness, bloom, hardiness, stamina, energy, strength

healthy *adj.* sound, trim, robust, vigorous, well, hearty, athletic, able–bodied, virile, blooming, firm, sturdy, lively, flourishing, fit, rugged

heap *n.* pile, mass, stack, quantity

heap *v.* pile, add, lump, load, pack

hear *v.* **LISTEN:** attend, catch, apprehend, eavesdrop, perceive, overhear; **TRY:** judge, examine, referee

hearsay *n.* rumor, scandal, gossip

heart *n.* **FEELING:** response, sympathy, sensitivity, emotion; **CENTER:** core, middle, pith; **SPIRIT:** courage, fortitude, gallantry

heartache *n.* sorrow, pain, despair, anguish, grief

heartless *adj.* cruel, unkind, insensitive, ruthless

hearty *adj.* warm, zealous, sincere, cheery, cheerful, jovial, animated, ardent, genial, enthusiastic, genuine, passionate, intense, exuberant, devout, unfeigned, fervent, responsive, friendly

heat *n.* **WARMTH:** fever, sultriness; **FERVOR:** ardor, passion, excitement, desire

heat *v.* warm, inflame, kindle, thaw, boil, sear, singe, scorch, ignite

heated *adj.* **WARMED:** cooked, fried, baked **FERVENT:** fiery, ardent, avid, excited, passionate

heathen *adj.* infidel, atheist, barbarian

heave *v.* **THROW:** toss; **MOVE:** rock, bob, pitch, lurch, roll, reel, sway, throb, slosh

heavenly *adj.* **DIVINE:** celestial, supernal, angelic, holy; **BLISSFUL:** sweet, enjoyable, excellent, pleasant

heavy *adj.* **WEIGHTY:** ponderous, huge, stout, dense, substantial, hefty, large; **BURDENSOME:** troublesome, oppressive, vexatious, difficult, disturbing, onerous; **DULL:** listless, slow, apathetic, indifferent; **GLOOMY:** dejected, cloudy, overcast, dismal, dark, sad

heavy-handed *adj.* oppressive, harsh, cruel, severe

heckle *v.* torment, disturb, pester, ridicule, bother

hectic *adj.* frantic, unsettled, boisterous, restless, confused, disordered

hector *v.* bully, annoy, tease, vex

heed *n.* notice, care

height *n.* altitude, elevation, prominence, loftiness, highness, tallness, stature, expanse, extent, length

heighten *v.* **INCREASE:** sharpen, strengthen, emphasize; **RAISE:** uplift, elevate, lift

heinous *adj.* hateful, atrocious, wicked

heir *n.* inheritor, successor, descendent, heiress, beneficiary, inheritor, prince

heirloom *n.* legacy, inheritance, bequest, gift, antique

heist *n.* robbery, burglary

helm *n.* leadership, control

help *n.* ASSISTANCE: advice, comfort, aid, support, gift, charity, encouragement, subsidy, service, relief, endowment, cooperation, guidance; EMPLOYEE: aid, representative, assistant, faculty, staff; RELIEF: maintenance, sustenance, nourishment, remedy

help *v.* assist, advise, encourage, cooperate, intercede, befriend, accommodate, sustain, benefit, bolster, promote, back, advocate, abet, stimulate, uphold, further, boost, support

helpful *adj.* USEFUL: valuable, serviceable, profitable, advantageous, favorable, convenient, suitable, practical, usable, applicable, desirable, convenient; CURATIVE: healthy, salutary, restorative, healthful; OBLIGING: accommodating, considerate, neighborly, kind

helping *n.* portion, serving, plateful, share

helpless *adj.* DEPENDENT: feeble, unable, weak, vulnerable; INCOMPETENT: incapable, unfit, inexpert

hem *n.* border, skirting, edging, edge, fringe, rim

henpeck *v.* nag, bully, suppress, intimidate, bother

herald *n.* proclaimer, forerunner

herd *n.* flock, group, drove, pack, brood, swarm, lot, bevy, covey, gaggle, nest, brood, flight, school

herdsman *n.* shepherd, herder, rancher

hereditary *adj.* inherited, genetic, paternal

heredity *n.* ancestry, inheritance, genetic

heresy *n.* dissent, nonconformity, dissidence, sectarianism, schism, unorthodoxy, secularism

heretic *n.* schismatic, apostate, sectarian, cynic

heritage *n.* **TRADITION:** culture, custom, fashion, system; **INHERITANCE:** legacy, birthright, ancestry, dowry, share, endowment, status, heredity

hermit *n.* ascetic, recluse

hero *n.* champion, model, martyr, conqueror, god, warrior, saint, knight-errant, star

heroic *adj.* valiant, valorous, fearless, brave, noble

heroism *n.* fortitude, valor, bravery, courage, strength

hesitancy *n.* indecision, wavering, procrastination, delay, pause

hesitant *adj.* **SLOW:** delaying, wavering, dawdling, lazy; **DOUBTFUL:** skeptical, irresolute, uncertain;

hesitate *v.* pause, stop, falter, vacillate, flounder, ponder, delay, weigh, consider, deliberate, linger

hesitation *n.* **DOUBT:** equivocation, skepticism, irresolution, uncertainty; **DELAY:** wavering, dawdling

hex *n.* spell, curse

hex *v.* curse, enchant, charm, bewitch

hiatus *n.* break, pause

hidden *adj.* secluded, private, covert, concealed, occult, masked, screened, veiled, clouded, obscured, disguised, unseen, camouflaged, shrouded, shadowy, clandestine, cloistered, surreptitious

hide *n.* skin, pelt, rawhide, fur, leather

hide *v.* conceal, shroud, curtain, veil, camouflage, cover, mask, cloak, screen, suppress, withhold, shield, secrete, hoard, closet, obscure, disguise

hideous *adj.* frightful, shocking, revolting, hateful, ghastly, grisly, ugly

hideout *n.* lair, den, refuge, retreat, shelter

hierarchy *n.* government, authority, ministry, regime

high *adj.* **TOWERING:** tall, gigantic, big, colossal, tremendous; great, giant, huge, formidable, immense, elevated, lofty, soaring, raised; **EXALTED:** eminent, powerful, distinguished, leading, noble; **EXPENSIVE:** costly, precious, **EXTRAORDINARY:** great, special, unusual; **SHRILL:** piercing, sharp, penetrating; **DRUNK:** intoxicated; tipsy, inebriated

high-pressure *adj.* forceful, compelling, powerful

high-spirited *adj.* daring, dauntless, reckless, brave

high-strung *adj.* nervous, tense, impatient, restless

highway *n.* roadway, parkway, freeway, turnpike

hijack *v.* rob, steal, privateer, capture, seize

hike *n.* walk, tour, trek, trip, backpack, journey

hike *v.* **TRAMP:** tour, explore, travel, walk; **RAISE:** lift, advance, increase

hilarious *adj.* gay, merry, funny, amusing, lively, witty, entertaining

hill *n.* mound, knoll, butte, bluff, promontory, precipice, rising, headland, upland, inclination, slope, ascent, grade, incline, rise, foothill, dune, climb, elevation, hillside, hilltop

hinder *v.* stop, impede, obstruct, check, retard, fetter, block, thwart, bar, clog, encumber, burden, inhibit, shackle, interrupt, arrest, curb, oppose, deter, hamper, frustrate, intercept, prohibit, stall, slow, down, smother, disappoint, spoil, gag

hindrance *n.* obstacle, barrier, interference

hinge *n.* joint, pivot, juncture, articulation, link

hinge *v.* hang, turn, depend, connect, couple, join

hint *n.* allusion, mention, inkling, implication, reference, observation, notice, tip, clue, omen, scent, notion, taste, suspicion, innuendo, sign, impression, indication, suggestion

hint *v.* intimate, inform, imply, infer, acquaint, remind, recall, cue, prompt, insinuate, indicate, wink, advise, suggest

hip *n.* **AWARE:** informed, enlightened, knowledgeable, cognizant; **FASHIONABLE:** modern, stylish

hire *v.* engage, secure, enlist, appoint, delegate, authorize, retain, commission, empower, select, pick, contract, procure

historic *adj.* factual, traditional, chronicled, old

history *n.* account, annals, records, archives, chronicle, writings, evidence, record

hit *adj.* struck, slugged, smacked, cuffed, smashed, clouted, hurt, tapped, rapped, swatted

hit *n.* **STROKE:** blow, slap, rap, punch; **SUCCESS:** favorite, sellout, knockout

hit *v.* **STRIKE:** knock, sock, slap, bump, thump, collide, punch, hammer, whack, jab, tap, pelt, cuff, clout, club; **REACH:** find, win

hitch *n.* KNOT: loop, noose, tie; DIFFICULTY: obstacle, hindrance, block

hitch *v.* hook, unite, yoke, hook, fasten, join

hoard *n.* cache, treasure, store, stockpile

hoard *v.* amass, acquire, keep, accumulate, save

hoary *adj.* white, old

hoax *n.* trick, fabrication, deceit, deception, lie

hobby *n.* pursuit, avocation, pastime, diversion, interest, activity, pursuit, sport, amusement, craft

hobo *n.* vagrant, vagabond, wanderer, beggar, bum

hock *v.* sell, pledge, deposit, pawn

hod *n.* trough, scuttle

hodgepodge *n.* mixture, jumble, combination, mess

hoist *n.* lift, crane, derrick, elevator

hoist *v.* raise, lift

hokum *n.* nonsense, trickery, chicanery

hold *v.* POSSESS: keep, retain, have, accept; SUPPORT: sustain, brace, buttress, prop; GRASP: grip, clutch, embrace, squeeze, hug, seize; CONFINE: imprison, enclose, restrain; RESIST: persevere, continue, endure; ADHERE: cling, fasten, stick

holdout *n.* die–hard, objector, resister, resistance, objector, dissenter

holdover *n.* remnant, relic, surplus, remainder

holdup *n.* robbery, burglary, stick–up, crime, theft

hole *n.* CAVITY: perforation, puncture, slot, eyelet, split, tear, cleft, opening, fissure, gap, gash, rift, rupture, aperture, breach, eye, crater, gorge, hollow, chasm, crevasse, BURROW: den, lair; DIFFICULTY: impasse, tangle, mess, crisis, emergency

holiday *n.* festival, fiesta, carnival, jubilee, anniversary, celebration

holiness *n.* devoutness, humility, saintliness, devotion

hollow *adj.* **CONCAVE:** sunken, depressed, excavated, indented; **CAVERNOUS:** deep, resonant, booming, rumbling, reverberating, muffled, dull, resounding; **UNSOUND:** empty, pretentious

hollow *n.* cavity, dale, bowl, basin, valley

hollow *v.* scoop, excavate, indent, dig, shovel

holocaust *n.* loss, fire, destruction, annihilation, catastrophe

holy *adj.* devout, pious, righteous, moral, just, good, angelic, godly, reverent, venerable, humble, innocent, saintly, godlike, saintlike, perfect, faultless, chaste, upright, virtuous, dedicated, devoted, spiritual, religious

homage *n.* loyalty, worship, respect, adoration, deference, devotion, reverence

home *n.* **DWELLING:** residence, habitation, abode, lodging, quarters, domicile, shelter; **ASYLUM:** orphanage, sanitarium, hospital

homecoming *n.* welcome, celebration, entry, arrival

homely *adj.* **PLAIN:** unattractive, uncomely; **UNPRETENTIOUS:** plain, snug, simple, cozy, modest

homespun *adj.* handcrafted, domestic, homemade

homestead *n.* property, house, ranch, estate, home

homogenize *v.* blend, combine

homologous *adj.* equivalent, associated

honest *adj.* **TRUTHFUL:** trustworthy, unimpeachable, legitimate; **FRANK:** aboveboard, candid, straightforward; **FAIR:** just, equitable, impartial

honesty *n.* fidelity, scrupulousness, candor, openness, goodness, virtue

honk *v.* blare, trumpet, bellow, sound

honor *n.* distinction, recognition, attention, reputation, tribute, integrity

honor *v.* **RESPECT:** worship, sanctify, venerate, praise; **VALUE:** admire, esteem, compliment; **ACCEPT:** clear, pass, acknowledge

honorable *adj.* reputable, creditable, distinguished, noble

honorary *adj.* titular, nominal, complimentary

hood *n.* **COVERING:** cowl, shawl, bonnet, veil, capuchin, mantle; **CANOPY:** awning, cover; **HOODLUM:** gangster, criminal, crook

hoodlum *n.* rowdy, thug, gangster, crook, criminal

hook *n.* lock, catch, clasp, fastener

hook *v.* **BEND:** curve, angle, crook, arch; **CATCH:** pin, secure, fasten

hoot *n.* howl, whoop, boo, cry

hop *v.* leap, jump, skip, bounce

hope *n.* **FAITH:** expectation, anticipation; **DREAM:** desire, purpose, wish, goal

hope *v.* expect, desire, await, suppose, believe, anticipate, trust

hopeful *adj.* **OPTIMISTIC:** expectant, trustful, anticipating, trusting, confident; **ENCOURAGING:** promising, reassuring, favorable, propitious, cheering, auspicious, uplifting, heartening, inspiring

hopeless *adj.* unfortunate, bad, incurable, vain, irreversible, irreparable, disastrous, tragic, desperate

horde *n.* crowd, swarm, pack, throng

horizon *n.* range, border, limit, boundary, extent

horizontal *adj.* **LEVEL:** aligned, parallel, flat, straight; **EVEN:** flush, uniform, regular, smooth

horrible *adj.* repulsive, dreadful, disgusting, terrible, frightful, shameful, shocking

horrid *adj.* shocking, hideous, disturbing, shameful, offensive, pitiful

horrify *v.* shock, terrify

horror *n.* fear, terror, awe, fright

hors d'oeuvre *n.* appetizer, canapé

horseman *n.* cavalryman, knight, dragoon, equestrian, jockey, cowboy, rider

horticulture *n.* cultivation, agriculture, farming

hospitable *adj.* kind, receptive, courteous, cordial, open, friendly

hospital *n.* clinic, infirmary, sanitarium, dispensary

hospitality *n.* companionship, fellowship, entertainment, welcome

hostile *adj.* unfriendly, antagonistic, hateful, opposed

hostility *n.* abhorrence, aversion, bitterness, hatred

hot *adj.* **BURNING:** fiery, flaming, blazing, baking, roasting, scorching, blistering, searing, sizzling, broiling, scalding, parching; **AROUSED:** furious, ill–tempered, indignant, angry

hotel *n.* motel, lodging, inn, hostel, resort, tavern

hotrod *n.* car, racer, dragster

hound *n.* dog, cur

hound *v.* bully, pester, badger, provoke, annoy

house *n.* **HOME:** habitation, dwelling, residence; **FAMILY:** line, tradition, ancestry; **LEGISLATURE:** congress, council, parliament

housekeeper *n.* caretaker, servant

hover *v.* remain, wait, float, linger

howl *v.* cry, wail, bawl, lament, yell

hub *n.* center, core, middle, focus, heart

huddle *v.* crowd, cluster, group, conference

hue *n.* color, tint, value, dye

huff *n.* anger, annoyance, pique

huff *v.* puff, blow, bluster, bully

huffy *adj.* offended, piqued, angry, insulted, irritable

hug *v.* embrace, hold, squeeze, clasp, press, cling, clutch, envelop, enfold, nestle, cuddle

huge *adj.* large, tremendous, enormous, immense

hulking *adj.* bulky, massive

humane *adj.* merciful, kind, sympathetic, benevolent, understanding, compassionate, kindhearted, forgiving, charitable, tender, lenient, tolerant, altruistic, philanthropic, magnanimous, unselfish, warmhearted

humanitarian *adj.* altruist, benfactor, philanthropist

humble *adj.* MEEK: submissive, gentle, diffident, retiring, reserved, bashful, shy, timid, deferential, hesitant, mild, withdrawn, fearful, tentative, obedient, passive, tame, restrained, subdued; UNPRETENTIOUS: unassuming, modest, seemly, becoming, homespun, natural, servile, shabby, insignificant, plain, common, homely, simple

humble *v.* humiliate, shame, chasten, mortify, demean, demote, lower, crush, degrade, discredit, squelch, deflate, squash

humbug *n.* hoax, fraud, lie, deception, nonsense

humdrum *adj.* monotonous, common, uninteresting, dull

humid *adj.* moist, damp, stuffy, sticky, muggy, close

humiliate *v.* humble, shame, debase, mortify, chasten, dishonor, demean, conquer, vanquish, disgrace, embarrass
humiliation *n.* chagrin, mortification, disgrace, embarrassment, shame
humility *n.* meekness, timidity, servility, subservience, resignation, shyness
humor *n.* COMEDY: entertainment, amusement, jesting, raillery; WITTICISM: pleasantry, banter, joke, mirth; DISPOSITION: gaiety, wittiness, joyfulness, playfulness
humor *v.* indulge, pamper, gratify, placate, appease, comfort
humorous *adj.* amusing, funny, comical, entertaining
hunch *n.* intuition, notion, feeling, premonition, instinct, foreboding, portent, apprehension, misgiving, qualm, suspicion, inkling
hunger *n.* longing, yearning, lust, want
hunger *v.* crave, desire
hungry *adj.* starved, famished, ravenous, desirous, unsatisfied, unfilled, starving, voracious
hunk *n.* lump, chunk, mass, clod, slice, morsel
hunt *v.* PURSUE: follow, stalk, hound, trail, seek, track, chase; INVESTIGATE: search, probe, seek
hurdle *n.* obstacle, barricade, blockade, barrier
hurl *v.* throw, cast, fling, heave
hurrah *v.* applaud, cheer, approve
hurry *v.* HASTEN: scurry, scuttle, dash, sprint, rush, scoot, dart, spring, speed, fly, bustle, race; URGE: drive, push, spur, goad
hurt *adj.* injured, harmed, wounded, disfigured, suffering, distressed, tortured, unhappy

hurt *v.* INJURE: cut, bruise, slap, abuse, flog, whip, harm, wound, lacerate, bite, burn, punch, scourge, lash, cane, switch; HARM: maltreat, injure, spoil, damage, destroy; PAIN: ache, throb, sting

hurtful *adj.* aching, injurious, deadly, harmful

husband *v.* economize, conserve

hush *v.* calm, soothe, quiet, silence, gag, stifle

husky *adj.* HOARSE: rough, throaty, gruff, growling; STRONG: muscular, sinewy, strapping

hustle *v.* rush, push, hurry, race, run, speed

hut *n.* shanty, lean–to, shack, dugout, hovel

hygiene *n.* health, sanitation, cleanliness

hygienic *adj.* healthful, sanitary, clean, pure, sterile

hyperbole *n.* metaphor, exaggeration

hypnotic *adj.* narcotic, soporific, soothing

hypnotize *v.* mesmerize, fascinate, captivate, stupefy

hypocrisy *n.* pretense, affectation, bigotry, sanctimony, dishonesty, lie

hypocrite *n.* pretender, fraud, faker, deceiver, charlatan, trickster

hypothesis *n.* theory, supposition, assumption, guess, opinion

hypothetical *adj.* SUPPOSED: imagined, uncertain, assumed, likely, POSTULATED: academic, philosophical, logical

hysteria, hysterics *n.* neurosis, emotionalism, delirium, agitation, confusion, excitement, nervousness

hysterical *adj.* frantic, raving, delirious, emotional, neurotic, distraught, uncontrollable, frenzied, unrestrained, tempestuous, impassioned, overwrought

icon *n.* image, picture

iconoclast *n.* dissenter, rebel

idea *n.* **CONCEPT:** belief, theory, hypothesis, assumption, conjecture, notion, thought; **FANCY:** imagination, whimsy, whim, fantasy

ideal *adj.* **TYPICAL:** model, archetypal; **PERFECT:** best, theoretical, supreme, fitting, exemplary, excellent

ideal *n.* concept, paragon, goal, prototype, model

idealism *n.* principle, conscience, philosophy, ethics, visionary, conscience

identical *adj.* same, alike, twin, indistinguishable

identification *n.* **CLASSIFYING:** naming, cataloguing, description, classification; **CREDENTIALS:** passport, testimony, papers, badge

ideal *adj.* **TYPICAL:** model, archetypal; **PERFECT:** best, theoretical, supreme, fitting, exemplary, excellent

ideal *n.* concept, paragon, goal, prototype, model

idealism *n.* principle, conscience, philosophy, ethics

identical *adj.* same, alike, twin, indistinguishable

identification *n.* **CLASSIFYING:** naming, cataloguing, description, classification; **CREDENTIALS:** passport, testimony, papers, badge

identify *v.* classify, catalog, analyze, describe, name

identity *n.* characteristics, identification, individuality, uniqueness, name

ideology *n.* philosophy, belief, doctrine, ethics

idiom *n.* expression, usage, jargon, argot

idiot *n.* simpleton, nincompoop, booby, fool

idiotic *adj.* dull, moronic, stupid

idle *adj.* unemployed, unoccupied, uncultivated, fallow, motionless, inert, resting

idle *v.* loiter, slack, shirk, loaf

idol *n.* image, icon, figurine, fetish, totem

idolatry *n.* worship, love, infatuation, fervor, zeal

idolize *v.* worship, glorify, adore, canonize

ignite *v.* fire, light, enkindle, burn

ignoble *adj.* mean, dishonorable

ignominy *n.* shame, disgrace

ignorance *n.* incomprehension, incapacity, inexperience, illiteracy, shallowness, simplicity

ignorant *adj.* **UNAWARE:** superficial, unconscious, shallow, inexperienced, unwitting, obtuse, unintelligent, dense, shallow; **UNTRAINED:** illiterate, uneducated, misguided, naïve

ignore *v.* overlook, disregard, reject, neglect

ilk *n.* type, kind

ill *adj.* **BAD:** harmful, evil, noxious, unfavorable; **SICK:** unwell, unhealthy, ailing

ill *n.* evil, depravity, misfortune, mischief, wrong

illegal *adj.* unlawful illicit banned outlawed unauthorized unlicensed, illegitimate, prohibited, forbidden, criminal

illegible *adj.* unreadable, faint, unintelligible, confused, obscure

illicit *adj.* unlawful, prohibited, unauthorized, illegal

illiteracy *n.* ignorance, stupidity, idiocy

illiterate *adj.* ignorant, uneducated, unenlightened

illness *n.* sickness, infirmity, disorder, attack, convalescence, complaint, collapse, breakdown, confinement, weakness, disease, ailment, malady

illogical *adj.* irrational, unreasonable, fallacious, absurd, incorrect, inconsistent, unscientific, contradictory, unsound, implausible

ill–tempered *adj.* cross, touchy, querulous, irritable

illuminate *v.* CLARIFY: illustrate, explain, interpret, elucidate; BRIGHTEN: lighten, illumine, decorate, light

illumination *n.* LIGHT: brilliance, lighting, flame; CLARIFICATION: instruction, teaching, education, information, knowledge

illusion *n.* deception, fancy, hallucination, mirage, apparition, delusion, trick, dream

illusory *adj.* deceiving, unreal

illustrate *v.* explain; picture, portray, depict

illustration *n.* explanation, picture, engraving, vignette, inset, chart, diagram

illustrative *adj.* symbolic, representative, pictorial, descriptive, explanatory, graphic

illustrious *adj.* distinguished, famous

image *n.* LIKENESS: idol, representation, effigy, form, drawing, portrait, photograph, replica, picture; CONCEPT: conception, perception, thought, idea

imagery *n.* metaphor, representation, comparison

imaginable *adj.* conceivable, comprehensible, possible, plausible, believable, reasonable, likely

imaginary *adj.* fancied, illusory, visionary, hypothetical, theoretical, imagined, hallucinatory, whimsical, fabulous, nonexistent, mythological, legendary, fictitious, unreal

imagination *n.* inventiveness, conception, sensitivity, visualization, awareness, insight

imaginative *adj.* creative, inventive, artistic, original

imagine *v.* conceive, invent, picture, conjure, envision, invent, fabricate, formulate, devise, conceptualize, dream, perceive, create

imbalance *n.* unevenness, inequality, irregularity

imbecilic *adj.* foolish, silly

imbibe *v.* ingest, gorge, guzzle, drink, swallow

imbroglio *n.* commotion, entanglement, fracas

imbue *v.* permeate, invade, absorb, saturate, teach

imitate *v.* **MIMIC:** impersonate, mirror, simulate, ape, mime, parody; **COPY:** duplicate, counterfeit, reproduce, falsify; **RESEMBLE:** simulate, parallel

imitation *n.* **SIMULATION:** duplication, mimicry, impersonation, copy; **COUNTERFEIT:** likeness, replica, substitution, forgery

imitative *adj.* deceptive, false, forged, sham

immaculate *adj.* pure, unsoiled, unsullied, spotless, stainless, bright, clean

immanent *adj.* deep-seated, inherent, natural, instinctive

immaterial *adj.* unimportant, insignificant

immature *adj.* childish, youthful, sophomoric, naïve

immediate *adj.* now, next, prompt, following

immense *adj.* large, gigantic, tremendous, enormous

immerse *v.* plunge, involve, submerge, douse, steep, soak, drench, dunk, souse

immigrant *n.* outsider, newcomer, alien

immigrate *v.* move, enter

immigration *n.* colonization, settlement, migration

imminent *adj.* impending, approaching, coming

immobility *n.* firm, fixed, motionless

immodest *adj.* brazen, shameless, bold, egotistic

immoral *adj.* sinful, corrupt, shameless, bad

immorality *n.* vice, depravity, dissoluteness, evil

immortal *adj.* DEATHLESS: undying, imperishable, endless, timeless, everlasting, enduring, eternal; ILLUSTRIOUS: celebrated, eminent, glorious, famous

immovable *adj.* solid, stable, fixed, firm

immune *adj.* exempt, free, unsusceptible, privileged, excused, safe

immunity *n.* EXEMPTION: privilege, license, freedom; IMMUNIZATION: resistance, protection

immure *v.* confine, imprison

impact *n.* shock, impression, contact, collision

impair *v.* lessen, diminish, spoil, blemish, injure, hurt, break, damage

impart *v.* GIVE: bestow, grant, present, allow; INFORM: tell, announce, divulge, admit, reveal

impartial *adj.* unbiased, equitable, disinterested, dispassionate, equal, fair

impartiality *n.* objectivity, candor, equality, fairness

impasse *n.* deadlock, standstill, cessation, pause

impassioned *adj.* ardent, fervent, passionate

impassive *adj.* emotionless, unemotional, unmoved

impatience *n.* agitation, restlessness, anxiety, excitement, nervousness

impatient *adj.* anxious, eager, feverish, restless

impeach *v.* charge, arraign, denounce, indict, discredit, reprimand, blame, incriminate

impeccable *adj.* flawless, perfect

impede *v.* hinder, obstruct, slow

impediment *n.* obstruction, hindrance, obstacle, difficulty, barrier

impel *v.* drive, force, urge

impend *v.* approach, threaten

impenetrable *adj.* **DENSE:** impervious, compact, hard, firm, thick, compressed; **INCOMPREHENSIBLE:** unintelligible, inscrutable, unfathomable, obscure, unexplainable

impenitent *adj.* unrepentant, remorseless

imperative *adj.* **NECESSARY:** obligatory, mandatory; **AUTHORITATIVE:** masterful, commanding, dominant, aggressive, powerful

imperfect *adj.* flawed, incomplete, deficient, faulty

imperfection *n.* fault, flaw, stain, blemish

imperious *adj.* haughty, arrogant

impersonal *adj.* detached, disinterested, indifferent

impersonate *v.* portray, mimic, represent, imitate

impersonation *n.* role, enactment, performance

impertinent *adj.* impudent, saucy, insolent, rude

impervious *adj.* impassable, impenetrable, watertight, impermeable

impetuous *adj.* hasty, impulsive, rash, spontaneous

impetus *n.* force, momentum, stimulus, incentive, purpose, reason

impinge *v.* encroach, infringe, strike, touch

impious *adj.* sinful, profane, blasphemous, bad

implement *n.* tool, instrument, appliance, utensil

implicate *v.* involve, connect, associate, link, relate

implication *n.* indication, inference, guess

implicit *adj.* **UNDERSTOOD:** implied; **DEFINITE:** certain, absolute, accurate, inevitable

imply *v.* indicate, intimate, suggest, hint, implicate, signify, mean, indicate

impolite *adj.* discourteous, churlish, rude, sullen

impolitic *adj.* imprudent, unwise

import *n.* meaning, signification

importance *n.* import, consequence, bearing, influence, emphasis, weight, relevance

important *adj.* **WEIGHTY:** significant, momentous, essential, critical, primary, foremost, valuable, crucial, vital, serious, consequential; **EMINENT:** illustrious, well–known, influential, famous

importune *v.* urge, entreat, press, implore

impose *v.* force, presume, burden, compel

imposing *adj.* stirring, overwhelming, impressive

imposition *n.* burden, pressure, encumbrance, demand, restraint

impossibility *n.* hopelessness, difficulty, futility

impossible *adj.* inconceivable, vain, unattainable, insurmountable, unworkable, futile, hopeless

impostor *n.* fraud, deceiver, pretender, charlatan

imposture *n.* ruse, deceit, hoax, sham

impotent *adj.* **WEAK:** powerless, inept, infirm, unable; **STERILE:** barren, frigid, unproductive

impound *v.* appropriate, take, usurp, seize

impoverish *v.* bankrupt, exhaust, ruin, destroy

impoverished *adj.* bankrupt, broke, poor, insolvent, destitute, ruined

impractical *adj.* unrealistic, unworkable, improbable, illogical, absurd, wild, impossible, idealistic

impregnable *adj.* invulnerable, unassailable, impenetrable

impregnate *v.* **PERMEATE:** fill, pervade, soak, infuse; **BEGET:** conceive, reproduce, fertilize

impress *v.* **MARK:** indent, emboss, imprint, dent, stamp; **FASCINATE:** affect, dazzle, stir, fascinate

impression *n.* **MARK:** imprint, dent, indentation, depression; **EFFECT:** response, reaction; **NOTION:** theory, conjecture, supposition, opinion

impressionable *adj.* perceptive, receptive, affected

impressive *adj.* stirring, moving, inspiring, thrilling, intense, dramatic, absorbing, profound, remarkable, extraordinary, notable, momentous

imprint *n.* **IDENTIFICATION:** emblem, banner, trademark; **IMPRESSION:** dent, indentation

imprint *v.* print, stamp, mark, designate

imprison *v.* jail, confine, incarcerate, detain, hold, intern, cage, enclose

improbable *adj.* doubtful, unlikely

improper *adj.* indecent, incongruous, inadvisable, untimely, inappropriate, unbefitting, unsuitable

improve *v.* update, refine, enrich, enhance, augment

improvement *n.* betterment, advancement, development, growth, enrichment, renovation, reorganization, amendment, revision, refinement, modernization, enhancement

impudent *adj.* bold, insolent, rude

impulse *n.* **THROB:** surge, beat, pulsation; **FANCY:** urge, stimulus, whim, caprice, notion, spontaneity, inclination, disposition

impulsive *adj.* impetuous, spontaneous

impure *adj.* adulterated, diluted, debased, tainted, contaminated, polluted, corrupted, doctored

impute *v.* ascribe, assign, charge

inability *n.* incompetence, incapacity, shortcoming, failure, weakness, lack, frailty

inaccessible *adj.* distant, rare, remote, separated

inaccuracy *n.* mistake, exaggeration, deception, error

inaccurate *adj.* incorrect, inexact, fallacious, incorrect, mistaken, wrong

inactive *adj.* idle, lazy, dormant, still, motionless

inadequacy *n.* inferiority, weakness, defect, flaw, drawback, shortcoming, blemish, lack

inadequate *adj.* insufficient, lacking, scanty, meager, deficient, imperfect, defective, unsatisfactory

inane *adj.* senseless, pointless, foolish, silly

inanimate *adj.* lifeless, dull, inert, idle, motionless

inappropriate *adj.* improper, unsuitable

inapt *adj.* unfit, unsuitable

inarticulate *adj.* **MUTE:** reticent, speechless, wordless; **INCOMPREHENSIBLE:** obscure, unintelligible, vague

inattentive *adj.* preoccupied, indifferent, negligent, careless, diverted

inaugurate *v.* induct, begin, introduce, initiate, begin

incalculable *adj.* unpredictable, uncertain
incantation *n.* chant, charm, recitation, supplication
incapable *adj.* inadequate, incompetent, inexperienced, naïve, poor, unqualified, unsuited
incapacitate *v.* disable, disqualify, invalidate
incarcerate *v.* confine, imprison
incarnate *adj.* bodily, manifest, personified
incense *n.* scent, fragrance, essence, perfume
incense *v.* inflame, anger, infuriate
incentive *n.* motive, spur, inducement, stimulus, impetus, enticement, temptation, inspiration, encouragement, reason
incessant *adj.* continual, ceaseless, constant
inchoate *adj.* shapeless, formless
incidence *n.* range, occurrence, scope
incident *n.* occurrence, happening, episode, event
incidental *adj.* subsidiary, related, subordinate
incinerate *v.* burn, cremate
incise *v.* cut, engrave, dissect, chop, split, divide
incision *n.* cut, gash, slash, surgery
incisive *adj.* cutting, keen, sarcastic, trenchant
incite *v.* rouse, stir, stimulate, provoke, spur, goad, persuade, induce, urge, inspire
inclement *adj.* stormy, severe; cruel, merciless
inclination *n.* **TENDENCY:** bias, bent, propensity, predilection, penchant, leaning, disposition, preference, drift, trend; **SLANT:** pitch, slope, incline, angle, ramp, bank, lean, list, grade
incline *v.* **LEAN:** tilt, bow, nod; **TEND:** prefer, favor

inclined *adj.* SLOPING: leaning, slanted, angled; TENDING: likely, prone

include *v.* contain, embrace, involve, incorporate, constitute, interject, insert

inclusive *adj.* including, incorporating

incoherent *adj.* UNCONNECTED: disorganized; INDISTINCT: unintelligible, muddled, muttered, muffled

income *n.* revenue, earnings, commission, salary, wages, profit, dividends, proceeds, receipts

incommensurate *adj.* disproportionate, inadequate

incomparable *adj.* excellent, exceptional, matchless, perfect, superior, unequaled, unique, unusual

incompatible *adj.* irreconcilable, incongruous, contrary, clashing, contradictory, inconstant, discordant

incompetent *adj.* incapable, unfit, unskilled, bungling, ineffectual, clumsy, awkward, inexperienced

incomplete *adj.* imperfect, rough, unfinished

inconceivable *adj.* unthinkable, unbelievable

incongruous *adj.* inconsistent, contradictory

inconsequential *adj.* irrelevant, trivial, unnecessary

inconsiderate *adj.* thoughtless, boorish, impolite, discourteous, rude

inconsistent *adj.* illogical, contradictory, incoherent

inconspicuous *adj.* concealed, hidden, obscure

inconstant *adj.* varying, fickle

inconvenience *n.* trouble, discomfort, bother

incorporation *n.* embodiment, addition

incorrect *adj.* false, mistaken, unreliable, wrong
incorrigible *adj.* bad, difficult
increase *n.* growth, addition, development, spread, enlargement, expansion, escalation
increase *v.* extend, enlarge, expand, dilate, broaden, widen, thicken, deepen, build, lengthen, augment, escalate, amplify, supplement
incredible *adj.* unbelievable, improbable, ridiculous
incredulous *adj.* disbelieving, skeptical
incriminate *v.* charge, involve, implicate, blame
incumbent *adj.* binding, obligatory
incurable *adj.* fatal, serious, hopeless, deadly
incursion *n.* inroad, invasion
indebted *adj.* obligated, grateful, appreciative
indecent *adj.* offensive, immoral, bad, lewd, shameful
indecency *n.* vulgarity, impropriety
indecision *n.* hesitation, doubt, uncertainty
indecisive *adj.* irresolute, unstable
indefinite *adj.* vague, uncertain, unsure, unsettled
indelible *adj.* ingrained, enduring, strong, permanent
indemnify *v.* compensate, protect
indentation *n.* imprint, recession, depression, dent
independence *n.* freedom, sovereignty, license
indestructible *adj.* durable, immortal, permanent
index *v.* list, catalog, alphabetize, arrange, tabulate
indicate *v.* **SIGNIFY:** symbolize, betoken, intimate, mean; **DESIGNATE:** show, name, point

indication *n.* symptom, evidence, sign, hint
indicator *n.* dial, pointer
indictment *n.* accusation, detention, incrimination
indifferent *adj.* unconcerned, cool, unemotional, unsympathetic, heartless, unresponsive, unfeeling, nonchalant, impassive, detached, callous, stony, remote, reserved, distant, arrogant, unmoved
indigent *adj.* destitute, impoverished, poor
indignant *adj.* angry, upset, displeased, piqued
indignity *n.* affront, humiliation, injury, insult
indirect *adj.* devious, roundabout, tortuous, twisting, devious, sinister, rambling, oblique
indiscreet *adj.* imprudent, rash, misguided, tactless
indiscriminate *adj.* random, chaotic, aimless
indispensable *adj.* necessary, required, essential
indisposed *adj.* ILL: ailing, sickly, weak; DISINCLINED: reluctant, unwilling
indisputable *adj.* incontrovertible, undeniable, undoubted, unquestionable, certain
indistinct *adj.* vague, confused, indefinite, obscure
individual *adj.* personal, particular, solitary, distinctive, personalized, sole, private
indoctrinate *v.* instruct, implant, influence, teach
indomitable *adj.* invincible, unconquerable
induce *v.* begin, cause, effect, persuade, instigate, produce
inducement *n.* incentive, influence, motive, stimulus

induct *v.* admit, recruit, enroll, conscript, draft

induction *n.* **REASONING:** rationalization, conjecture, reason; **INITIATION:** ordination, consecration

indulge *v.* humor, coddle, entertain, gratify

indulgence *n.* **HUMORING:** coddling, pampering, spoiling, placating, gratifying; **REVELRY:** intemperance, greed, waste

industrious *adj.* diligent, intent, involved, active, busy

industry *n.* perseverance, persistence, application, enterprise, zeal, attention

inebriate *v.* exhilarate, intoxicate, stupefy

ineffective *adj.* inadequate, incompetent, weak

inefficient *adj.* prodigal, wasteful, improvident

ineligible *adj.* unqualified, unsuitable, unfit

inept *adj.* bungling, clumsy, incompetent, awkward

inert *adj.* inactive, sluggish, still, dormant, idle

inevitable *adj.* unavoidable, irresistible, fated, sure, inescapable, destined, unalterable, ordained

inexorable *adj.* rigid, stubborn, inflexible

inexperienced *adj.* unskilled, untried, youthful, new, immature, tender, raw, green

infallible *adj.* perfect, accurate, certain

infamous *adj.* notorious, wicked, heinous, offensive

infant *n.* baby, minor, child, tot

infantile *adj.* childlike, juvenile, childish, naïve

infect *v.* taint, defile, spoil

infer *v.* deduce, conclude, gather, assume

inferior *adj.* subordinate, mediocre, common, poor

inferiority *n.* deficiency, inadequacy, weakness

infernal *adj.* fiendish, devilish

infest *v.* **CONTAMINATE:** pollute, infect, corrupt; **INVADE:** crowd, jam, teem, flood, flock, overwhelm

infidelity *n.* unfaithfulness, disloyalty, adultery

infiltrate *v.* permeate, pervade, penetrate, join

infinite *adj.* endless, limitless, countless, incalculable, boundless, immense, endless

infinitesimal *adj.* tiny, small

infirm *adj.* sickly, decrepit, weak

infirmary *n.* clinic, sickroom, hospital

infirmity *n.* disease, weakness, frailty, debility

inflame *v.* **AROUSE:** incense, disturb, excite; **HURT:** redden, swell; **BURN:** kindle, scorch, ignite

inflate *v.* **DISTEND:** expand, swell, bloat, balloon; **EXAGGERATE:** magnify, overestimate, raise

inflection *n.* tone, enunciation, intonation, accent

inflexibility *n.* toughness, rigidity, stiffness, firmness

inflexible *adj.* rigid, unyielding, taut, firm, stiff

inflict *v.* impose, administer, deliver, strike, cause

influence *n.* power, authority, control, command, esteem, prominence, prestige, reputation

influence *v.* affect, impress, compel, urge, shape, convince, persuade, motivate

influential *adj.* prominent, substantial, powerful, important, significant

inform *v.* tell, betray, instruct, relate, teach

informal *adj.* casual, intimate, relaxed, natural, unofficial

information *n.* NEWS: report, notice, message; KNOWLEDGE: facts, evidence, details, statistics, data

infraction *n.* violation, breach

infrequent *adj.* seldom, occasional, scarce, rare

infringe *v.* encroach, trespass, transgress, meddle

infuriate *v.* aggravate, enrage, provoke, anger

infuse *v.* fill, inspire; steep

ingenious *adj.* able, clever, cunning, intelligent, gifted, original, resourceful, shrewd, skillful

ingenuity *n.* cleverness, imagination, inventiveness, originality, productiveness, resourcefulness

ingenuous *adj.* candid, innocent, straightforward

ingrain *v.* imbue, fix, instill, teach

ingratiate *v.* charm, seduce, disarm

ingredient *n.* component, constituent, element

inhabit *v.* dwell, occupy, reside, stay

inhabitant *n.* occupant, dweller, lodger, roomer, boarder, tenant, resident

inherent *adj.* inborn, inbred, inherited, innate, intrinsic, native, natural

inherit *v.* acquire, receive, succeed, get

inheritance *n.* bequest, legacy, heritage, gift

inhibit *v.* check, restrain, repress, frustrate, hinder

inhibition *n.* restraint, hindrance, interference, constraint

inhuman *adj.* mean, heartless, cruel, fierce, ruthless

iniquity *n.* crime, evil, injustice, sin, wickedness, wrong, abomination

initial *adj.* beginning, starting, basic, primary, elementary, first, fundamental

initiate *n.* beginner, learner, novice
initiation *n.* beginning, introduction; indoctrination, induction, orientation
initiative *n.* enterprise, responsibility, enthusiasm, ambition
injure *v.* harm, damage, wound, abuse, hurt, wrong
injurious *adj.* harmful, detrimental, damaging
injury *n.* hurt, abrasion, wound, laceration, affliction
injustice *n.* infringement, transgression, violation, breach, infraction, wrong
inkling *n.* hint, indication, notion, innuendo, suspicion, suggestion
inmate *n.* occupant, patient, convict, prisoner
inn *n.* tavern, hostel, hotel, motel, resort
innate *adj.* inborn, native
innermost *adj.* intimate, private, secret
innocence *n.* honesty, simplicity, purity, naïveté, chastity, ignorance, virtue
innocent *adj.* **PURE:** unblemished, wholesome, upright, virtuous, righteous, angelic; **GUILTLESS:** honest, blameless, faultless; **OPEN:** guileless, frank, childish, naïve, natural, simple; **HARMLESS:** innocuous, inoffensive, safe
innovation *n.* change, newness, addition
innuendo *n.* hint, insinuation, aside, intimation
innumerable *adj.* countless, incalculable, infinite
inopportune *adj.* disadvantageous, ill–timed, inappropriate, awkward, untimely
input *n.* data, information, knowledge, facts
input *v.* add, enter
inquest *n.* inquiry, investigation
inquire *v.* ask, investigate, probe

inquiry *n.* probe, analysis, hearing, examination

inquisitive *adj.* curious, questioning, analytical, meddling, prying, snoopy, nosy, interested

inquisitor *n.* examiner, questioner

inroad *n.* encroachment, invasion

insane *adj.* DEMENTED: crazed, frenzied, lunatic, balmy, psychotic, raving, deluded, possessed, obsessed

insanity *n.* abnormality, dementia, psychosis, neurosis, phobia, mania

insatiate *adj.* ravenous, voracious

inscribe *v.* address, carve, dedicate, engrave, write

inscription *n.* dedication, engraving, legend

insecure *adj.* anxious, vague, uncertain, troubled

insert *v.* introduce, place, inject, include

insidious *adj.* treacherous, deceitful, corrupting, harmful

insight *n.* perspicacity, shrewdness, intelligence, intuition, wisdom, understanding

insignia *n.* badge, rank, ensign, symbol, decoration, emblem

insignificant *adj.* trivial, unimportant, irrelevant, petty, trifling

insincere *adj.* deceitful, pretentious, dishonest, shifty, false, hypocritical, sly

insinuate *v.* hint, suggest, imply, purport, mention

insipid *adj.* dull, flat, tasteless, uninteresting, bland

insist *v.* persist, demand, exhort, urge

insolent *adj.* disrespectful, insulting, rude, impertinent, overbearing

insolvent *adj.* bankrupt, broke, failed, ruined

inspect *v.* examine, probe, scrutinize, scan, audit

inspiration *n.* **IDEA:** notion, whim, fancy, impulse, thought; **STIMULUS:** spur, influence, incentive

inspire *v.* encourage, enthuse, invigorate, motivate, stimulate

install *v.* establish, introduce, inaugurate

installation *n.* induction, ordination, inauguration, launching, establishment

installment *n.* payment, part

instance *n.* example, case, situation, occurrence

instant *adj.* momentary, quick, pressing, current

instantly *adv.* urgently, directly, immediately

instigate *v.* incite, initiate, spur, urge

instill *v.* infuse, indoctrinate, implant, teach

instinct *n.* impulse, sense, intuition

instinctive *adj.* intuitive, spontaneous, natural

institute *n.* establishment, foundation, organization

institute *v.* establish, found, launch, organize

institution *n.* establishment, organization, company, association, business, university

instruct *v.* inform, teach, order, direct, educate

instruction *n.* guidance, direction, education

instructor *n.* professor, tutor, lecturer, teacher

instrument *n.* **UTENSIL:** apparatus, implement, device, tool; **CONTRACT:** deed, document

insubordinate *adj.* disobedient, mutinous, treacherous, defiant, rebellious

insufferable *adj.* difficult, intolerable, unbearable

insufficient *adj.* meager, skimpy, inadequate

insular *adj.* detached, isolated, narrow, provincial

insult *n.* affront, indignity, abuse, impudence, impertinence, insolence, mockery, derision, invective

insult *v.* offend, mock, annoy, taunt, ridicule, provoke

insurance *n.* security, indemnity, assurance, warrant

insure *v.* secure, warrant, protect, guarantee

insurrection *n.* uprising, rebellion, insurgence, revolt

intact *adj.* entire, whole, together

intangible *adj.* indefinite, uncertain, vague

integral *adj.* **WHOLE:** entire; **NECESSARY:** essential

integrate *v.* blend, combine, mix

integrity *n.* morality, honesty, uprightness, honor

intellect *n.* understanding, intelligence, mentality

intellectual *adj.* smart, creative, intelligent, learned, reasonable, sensible

intellectual *n.* highbrow, genius, philosopher, academician, egghead, brain

intelligence *n.* **UNDERSTANDING:** discernment, comprehension, judgment; **INTELLECT:** mind, brain, mentality; **INFORMATION:** statistics, facts, news

intelligent *adj.* clever, bright, smart, brilliant, keen, perceptive, imaginative, discerning, knowledgeable, understanding, quick, sharp, comprehending

intelligentsia *n.* intellectuals, elite, literati, aristocrats

intelligible *adj.* understandable, comprehensible, plain, clear, obvious

intend *v.* **PROPOSE:** purpose, aspire, aim, plan; **MEAN:** indicate, signify, denote

intense *adj.* deep, profound, heightened, impassioned, exaggerated, violent, excessive, keen, piercing, cutting, severe

intensify *v.* enhance, heighten, sharpen, emphasize, increase, strengthen

intensity *n.* concentration, strength, fervor, power, force, passion, ardor, severity

intensive *adj.* accelerated, hard, fast, severe

intent *adj.* fixed, absorbed

intent *n.* design, plan

intention *n.* purpose, aim, end, plan

intentional *adj.* deliberate, planned

inter *v.* bury, entomb

intercept *v.* obstruct, ambush, block, hijack

intercession *n.* entreaty, petition, mediation, plea

interchange *n.* **BARTER:** trade, exchange, substitution; **INTERSECTION:** cloverleaf, off–ramp

interest *n.* **CONCERN:** attention, excitement, curiosity, enthusiasm; **SHARE:** claim, right, stake

interest *v.* arouse, involve, fascinate, intrigue, attract, amuse, please, entertain

interested *adj.* **AROUSED:** stimulated, curious, responsive, roused, stirred, attracted; **OCCUPIED:** engrossed, obsessed, absorbed, involved

interesting *adj.* intriguing, fascinating, engaging, absorbing, captivating

interfere *v.* meddle, intervene, interpose, interlope

interference *n.* **MEDDLING:** interruption, trespassing, tampering; **OBSTRUCTION:** check, obstacle, restraint

interior *adj.* within, inside, inland, inner, internal, inward, central, inside

interlope *v.* interfere, intrude, meddle

intermediate *adj.* intervening, medium, intermediary, median, central, middle

intermediary *n.* mediator, agent

intermission *n.* pause, interval, interim

intermix *v.* mix, mingle, blend

intermittent *adj.* cyclic, recurring, periodic, recurrent, changing, irregular

intern *v.* confine, detain, imprison

internal *adj.* interior, inner, domestic, inside, inward, intrinsic, innate, inherent

interpret *v.* translate, explain, render, delineate, define, describe

interpretation *n.* rendition, description, representation, presentation, explanation

interrogate *v.* question, ask, examine

interrogation *n.* inquiry, investigation, examination

interrupt *v.* intervene, interfere, infringe

intersperse *v.* scatter, strew

interval *n.* time, period, interlude, interim, pause

intervene *v.* intercede, mediate, negotiate, reconcile

intervention *n.* intercession, interruption, interference, intrusion

interview *n.* meeting, audience, conference

interview *v.* interrogate, question, examine

intimacy *n.* closeness, familiarity, affection

intimate *adj.* familiar, close, trusted, secret, special

intimate *n.* friend, associate, companion, lover

intimate *v.* hint, allude

intimidate *v.* frighten, threaten

intolerable *adj.* insufferable, unendurable, unbearable, impossible, offensive, painful, undesirable

intolerant *adj.* dogmatic, bigoted, prejudiced

intoxicate *v.* inebriate, muddle, befuddle
intransigence *n.* obstinacy, stubbornness
intransigent *adj.* intolerant, uncompromising, stubborn
intricacy *n.* elaborateness, complexity, difficulty
intricate *adj.* involved, complex, tricky, abstruse, difficult, obscure
intrigue *v.* **SCHEME:** plot, devise; **DELIGHT:** please, attract, fascinate, charm, entertain
intrinsic *adj.* essential, inborn, inherent
introduce *v.* **PRESENT:** submit, advance, offer, propose, acquaint; **INSERT:** add, enter, include
introduction *n.* **ADMITTANCE:** initiation, installation, entrance; **PRESENTATION:** debut, acquaintance, start, awakening, baptism; **PREFACE:** preamble, foreword, prologue, overture
introductory *adj.* opening, early, starting, beginning, preparatory, primary, original
introvert *n.* loner, recluse
intrude *v.* encroach, trespass, interfere, meddle
intuition *n.* instinct, hunch, feeling, foreknowledge
intuitive *adj.* instinctive, natural
inure *v.* acclimate, accustom
inured *adj.* hardened, cold, unfeeling
invade *v.* attack, intrude. infringe, trespass, interfere
invader *n.* trespasser, alien, attacker, enemy
invalidate *v.* void, revoke, annul, refute, nullify
invaluable *adj.* priceless, expensive, dear, valuable
invariable *adj.* unchanging, uniform, static, constant
invective *adj.* railing, abusive

inveigh *v.* protest, declaim, harangue, rant
inveigle *v.* coax, entice, flatter
invent *v.* create, discover, originate, devise, fashion, form, design, improvise, contrive, build
invention *n.* contrivance, contraption, design, innovation
inventory *n.* **LIST:** itemization, register, index, record; **INSPECTION:** examination, summary
inverse *adj.* reversed, contrary
invert *v.* **UPSET:** overturn, tip; **REVERSE:** change, transpose, exchange
investigate *v.* inquire, review, examine, analyze, scrutinize, study
investigation *n.* inquiry search research examination
inveterate *adj.* addicted, well–established, persisting
invidious *adj.* envious, malicious, spiteful
invigorate *v.* animate, energize, enervate, enliven, excite, exhilarate, freshen, stimulate
invincible *adj.* impregnable, invulnerable, powerful, strong, unconquerable
inviolate *adj.* hallowed, holy, intact, pure, sacred
inviting *adj.* appealing, attractive, encouraging, tempting
invocation *n.* prayer, appeal
invoice *n.* notice, statement, bill, receipt
invoke *v.* implore, solicit, summon
involuntary *adj.* unintentional, uncontrolled, instinctive, automatic, habitual
involve *v.* associate, commit, connect, comprise, connect, entangle, implicate, include, link
involved *adj.* **COMPLICATED:** elaborate, entangled, intricate, sophisticated;

IMPLICATED: connected, emotional, engrossed, incriminated

invulnerable *adj.* secure, strong, invincible, indestructible, formidable, safe

iota *n.* jot, particle, trace, scrap, grain, bit, speck

irascible *adj.* irritable, temperamental, testy, touchy, petulant, cranky

irate *adj.* enraged, furious, incensed, agitated, angry

irk *v.* vex, annoy, harass, disturb, bother

irony *n.* satire, ridicule, mockery, derision, sarcasm

irrational *adj.* illogical, unreasoning, specious, fallacious, wrong, senseless, silly, ridiculous

irreconcilable *adj.* implacable, incompatible

irrefutable *adj.* conclusive, evident, indisputable, obvious, undeniable

irregular *adj.* **UNEVEN:** rough, fitful, random, occasional, fluctuating, wavering, intermittent, variable, sporadic; **QUESTIONABLE:** strange, debatable, suspicious; **UNIQUE:** abnormal, extraordinary, unusual

irrelevant *adj.* immaterial, unrelated, extraneous, pointless, trivial, unnecessary

irreparable *adj.* incurable, hopeless, irreversible, destroyed, ruined

irresistible *adj.* compelling, overpowering, overwhelming, powerful

irresponsible *adj.* capricious, thoughtless, flighty, fickle, rash, unstable, lax, shiftless, unreliable

irrevocable *adj.* permanent, indelible, inevitable

irritable *adj.* cranky, testy, touchy, huffy, peevish, petulant, surly, moody, churlish, grouchy, grumpy

irritant *n.* annoyance, bother, nuisance

irritate *v.* **BOTHER:** exasperate, pester, disturb, annoy; **INFLAME:** redden, chafe, sting, burn, hurt, itch

irritated *adj.* annoyed, disturbed, upset, bothered

island *n.* isle, bar, archipelago

isolate *v.* detach, insulate, confine, seclude, divide

isolation *n.* solitude, seclusion, segregation, confinement, separation

issue *n.* **DISTRIBUTION:** publication; **TOPIC:** subject, concern, argument; **EDITION:** number, copy

issue *v.* **EMERGE:** proceed, appear, begin; **RELEASE:** circulate, announce, advertise, declare, publish

itemize *v.* list, catalog, enumerate, number, detail

itinerant *adj.* traveling, roving, nomadic, wandering

itinerant *n.* wanderer, nomad, vagrant, tramp

jab *v.* poke, punch, hit, blow

jacket *n.* coat, tunic, jerkin, parka, cape

jackpot *n.* bonanza, winnings, luck, profit, success

jaded *adj.* cold, impassive, indifferent, nonchalant, world–weary

jail *n.* penitentiary, cage, cell, dungeon, bastille, stockade, prison, lockup

jam *n.* **PRESERVES:** conserve, marmalade, jelly; **TROUBLE:** dilemma, problem, difficulty

jam *v.* compress, bind, squeeze, push, pack, press

jar *n.* **CONTAINER:** crock, vessel, beaker, cruet, bottle, flagon, flask; **JOLT:** jounce, thud, thump, bump

jargon *n.* argot, patois, idiom, vernacular, colloquialism, localism, dialect, slang

jaunt *n.* excursion, trip, tour, journey, walk

jaunty *adj.* buoyant, chipper, dashing, frisky, rakish

jealous *adj.* envious, possessive, resentful

jeer *n.* derision, ridicule, taunt

jeer *v.* deride, insult, mock, ridicule, taunt

jell *v.* set, harden, stiffen, thicken

jeopardize *v.* endanger, imperil, expose, venture, risk

jeopardy *n.* danger, peril, hazard, chance

jerk *n.* **TWITCH:** tic, shake, quiver; **DOLT:** scamp, scoundrel, fool, rascal

jerk *v.* **SPASM:** quiver, shiver, shake, twitch; **PULL:** yank, snatch, seize

jest *v.* joke, tease, spoof, scoff, deride

jester *n.* comedian, buffoon, joker, actor, clown, fool

jetty *n.* pier, wharf

jewel *n.* prize, bauble, gem, trinket

jewelry *n.* bangles, gems, baubles, trinkets, adornment

jiggle *v.* shake, twitch, wiggle, jerk

jingle *n.* rhyme, verse

jingle *v.* tinkle, clink, rattle

jinx *n.* hex, spell

job *n.* **EMPLOYMENT:** situation, position, calling, vocation, career, pursuit, business, profession, trade; **TASK:** assignment, undertaking, project, chore, errand, duty; **ASSIGNMENT:** output, duty

jobber *n.* broker, wholesaler

jocular *adj.* comic, frolicsome, funny, witty

jocund *adj.* cheerful, happy, joyful, lighthearted

jog *v.* **TROT:** canter, lope, nudge, run; **NUDGE:** bump, jar, jostle, shake

join *v.* unite, blend, combine, connect, couple, attach, link, fuse, associate

joint *adj.* joined, shared, united

joint *n.* juncture, union, coupling, hinge, link, seam, connection; **DIVE:** hangout, bar, tavern

joke *v.* jest, quip, banter, laugh, play, frolic, wisecrack

jolly *adj.* gay, merry, joyful, happy

jolt *n.* **BUMP:** jar, bounce, blow, jerk; **SURPRISE:** jar, start, shock, surprise

jostle *v.* push, elbow, nudge

jot *n.* bit, iota

jot *v.* write, note, scribble, record

journal *n.* **DIARY:** almanac, chronicle, record; **PERIODICAL:** publication, newspaper, magazine, daily

journalist *n.* columnist, commentator, reporter

journey *n.* trip, tour, excursion, jaunt, travel

jovial *adj.* affable, amiable, merry, happy

joy *n.* mirth, delight, playfulness, gaiety, geniality, merriment, levity, jubilation, laughter

joyful *adj.* elated, glad, happy, joyous, jubilant

joyous *adj.* blithe, glad, gay, happy

jubilant *adj.* ecstatic, elated, exuberant, delighted, rapturous, joyous

jubilee *n.* anniversary, celebration

judge *n.* **MODERATOR:** arbiter, referee, umpire; **CONNOISSEUR:** analyst, critic, expert, specialist

judge *v.* hear, decide, adjudicate, rule

judgment *n.* **DISCERNMENT:** discrimination, taste; **DECISION:** determination, analysis, pronouncement, conclusion, verdict

judgmental *adj.* biased, prejudiced, unfair

judicial *adj.* legalistic, administrative, lawful

judicious *adj.* prudent, discreet, sound, sensible, practical, reasonable
jug *n.* crock, flask, pitcher, container
juice *n.* sap, extract, fluid, liquid
juicy *adj.* succulent, moist, watery, syrupy
jumble *n.* clutter, mess, hodgepodge, confusion
jump *v.* **LEAP:** vault, spring, lunge, bound, skip, hurdle; **ACCOST:** attack; **PLUMMET:** plunge, dive, fall
junction *n.* **MEETING:** joining, coupling, joint; **CROSSROADS:** crossing, intersection
juncture *n.* joining, junction
jungle *n.* tangle, wilderness, undergrowth, forest
junior *adj.* younger, lower
junk *n.* scrap, waste, garbage, filth, trash
junk *v.* abandon, discard
junket *n.* picnic, excursion, trip
jurisdiction *n.* authority, range, province, scope, domain, empire, sovereignty
jurist *n.* judge, attorney, adviser, lawyer
jury *n.* council, committee, tribunal, panel
just *adj.* **PRECISE:** exact, correct, perfect, accurate; **HARDLY:** barely, scarcely; **ONLY:** merely, simply, plainly; **FAIR:** impartial, equal, righteous
justice *n.* **FAIRNESS:** right, truth, equity; **LAWFULNESS:** legality, legitimacy, sanction, constitutionality, authority, custom; **ADMINISTRATION:** adjudication, arbitration, hearing, trial, litigation, judgment; **JUDGE:** magistrate, umpire, chancellor
justification *n.* excuse, defense, reason, explanation
justify *v.* **VINDICATE:** absolve, acquit, clear, excuse, exonerate; **EXPLAIN:** apologize, excuse, defend

jut *adj.* extend, bulge, project
juvenile *adj.* childish, youthful, adolescent, teenage
juxtapose *v.* compare, contrast

keen *adj.* **ASTUTE:** clever, intelligent, shrewd; **EAGER:** ardent, intent, zealous; **SHARP:** pointed, edged
keep *v.* **HOLD:** retain, possess, have, seize, save; **MAINTAIN:** preserve, retain, conserve; **STORE:** hoard, stash, cache, preserve; **REMAIN:** stay, continue, abide, settle; **CONTINUE:** sustain, endure;
keepsake *n.* memento, token, remembrance
keg *n.* cask, drum, vat, barrel
kernel *n.* seed, grain, core, nut, germ
kettle *n.* vessel, cauldron, saucepan, pot
key *n.* **OPENER:** latchkey, passkey; **SOLUTION:** clue, code, indicator, answer
kickback *n.* **BRIBE:** grease, payback, tribute; **BACKLASH:** backfire, reaction, recoil
kickoff *adj.* start, opening, beginning, launching
kid *n.* child, son, daughter, tot, boy, girl
kid *v.* mock, tease
kidnap *v.* abduct, capture, shanghai
kill *v.* **SLAY:** slaughter, murder, assassinate, massacre, butcher, finish, execute, liquidate, dispatch; **VETO:** cancel, prohibit, refuse, forbid; **CANCEL:** annul, nullify, counteract
killer *n.* murderer, gangster, assassin, cutthroat
killjoy *n.* grouch, sourpuss, spoilsport
kiln *n.* dryer, oast, oven
kind *adj.* accommodating, agreeable, considerate, charitable, compassionate, generous, loving, tender, tactful, kindhearted, sensitive

kind *n.* **CLASS:** classification, species, genus; **TYPE:** sort, variety, description, designation

kindhearted *adj.* amiable, generous, good, humane

kindle *v.* fire, excite, light, ignite

kindly *adj.* generous, helpful, good, humane, kind

kindness *n.* **TENDERNESS:** consideration, thoughtfulness, humanity, understanding, compassion, graciousness, kindheartedness; **SERVICE:** benevolence, philanthropy, lift, boost, help

kindred *adj.* alike, kin, connected, related, similar

kingdom *n.* realm, domain, country, empire, principality, dominions, territory

kink *n.* bend, obstacle, hitch

kinship *n.* affiliation, relationship, connection, alliance, family

kit *n.* **EQUIPMENT:** material, tools, outfit; **PACK:** poke, knapsack, satchel, bag, container

knack *n.* dexterity, trick, skill, faculty, ability

knapsack *n.* sack, bag, pack, kit, rucksack

knead *v.* work, shape, twist, press

kneel *v.* genuflect, bend, stoop, bow, curtsey

knickknack *n.* bric–a–brac, curio, ornament, trifle, bauble, trinket, showpiece, gewgaw

knife *n.* blade, dagger, stiletto, lancet, machete, scalpel, dirk

knit *v.* unite, join, intermingle, affiliate

knob *n.* **PROJECTION:** bulge, protuberance, bulge, node, bump; **HANDLE:** doorknob, latch

knock *v.* rap, strike, thump, whack, beat, tap, hit

knoll *n.* mound, hill, hillock

knot *n.* FASTENING: bond, cinch, hitch, tie, splice; CLUSTER: group, crowd, gang; SNARL: snag tangle twist
know *v.* UNDERSTAND: comprehend, apprehend; RECOGNIZE: perceive, discern, acknowledge
knowing *adj.* SHREWD: acute, clever, intelligent, reasonable, sharp; DELIBERATE: conscious, intentional
knowledge *n.* information, learning, lore, wisdom, enlightenment, expertise, awareness, insight

label *n.* tag, marker, identification, name
label *v.* identify, mark, name, specify
labor *n.* TASK: work, activity, toil, operation, employment, undertaking, job; EXERTION: energy, industry, diligence, strain, stress, effort
labor *v.* work, toil, strive
laborious *adj.* arduous, difficult, exhausting, onerous
lace *v.* fasten, tie, adorn, strap, bind, close
lacerate *v.* wound, tear, injure, damage
lacing *n.* bond, hitch, tie, fastener, knot
lack *n.* ABSENCE: deficiency, scarcity, insufficiency, inadequacy; WANT: need, privation, poverty, distress
lack *v.* need, want, require
lackadaisical *adj.* halfhearted, indifferent, languid
lackey *n.* MENIAL: servant; FLUNKY: toady, underling
laconic *adj.* concise, curt, succinct, terse
lad *n.* fellow, youth, stripling, boy, child
ladle *n.* spoon, skimmer, scoop
lady *n.* woman, female, matron, gentlewoman
ladylike *adj.* cultured, well-bred, polite, refined

lag *v.* tarry, straggle, falter, delay

laggard *n.* loiterer, idler

lair *n.* den, cave, home, pen

lame *adj.* halt, impaired, handicapped, limping

lament *v.* grieve, deplore

lamentation *n.* dirge, mourning, tears, wailing

lampoon *v.* satirize, burlesque

lance *v.* foil, point, spear

land *n.* PROPERTY: estate, tract, ranch, farm, lot; COUNTRY: province, region, nation

landing *n.* ARRIVING: docking, anchoring, arrival; DOCK: marina, pier, wharf

landlord *n.* innkeeper, landowner, lessor, owner

landscape *n.* countryside, scenery, panorama, view

lane *n.* way, alley, passage, path, road

language *n.* expression, tongue, word, sign, signal, gesture, vocabulary, diction, dialect, idiom, patois, vernacular, speech, jargon

languid *adj.* spiritless, sluggish

languish *v.* weaken, decline

lank *adj.* angular, bony, gaunt. lean, slender, spare

lanky *adj.* lean, rangy

lantern *n.* light, torch, lamp

lap *n.* EXTENSION: fold, flap, projection; RACECOURSE: circuit, round, course, distance

lapidary *n.* jeweler, engraver

lapse *v.* pass, void, slip, deteriorate, decline, weaken

larceny *n.* theft, burglary, thievery, robbery, crime

large *adj.* huge, wide, grand, great, considerable, substantial, vast, massive, immense, spacious

largely *adv.* **MOSTLY:** mainly, chiefly, principally; **EXTENSIVELY:** abundantly, comprehensively, widely

lariat *n.* lasso, riata, tether, line, rope

lascivious *adj.* bawdy, carnal, immoral, lewd, licentious, lurid, sensual, sexual

lash *n.* whip, stroke

lash *v.* strike, flog, thrash, scourge, beat, hit

lass *n.* girl, woman, lady, damsel, maiden

lassitude *adj.* weariness, listlessness

lasso *n.* rope, lariat, tether, noose

lasso *v.* rope, catch

last *adj.* **FINAL:** ultimate, concluding, ending, terminal, decisive, crowning, climactic, closing; **RECENT:** latest, newest, freshest

last *v.* **ENDURE:** continue, maintain, persist, remain, stay, survive, sustain; **SUFFICE:** do, satisfy, serve

lasting *adj.* enduring, abiding, constant, permanent

latch *n.* catch, hasp, hook, bar, fastener, lock

latch *v.* fasten, lock, cinch, close

late *adj.* **OVERDUE:** tardy, lagging, delayed; **DEFUNCT:** deceased, dead, departed; **RECENT:** new, fresh

latent *adj.* potential, undeveloped, dormant

lather *n.* foam, froth, suds, bubbles

lather *v.* foam, froth, soap

latitude *n.* freedom, degree, measure, extent, scope

latter *adj.* after, following, late, last, recent

lattice *n.* arbor, framework, trellis

laud *v.* glorify, honor, praise

laugh *v.* chuckle, guffaw, snicker, titter, chortle, cackle, giggle, roar

launch *v.* initiate, originate, start, begin

launder *v.* cleanse, wash, clean
lavatory *n.* basin, privy, bathroom, washroom, toilet
lave *v.* clean, wash
lavish *adj.* profuse, extravagant, generous, unstinted, unsparing, plentiful, improvident, excessive
lawful *adj.* **LEGAL:** legitimate, decreed, permitted, constitutional; **LEGISLATED:** enacted, official, enforced, protected, legitimized, established
lawless *adj.* **WILD:** untamed, uncivilized, uncontrolled, barbarous, savage, disordered; **UNRESTRAINED:** riotous, insubordinate, disobedient, unruly, revolutionary, mutinous
lawsuit *n.* action, suit, case, prosecution, claim, trial
lawyer *n.* attorney, solicitor, jurist, defender, prosecuting, counsel, solicitor, barrister, advocate
lax *adj.* slack, loose, remiss, soft, careless, indifferent
laxity, laxness *n.* slackness, negligence, indifference, neglect
layer *n.* stratum, thickness, fold, lap, floor, story, tier
layman *n.* nonprofessional, novice, dilettante, amateur, recruit
layout *n.* arrangement, design, organization, plan, proposal, draft, schematic
lazy *adj.* indolent, idle, sluggish, apathetic, loafing, flagging, slothful, lethargic
lead *n.* **GUIDANCE:** leadership, direction; **CLUE:** evidence, trace, hint, proof, sign; **ROLE:** part, character
lead *v.* **CONDUCT:** steer, pilot, show, guide; **DIRECT:** manage, supervise
leaden *adj.* heavy, burdensome, oppressive, weighty
leader *n.* **GUIDE:** conductor, pilot;

DIRECTOR: manager, officer, captain, master, ruler, boss, brains

leading *adj.* foremost, chief, dominating, best

leaflet *n.* brochure, handbill, circular, pamphlet

league *n.* union, alliance, group, unit, organization

leak *n.* **HOLE:** puncture, chink, crevice; **WASTE:** loss, leakage, seepage, expenditure, decrease; **NEWS:** exposé, slip

leak *v.* **ESCAPE:** drip, ooze, drool, flow

lean *v.* **INCLINE:** slant, sag, list, tip, veer, droop, pitch, tilt; **TEND:** favor, prefer

lean *adj.* **THIN:** lank, meager, slim, skinny; **FIBROUS:** muscular, sinewy

leaning *n.* inclination, preference, tendency

lean–to *n.* shelter, shanty, hut, hovel

leap *v.* jump, bound, spring, vault, bounce

learn *v.* acquire, read, master, ascertain, determine, unearth, hear, memorize; study

learned *adj.* scholarly, erudite, cultured, accomplished, well–informed, professorial, educated

learning *n.* lore, training, knowledge, education

lease *v.* let, rent, charter

least *adj.* **SMALLEST:** tiniest; **TRIVIAL:** piddling, unimportant; **MINIMAL:** bottom, lowest

leave *n.* **PARTING:** departure, farewell; **PERMISSION:** consent, dispensation, indulgence, authorization, consent; **LIBERTY:** furlough, vacation

leave *v.* **ABANDON:** forsake, desert; **DEPART:** withdraw, part, defect, flee, embark, emigrate, scram, split, vacate, go; **BEQUEATH:** transmit, will, give, dower; **OMIT:** drop, forget, neglect

leaving *n.* departure, exodus

lecher *n.* debaucher, rake

lecture *n.* **REPROOF:** dressing-down, rebuke, reprimand; **INSTRUCTION:** address, discourse, lesson, oration, speech, talk

lecture *v.* **INSTRUCT:** address, instruct, talk, teach; **REPROVE:** rebuke, reprimand

ledge *n.* shelf, mantle, bar, step, ridge, rim

ledger *n.* accounts, books, records, journal

leech *n.* **PARASITE:** tapeworm, hookworm, bloodsucker; **DEPENDENT:** hanger-on, sponger, weakling

leer *n.* glance, grin, look, smirk

leery *adj.* distrustful, doubting, suspicious, wary

leeway *n.* space, margin, latitude, extent

left *adj.* **REMAINING:** staying, continuing, over, extra; **RADICAL:** left-wing, liberal, progressive, revolutionary; **DEPARTED:** gone, absent, lacking

legacy *n.* bequest, inheritance

legal *adj.* lawful, constitutional, permissible, allowable, legalized, sanctioned, legitimate, authorized

legality *n.* legitimacy, lawfulness, authority, law

legalize *v.* authorize, sanction, approve

legate *n.* ambassador, envoy, deputy, representative, delegate

legation *n.* delegation, embassy

legend *n.* story, myth, saga, fable; inscription

legendary *adj.* fabulous, mythical, fanciful, allegorical

legerdemain *n.* deception, trickery

legible *adj.* readable, distinct, plain, sharp, clear

legion *n.* multitude, horde, throng, crowd

legislate *v.* enact, pass, constitute

legislation *n.* bill, enactment, act, law
legislature *n.* lawmakers, congress, parliament, senate, house, representatives
legitimate *adj.* **LICIT:** statutory, authorized, lawful, legal, honorable; **LOGICAL:** reasonable, probable, consistent, understandable; **AUTHENTIC:** real, verifiable, valid, reliable, genuine
leisure *n.* relaxation, recreation, holiday, vacation
leisurely *adj.* unhurried, lazily, calmly, listlessly
lend *v.* loan, advance, furnish, entrust, accommodate
length *n.* **DISTANCE:** measure, span, range, longitude, magnitude, dimension; **DURATION:** period, interval
lengthen *v.* extend, stretch, protract, increase;
lengthy *adj.* tedious, long, dull, protracted, prolonged
lenient *adj.* mild, merciful, tolerant, kind, sympathetic
lesion *n.* abrasion, injury, tumor, wound
less *adj.* fewer, smaller, reduced, declined, inferior, secondary, subordinate, diminished, shortened
lessen *v.* diminish, dwindle, decline, decrease; reduce
lesser *adj.* inferior, minor, secondary, subordinate
lesson *n.* learning, precept, assignment
let *v.* **PERMIT:** approve, authorize, consent, tolerate, allow; **LEASE:** rent, hire, sublet
letdown *n.* frustration, setback, disillusionment, disappointment
lethal *adj.* deadly, fatal, mortal, malignant, harmful
lethargic *adj.* apathetic, listless, sluggish
lethargy *n.* stupor, dullness, drowsiness
letter *n.* **MESSAGE:** memo, note, epistle,

memorandum, missive, line, mail; **SYMBOL:** character, type

letter *v.* inscribe, write

letup *n.* reduction, slowdown, pause, interval, respite

levee *n.* embankment, dike

level *adj.* **SMOOTH:** planed, even, flat; **REGULAR:** uniform, flush, straight, trim, precise, exact, matched, unbroken, aligned, continuous

level *v.* **STRAIGHTEN:** flatten, surface, bulldoze, smooth; **DEMOLISH:** destroy, ruin, wreck, raze

lever *n.* bar, fulcrum, pry, crowbar

leverage *n.* power, purchase; lift, hold, support

leviathan *n.* monster, beast

levity *n.* flippancy, frivolity

levy *n.* collection, seizure, toll, duty, custom, tax

levy *v.* collect, assess

lewd *adj.* **RIBALD:** smutty, indecent, sensual; **LUSTFUL:** wanton, lascivious, licentious, lecherous, dissolute, debauched, corrupt, depraved, vulgar

lexicon *n.* dictionary, vocabulary, glossary

liability *n.* obligation, responsibility, debt, indebtedness, responsibility

liable *adj.* **APT:** inclined, likely, tending; **RESPONSIBLE:** accountable, answerable, exposed, obliged

liaison *n.* **LINK:** agent, connection, emissary, proxy; **AFFAIR:** intrigue, romance, tryst

liar *n.* prevaricator, deceiver, perjurer, falsifier, fibber

libel *v.* defame, slander, smear, vilify

libelous *adj.* defamatory, derogatory, slanderous

liberal *adj.* **PROGRESSIVE:** broad-minded, nonconformist, permissive, radical, tolerant; **GENEROUS:** indulgent, lavish, magnanimous

liberate *v.* free, loose, release, lberate, extricate, disentangle

liberation *n.* rescue, freedom, deliverance, release

libertine *n.* lecher, pervert, rake, roué

liberty *n.* **DELIVERANCE:** emancipation, enfranchisement, rescue, freedom; **LEAVE:** relaxation, rest, leisure, recreation; **PRIVILEGE:** permission, decision, selection; **RIGHTS:** freedom, independence

libretto *n.* lyric, words

license *n.* **CONSENT:** authorization, permission, sanction; **DOCUMENT:** permit, certificate, registration; **FREEDOM:** looseness, excess, immoderation, latitude

license *v.* grant, authorize, permit, allow, sanction

licit *adj.* authorized, lawful, sanctioned

lick *v.* beat, thrash, whip, defeat, overcome, vanquish, conquer, frustrate

lid *n.* cover, cap, top, roof, hood

lie *n.* falsehood, untruth, misrepresentation, prevarication, falsification, fabrication, distortion

lie *v.* **FIB:** falsify, prevaricate, deceive, misinform, exaggerate, distort, concoct, misrepresent, dissemble, delude; **PROSTRATE:** recline, retire, rest, sleep; **ABIDE:** remain, exist

lieu *n.* place, stead

life *n.* **BEING:** entity, presence, consciousness, vitality; **BIOGRAPHY:** story, memoir; **DURATION:** lifetime, span, career, generation, season, cycle; **SPIRIT:** animation, excitement, zeal

lifeless *adj.* **INERT:** inanimate, departed, dead; **LACKING SPIRIT:** lackluster, listless, heavy, dull, slow

lifetime *n.* existence, endurance, continuance

lift *v.* **ELEVATE:** raise, hoist; **STEAL:** filch, pilfer, swipe; **RESCIND:** repeal, reverse, revoke, cancel

light *adj.* **ILLUMINATED:** radiant, luminous, bright; **SUPERFICIAL:** slight, frivolous, trivial, unimportant; **VIVID:** colorful, rich, clear; **LIVELY:** spirited, animated, active; **ETHEREAL:** airy, fluffy, downy, dainty, thin, sheer, insubstantial, graceful

light *v.* **ILLUMINATE:** illumine, lighten, brighten; **IGNITE:** inflame, spark, kindle, burn; **REST:** stop, arrive

lighten *v.* unburden, lessen, uplift, alleviate, reduce, shift, change, unload

light-headed *adj.* **GIDDY:** inane, fickle, frivolous, silly; **FAINT:** tired, delirious, dizzy, weak

light-hearted *adj.* gay, joyous, cheerful, happy

lightly *adj.* delicately, airily, daintily, gently, subtly, softly, tenderly

like *adj.* similar, resembling, close, matching, related, analogous, corresponding, comparable

like *v.* **ENJOY:** relish, savor, fancy; **ADMIRE:** esteem, approve; **PREFER:** choose, desire, fancy

likelihood *n.* possibility, probability

likely *adj.* probable, conceivable, rational, plausible, apt, tending, prone, liable

likeness *n.* **SIMILARITY:** resemblance, correspondence; **REPRESENTATION:** image, effigy, portrait, picture

liking *n.* desire, fondness, devotion, affection, love

limb *n.* **BRANCH:** arm, bough, offshoot; **APPENDAGE:** arm, leg, wing, fin, flipper

limber *adj.* flexible, pliant, supple, nimble
limit *n.* boundary, frontier, border, extent, extremity
limit *v.* confine, bound, curb, restrict
limitation *n.* **RESTRICTION:** restraint, control; **CONDITION:** qualification, stricture, inhibition, constraint; **SHORTCOMING:** inadequacy, deficiency, flaw, weakness, failing, frailty
limp *adj.* weak, pliant, flaccid, flabby, pliable, slack, loose, flimsy
limp *n.* hitch, hobble
limp *v.* halt, stumble, shuffle, stagger, totter, falter
line *n.* **BORDER:** limit, boundary, edge, boundary; **ROW:** rank, file, order, arrangement, sequence, column, groove, thread; **JOB:** profession, career, vocation; **ROPE:** cord, filament; **DESCENT:** pedigree, lineage, family, heredity; **WARES:** goods, merchandise, produce, material; **TALK:** speech, patter
line *v.* **ARRANGE:** align, order, dress, array, fix, place; **BORDER:** edge, bound, fringe; **PROTECT:** face, back, bind, trim, pad; **TRACE:** delineate, outline, draw
linear *adj.* successive, direct, straight
linger *v.* remain, loiter, tarry, lag, delay, dawdle, wait
linguist *n.* lexicographer, translator, grammarian
liniment *n.* ointment, lotion, balm, medicine
lining *n.* interlining, filling, quilting, stuffing, padding
link *n.* **LOOP:** ring, coupling; **CONNECTION:** seam, weld, intersection, fastening, splice, articulation, joint
link *v.* connect, associate, combine, join
lint *n.* fluff, raveling, fiber, dust

liquid *adj.* **WATERY:** molten, moist, aqueous, liquefied, dissolved, wet, melted, thawed; **FLOWING:** running, splashing, thin, viscous, fluid

liquidate *v.* **CHANGE:** sell, exchange, convert; **DESTROY:** eliminate, kill, cancel

list *n.* roll, record, agenda, slate, inventory, account, tally, roster, muster, menu, docket

list *v.* **ARRANGE:** catalogue, register, tally, inventory, index; **LEAN:** pitch, slant, incline

listen *v.* hear, heed, attend, overhear

listless *adj.* languid, sluggish, indolent, indifferent

litany *n.* form, ritual

literacy *n.* scholarship, education, knowledge

literal *adj.* precise, exact, verbatim, accurate

literally *adj.* actually, exactly, strictly, verbatim

literary *adj.* scholarly, learned, bookish, literate

literate *adj.* lettered, learned, scholarly, educated

lithograph *n.* print, copy

lithograph *v.* engrave, print

litter *n.* **DEBRIS:** mess, jumble, hodgepodge, trash, clutter; **BROOD:** piglets, puppies, kittens, offspring

litter *v.* scatter, confuse, jumble

little *adj.* **SMALL:** diminutive, tiny, wee, slight, miniature, puny; **INADEQUATE:** inconsiderable, insufficient; **TRIFLING:** shallow, petty, superficial, frivolous, paltry, trivial; **BASE:** weak, shallow, mean, petty

livable *adj.* **HABITABLE:** inhabitable, comfortable; **BEARABLE:** acceptable, adequate, tolerable

live *adj.* **ACTIVE:** energetic, vital, vivid;

AWARE: conscious, existing

live *v.* **EXIST:** subsist, survive, breathe, be; **RELISH:** savor, experience; **DWELL:** inhabit, abide; **CONTINUE:** remain, survive, endure, last

livelihood *n.* job, career, trade, vocation, occupation, means, subsistence

lively *adj.* active, animated, brisk, energetic, spirited, vigorous, vivacious

living *adj.* **ALIVE:** active, live, existing, breathing, being; **VIGOROUS:** awake, brisk, alert, active

living *n.* means, sustenance, maintenance, subsistence, work, vocation, business

load *n.* **BURDEN:** cargo, lading, shipment, capacity, payload, bundle; **RESPONSIBILITY:** charge, obligation, trust, duty

loaf *v.* loiter, idle, lounge, relax, shirk, dream

loafer *n.* malingerer, slacker, goldbrick, deadbeat

loan *v.* lend, provide, advance

loath *adj.* disinclined, unwilling

loathe *v.* detest, dislike

lobby *n.* **ENTRYWAY:** antechamber, foyer, hall, vestibule; **INFLUENCE:** pressure

lobby *v.* influence, promote

local *adj.* **LIMITED:** confined, restricted, bounded; **INDIGENOUS:** native, territorial, provincial, regional

locale *n.* vicinity, territory, district, area, region

locality *n.* district, section, sector, region, location, site, neighborhood, block, vicinity

locate *v.* **DISCOVER:** find, establish, determine, place; **SETTLE:** inhabit, dwell

lock *n.* **HOOK:** catch, latch, bolt, bar, hasp, bond; **TRESS:** tuft, ringlet, curl

lock *v.* fasten, bolt, bar

locker *n.* cabinet, wardrobe, cupboard, closet

locket *n.* case, pendant, jewelry

lodge *n.* **RETREAT:** inn, hostel, chalet, hotel, motel, resort, cabin, cottage; **SOCIETY:** club, fraternity

lodge *v.* **SHELTER:** board, harbor, quarter; **PLACE:** fix, leave, deposit, embed

lodging *n.* accommodation, refuge, shelter, residence, home, hotel, motel, resort

lofty *adj.* **HIGH:** elevated, tall, towering, raised; **EXALTED:** arrogant, commanding, haughty, proud

log *n.* **WOOD:** limb, timber, stick **JOURNAL:** account, register, ledger, diary, record

logic *n.* reasoning, deduction, induction, thought

logical *adj.* coherent, consistent, probable, sound, congruent, reasonable

logistics *n.* procurement, distribution, management

loiter *v.* linger, dawdle, idle, loll, tarry, wait

lone *adj.* solitary, deserted, alone

lonely *adj.* abandoned, homesick, forlorn, deserted, solitary, secluded

lonesome *adj.* forlorn, homesick, lonely

long *adj.* **ELONGATED:** extended, lengthy, outstretched; **PROLONGED:** protracted, meandering, lengthy, sustained; **TEDIOUS:** dull

long *v.* desire, yearn, wish, want

longing *n.* craving, yearning, pining, desire, wish

long-lived *adj.* perpetual, enduring, permanent

look *n.* **SIGHT:** glance, survey, glimpse, peek, peep, leer, stare; **APPEARANCE:** presence, mien, expression, looks, manner, aspect

look *v.* **EYE:** view, gaze, behold, contemplate, scrutinize, regard, inspect, observe, examine, watch; **SEEM:** resemble, appear

lookout *n.* **VIEW:** panorama, scene, observatory, station; **WATCHMAN:** watcher, sentinel, scout

loom *v.* **APPEAR:** rise, emerge; **MENACE:** threaten, hulk, hover, approach

loop *v.* curve, encircle, connect, bend

loophole *n.* escape, omission, avoidance

loose *adj.* **SLACK:** free, careless; **LICENTIOUS:** wanton, unrestrained, dissolute; **UNBOUND:** unattached, disconnected, baggy, free; **VAGUE:** random, obscure

loose *v.* **FREE:** release, liberate; **RELAX:** slack ease

loosen *v.* extricate, untie, undo, disentangle, free

loot *n.* plunder, spoils, take, booty

loot *v.* plunder, steal, thieve, rifle, rob

lop *v.* cut, trip, prune, chop

lope *v.* jog, run, trot

lopsided *adj.* uneven, unbalanced, tipped, irregular

lordly *adj.* grand, dignified, honorable, noble

lore *n.* enlightenment, wisdom, learning, knowledge

loss *n.* **RUIN:** destruction, calamity, disaster; **DEPRIVATION:** bereavement, destitution

lost *adj.* **MISPLACED:** mislaid, obscured, vanished, strayed; **BEWILDERED:** perplexed, puzzled; **DESTROYED:** demolished, wasted, ruined

lot *n.* **FATE:** destiny, fortune, chance; **PORTION:** cluster, array, bunch, group; **LAND:** tract, parcel, division, patch, field; **LOAD:** consignment; **ABUNDANCE:** plenty, loads, oodles

lotion *n.* cream, balm, salve, unguent, cosmetic

loud *adj.* **CLAMOROUS:** noisy, vociferous, boisterous, cacophonous, raucous, harsh; **BRASH:** offensive, vulgar, loud-mouthed, rude; **GARISH:** gaudy, flashy, tawdry, ornate

lounge *n.* **SOFA:** couch, divan; **ROOM:** bar, lobby, parlor, salon

lounge *v.* recline, ease, idle, repose, loaf, rest

lovable *adj.* winning, winsome, friendly

love *n.* **DEVOTION:** attachment, infatuation, rapture, ardor; **ESTEEM:** respect, regard, admiration

love *v.* adore, idolize, prize, treasure, cherish

lovely *adj.* beautiful, attractive, comely, fair, handsome, engaging, enchanting, captivating, pleasing

lover *n.* suitor, sweetheart, admirer, escort, paramour, fiancé, boyfriend, girlfriend

loving *adj.* devoted, thoughtful, passionate, amorous, affectionate, caring, considerate

low *adj.* **SQUAT:** flat, prostrate, crouched, sunken; **FAINT:** muffled, hushed, quiet; **SAD:** dejected, moody, blue; **ECONOMICAL:** moderate, inexpensive, cheap; **VULGAR:** base, mean, coarse

lower *adj.* inferior, beneath, under

lower *v.* diminish, fall, sink, depress, decrease, drop

lowering *adj.* threatening, dark, gloomy, menacing

lowly *adj.* unpretentious, meek, humble, unassuming

loyal *adj.* faithful, true, dependable, firm, faithful

loyalty *n.* fidelity, allegiance, faithfulness, constancy, attachment, support, devotion

lucid *adj.* **CLEAR:** obvious, unmistakable;

SHINING: bright, luminous; **SANE:** rational, normal

luck *n.* **FORTUNE:** prosperity, wealth, windfall, blessing; **CHANCE:** fate, opportunity, break, accident

lucky *adj.* **BLESSED:** wealthy, favored, successful, prosperous, fortunate; **AUSPICIOUS:** providential, propitious, magic

lucrative *adj.* profitable, fruitful, productive, gainful

ludicrous *adj.* absurd, ridiculous, laughable, farcical, incongruous

lug *v.* carry, tug, lift, draw

luggage *n.* baggage, trunks, bags, valises

lukewarm *adj.* cool, tepid, chilly

lull *n.* pause, hiatus, stillness, hush, silence

lull *v.* soothe, quiet, calm

lumber *v.* slog, plod

luminescence *n.* fluorescence, fire, radiance, light

luminous *adj.* lighted, glowing, radiant, bright

lump *n.* mass, clump, block, chunk, hunk

lunacy *n.* **INSANITY:** madness, dementia, mania; **FOOLISHNESS:** silliness

lunatic *adj.* **INSANE:** demented, deranged, psychotic; **FOOLISH:** irrational, idiotic, daft, stupid

lunge *v.* thrust, surge, bound, jump

lurch *v.* roll, stagger, weave, sway, totter

lure *n.* bait, decoy, trick

lure *v.* entice, enchant, bewitch, allure, attract, tempt

lurid *adj.* ghastly, gruesome, sensational

lurk *v.* skulk, slink, prowl, wait, crouch, conceal, hide

luscious *adj.* toothsome, palatable, delicious

lush *adj.* **GREEN:** verdant, dense, grassy; **DELICIOUS:** rich, juicy, succulent;

ELABORATE: extravagant, luxurious, ornamental, ornate

lust *n.* desire, appetite, passion, sensuality

luster *n.* brightness, radiance, glow, brilliance, light

lusty *adj.* hearty, boisterous, robust, vigorous

luxuriant *adj.* exuberant, overabundant

luxuriate *v.* indulge, bask, revel

luxurious *adj.* comfortable, affluent, expensive, rich

luxury *n.* indulgence, idleness, leisure, lavishness, extravagance, excess

lying *adj.* **FRAUDULENT:** deceitful, double–dealing, dishonest; **FALSIFYING:** prevaricating, misrepresenting; **UNRELIABLE:** unsound, tricky, treacherous, false

lynch *v.* punish, hang, murder

lyrical *adj.* melodious, sweet, rhythmical, poetic

machination *n.* conspiracy, plot

machine *n.* contrivance, device, implement

machinist *n.* operator, engineer, workman

macrocosm *n.* universe, world

mad *adj.* **INSANE:** demented, deranged, psychotic; **ANGRY:** provoked, enraged, exasperated

madden *v.* craze, infuriate, enrage, anger, annoy, irritate

maddening *adj.* annoying, infuriating, disturbing

made *adj.* fashioned, built, formed, manufactured

made–up *adj.* invented, concocted, devised, fictitious

madhouse *n.* bedlam, confusion

madman *n.* lunatic, maniac, screwball, oddball

magazine *n.* periodical, journal, publication

magic *adj.* enchanting, mystic, enchanting

magic *n.* occultism, legerdemain, wizardry, sorcery, divination, witchcraft, voodooism, soothsaying

magical *adj.* occult, enchanting, mystic, mysterious

magician *n.* conjurer, sorcerer, wizard, shaman

magnanimous *adj.* charitable, noble, unselfish, forgiving, generous

magnate *n.* tycoon, mogul

magnetic *adj.* alluring, appealing, attractive, irresistible, captivating, charming, fascinating

magnetism *n.* attraction, allure, charm, appeal

magnetize *v.* fascinate, attract

magnificence *n.* grandeur, majesty, stateliness, glory, radiance, luxuriousness, greatness, lavishness, brilliance, pomp, splendor, richness

magnificent *adj.* splendid, grand, exalted, majestic

magnify *v.* amplify, expand, increase, enlarge

magnitude *n.* **SIZE:** extent, quantity; **IMPORTANCE:** greatness, consequence, significance

maid *n.* **GIRL:** maiden, woman; **SERVANT:** nursemaid, housemaid, chambermaid

mail *v.* post, send, drop

maim *v.* disfigure, mutilate, disable, damage, hurt

main *adj.* principal, chief, leading, dominant, foremost

main *n.* conduit, channel, duct, pipe

mainly *adv.* chiefly, largely, predominantly, principally

maintain *v.* **UPHOLD:** support, sustain, affirm, defend; **ASSERT:** state, attest, declare, say; **PRESERVE:** keep, conserve, reserve, save, manage

majestic *adj.* stately, dignified, exalted, grand, noble

majesty *n.* grandeur, nobility, splendor, magnificence

major *adj.* important, significant, principal, main

make *v.* **MANUFACTURE:** construct, fabricate, assemble, fashion, produce, build, form; **CREATE:** originate, generate, devise, conceive, invent; **FORCE:** constrain, compel, coerce; **WAGE:** conduct, engage, act; **PREPARE:** ready, arrange, adjust, cook; **OBTAIN:** earn, gain; **ATTAIN:** reach, arrive

makeshift *adj.* temporary, expedient, stopgap

make–up *n.* **COSMETICS:** mascara, liner, rouge, powder; **COMPENSATION:** payment, conciliation, atonement; **COMPOSITION:** structure, formation, arrangement

maladroit *adj.* awkward, clumsy, inept, bungling

malady *n.* affliction, ailment, disease, sickness

malformation *n.* deformity, distortion

malfunction *n.* breakdown, slip, failure

malice *n.* hatred, spite, animosity, resentment

malicious *adj.* hateful, spiteful, bad

malign *v.* vilify, defame, slander

malignant *adj.* lethal, poisonous, deadly, harmful, destructive, deleterious, corrupt, dangerous

malinger *v.* lounge, loll, loaf, loiter

mall *n.* market, shop

malnutrition *n.* starvation, hunger

malodorous *adj.* stinking, fetid

malpractice *n.* negligence, neglect, carelessness

mammoth *adj.* huge, large

manacle *v.* chain, handcuff, shackle

manage *v.* **DIRECT:** control, lead, oversee, mastermind, engineer, handle, supervise; **CONTRIVE:** accomplish, achieve, effect; **ENDURE:** survive, withstand
manageable *adj.* docile, compliant, tractable, obedient, submissive, yielding
manager *n.* supervisor, administrator, director, superintendent, executive
managerial *adj.* executive, administrative
mandate *v.* decree, require
mandatory *adj.* imperative, compulsory, obligatory
mane *n.* hair, ruff, fur
maneuver *v.* plot, scheme, contrive, design, conspire
manger *n.* trough, tub
manhandle *v.* damage, maul, mistreat, abuse, beat
mania *n.* craze, lunacy, madness, desire, obsession
maniac *n.* madman, lunatic
manifest *adj.* apparent, clear, evident, obvious
manifest *v.* exhibit, express, show, reveal, prove, demonstrate
manifestation *n.* evidence, indication, sign
manipulate *v.* control, shape, mold, form manage
mankind *n.* humanity, society, man
mannequin *n.* model, dummy, display
manner *n.* **CONDUCT:** deportment, demeanor, behavior; **CUSTOM:** habit, use, way, practice
mannerism *n.* peculiarity, idiosyncrasy, quirk
mannerly *adj.* polished, considerate, charming
mansion *n.* house, villa, hall, estate, home
mantel *n.* shelf, ledge
mantle *n.* cloak, blanket

manual *n.* handbook, guidebook, reference, instructions

manufacture *v.* make, fabricate, produce, build, fashion, construct

manuscript *n.* book, paper, document, composition

many *adj.* numerous, multiple, innumerable, several

map *n.* chart, graph, drawing, portrayal, draft, plan

mar *v.* damage, spoil, deface, harm, disfigure, scratch

maraud *v.* raid, attack, plunder, pillage

march *v.* parade, proceed, tramp, advance

margin *n.* edge, border, lip, shore, boundary

marina *n.* dock, mooring, landing, harbor

marine *adj.* nautical, maritime, oceanic

maritime *adj.* nautical, marine, seafaring, aquatic

mark *n.* stamp, imprint, impression, emblem, label

mark *v.* **BRAND:** imprint, label, identify, earmark; **SIGNIFY:** denote mean characterize, qualify

marker *n.* ticket, trademark, seal, brand, stamp, pencil, pen, boundary, inscription, label

market *v.* sell, trade, exchange, barter

marquee *n.* awning, canopy

marry *v.* **WED:** espouse; **JOIN:** unite, combine

marsh *n.* swamp, morass, bog, quagmire

marshal *v.* arrange, gather, lead

martial *adj.* warlike, combative, aggressive

martyr *n.* saint, victim, sufferer, offering, scapegoat

marvel *v.* wonder, awe, stare

marvelous *adj.* fabulous, astonishing, spectacular

mash *v.* crush, bruise, squash, pulverize

mask *v.* disguise, cloak, conceal, veil, hide

mass *n.* **MATTER:** piece, portion, wad, hunk, lump; **HEAP:** volume quantity; **SIZE:** magnitude, extent

massacre *v.* slaughter, kill, exterminate, annihilate

massage *v.* rub, knead, stimulate, caress

massive *adj.* weighty, bulky, huge, cumbersome, large

master *n.* lord, teacher, mentor, maestro

master *v.* **CONQUER:** subdue, overcome, humble; **LEARN:** understand, comprehend

masterful *adj.* commanding, excellent

mastery *n.* **CONTROL:** dominance, sovereignty, superiority; **SKILL:** capacity, proficiency, ability

match *n.* **EQUAL:** peer, equivalent, counterpart, approximation; **CONTEST:** race, rivalry, competition

match *v.* equalize, liken, coordinate, even, balance

material *adj.* **REAL:** physical, tangible; **MEANINGFUL:** essential, substantial

materialize *v.* form, become, actualize

maternal *adj.* motherly, protective

mathematics *n.* arithmetic, geometry, algebra, computation, trigonometry, calculus, logarithms

matrimony *n.* marriage, wedlock, union

matrix *n.* mold, die

matron *n.* dame, dowager, lady, wife, mother, woman

matter *n.* **SUBSTANCE:** material, constituents, object, thing, element; **SUBJECT:** interest, focus, theme; **AFFAIR:** undertaking, circumstance, concern

mature *adj.* developed, ripe, grown, cultured

maturity *n.* competence, development, cultivation; adulthood, majority

maudlin *adj.* tearful, sentimental

maxim *n.* saying, proverb, aphorism, adage, epithet

maximum *adj.* greatest, supreme, highest, best

maybe *adv.* perhaps, possibly, conceivable

mayhem *n.* crime, violence

maze *n.* labyrinth, tangle, convolution, intricacy

meadow *n.* grass, pasture, field

meager *adj.* lean, scanty, spare, wanting

meal *n.* **FOOD:** repast, feast, chow, spread, banquet tea; **GRAIN:** fodder, provender, forage, feed

mean *adj.* **HUMBLE:** servile, pitiful, shabby; **VICIOUS:** contemptible, despicable, degenerate, knavish, unscrupulous; **BASE:** low, vulgar, common

mean *v.* **SIGNIFY:** denote, symbolize, imply, suggest, designate, intimate; **INTEND:** propose, expect

meander *v.* wander, wind, roam, ramble

meaning *n.* sense, import, definition, implication, intent, connotation, context, significance

meaningful *adj.* significant, essential, important

means *n.* **WEALTH:** resources, substance, property; **INSTRUMENTALITY:** machinery, method, system, agency

measure *n.* **EXTENT:** degree, dimension, capacity, weight, volume, distance, quantity, area, mass; **STANDARD:** rule, test, norm, criterion

measured *adj.* steady, systematic, deliberate, regular

mechanical *adj.* **AUTOMATED:** programmed, automatic; **PERFUNCTORY:** stereotyped, unchanging, monotonous

mechanism *n.* machine, device, process, tool

medal *n.* badge, award, decoration, commemoration

meddle *v.* interfere, interlope, intervene, encroach

meddlesome *adj.* intrusive, snoopy, prying, nosy

mediate *v.* arbitrate, negotiate, intercede, reconcile

medication *n.* remedy, pill, vaccination

mediocre *adj.* middling, average, common, ordinary

meditation *n.* contemplation, reflection, thought

medium *n.* **MEANS:** mechanism, tool, agency, device; **SPIRITUALIST:** seer, oracle, prophet

medley *n.* mixture, conglomeration, variety, melange, assortment

meek *adj.* humble, unassuming, passive, docile

meet *v.* **ENCOUNTER:** engage, battle, match, face; **TOUCH:** coincide, join, intersect; **CONVENE:** assemble, gather, converge, congregate; **SATISFY:** fulfill, suffice

melancholy *adj.* gloomy, depressed, dispirited, sad

mellow *v.* ripen, mature, age

melodramatic *adj.* artificial, sensational, exaggerated

melody *n.* song, tune, air, lyric, strain

melt *v.* **DISSOLVE:** liquefy, thaw, soften, **DWINDLE:** vanish, go, pass; **RELENT:** forgive, yield

member *n.* **LIMB:** organ, arm, leg; **ASSOCIATE:** constituent, affiliate; **PART:** segment, fragment, division

memento *n.* keepsake, reminder, souvenir

memoir *n.* autobiography, account

memorabilia *n.* memento, souvenir

memorable *adj.* unforgettable, notable, significant, monumental, eventful, exceptional, singular

memorial *n.* monument, tablet, tombstone, mausoleum, statue; celebration, ceremony

memorize *v.* retain, learn, remember

memory *n.* recollection, retrospection, reminiscence

menace *v.* threaten, intimidate, portend

mend *v.* repair, patch, fix, aid, remedy, cure, correct

menial *n.* servant, domestic, maid, lackey

mental *adj.* thoughtful, rational, intellectual, subconscious, telepathic, psychic

mentality *n.* intellect, comprehension, reasoning

mention *v.* remark, comment, infer, intimate, suggest

merchandise *n.* goods, wares, commodities, stock

merchandise *v.* advertise, sell

merchant *n.* trader, shopkeeper, dealer, jobber

merciful adj. lenient, softhearted, tolerant, compassionate, humane, kind

mercurial *adj.* changeable, volatile

mere *adj.* minor, insignificant, little

merge *v.* combine, fuse, join, blend, mix, unite

merit *n.* worth, excellence, honor, character, virtue

merit *v.* earn, warrant, justify, deserve

merriment *n.* mirth, joy, gaiety, happiness, humor

mesh *v.* engage, coincide, suit, agree, fit

mess *n.* confusion, disorder, jumble, clutter

message *n.* communication, tidings, information

messenger *n.* courier, envoy, minister, herald, runner, emissary, angel, prophet

metamorphosis *n.* change, transformation

metaphorical *adj.* figurative, symbolical, allegorical

method *n.* procedure, process, technique, system

meticulous *adj:* mindful, cautious

metropolitan *adj.* cosmopolitan, modern, urban

mettlesome *adj.* spirited, active

middle *adj.* median, mean, midway, equidistant, central, halfway, intermediate

middleman *n.* wholesaler, jobber

miff *v.* offend, annoy

might *n.* power, ability, strength, force, sway

mighty *adj.* powerful, great, imposing, impressive

migrate *v.* move, emigrate, leave

migration *n.* voyage, departure, journey, movement

mild *adj.* moderate, gentle, temperate

militant *adj.* aggressive, warlike, belligerent

millinery *n.* hats, bonnets

mimic *v.* **IMITATE:** copy, simulate, impersonate; **MOCK:** burlesque, caricature, ridicule

mind *n.* **MENTALITY:** perception, judgment, wisdom, intellect; **INTENTION:** inclination, determination

mind *v.* **OBEY:** heed, behave, attend, regard; **OBJECT:** complain, deplore, dislike

mindless *adj.* **CARELESS:** inattentive, oblivious, neglectful, indifferent; **FOOLISH:** senseless, rash

miniature *adj.* small, tiny, little, minute

minimize *v.* reduce, lessen, depreciate, decrease

minister *n.* clergyman, ambassador

minister *v.* attend, tend, help

ministration *n.* assistance, comfort, relief

minor *adj.* inferior, secondary, lesser, trivial

minor *n.* adolescent, child, infant, youth

minute *adj.* **SMALL:** tiny, microscopic; **TRIVIAL:** paltry, immaterial; **EXACT:** particular, detailed

minutiae *n.* trivia, particulars, details

miracle *n.* marvel, revelation, wonder, phenomenon

miraculous *adj.* supernatural, wonderful, marvelous, phenomenal, mysterious

mirage *n.* illusion, phantasm, hallucination, fantasy

mirth *n.* gaiety, laughter, frolic, jollity, fun

misbehave *v.* sin, trespass, err

miscalculate *v.* blunder, miscount, err, mistake

miscellaneous *adj.* **DIVERSE:** unmatched, unlike; **MIXED:** muddled, scattered, confused, disordered

mischievous *adj.* playful, roguish, naughty

misconduct *n.* misbehavior, wrongdoing, mischief

miser *n.* niggard, skinflint, money-grubber

miserable *adj.* distressed, wretched, troubled

misery *n.* **PAIN:** distress, suffering, agony; **TROUBLE:** grief, anxiety; **DESPAIR:** depression, sadness

misfortune *n.* calamity, adversity, unpleasantness

misgiving *n.* mistrust, doubt, uncertainty

misguided *adj.* misled, deceived, confused

misjudge *v.* miscalculate, overestimate, underestimate

mislead *v.* delude, trick, beguile, dupe, misrepresent

mismatched *adj.* incompatible, discordant, unfit

misrepresent *v.* distort, falsify, deceive, lie, mislead

miss *n.* **FAILURE:** slip blunder mishap mistake deviation **WOMAN:** lass maid female girl
mission *n.* purpose, charge, commission
missionary *n.* apostle, evangelist, messenger
mist *n.* vapor, cloud, rain, haze, fog
mistake *n.* **BLUNDER:** error, slip, omission; **MISUNDERSTANDING:** confusion, misinterpretation
mistake *v.* err, blunder, misjudge, botch, bungle
mistreat *v.* harm, injure, wrong, abuse
mistrust *v.* suspect, distrust, doubt
misunderstanding *n.* **MISAPPREHENSION:** misinterpretation; **DISAGREEMENT:** quarrel, dispute
mix *v.* **BLEND:** combine, mingle, stir, unite; **CONFUSE:** jumble, tangle; **ASSOCIATE:** fraternize
mixture *n.* combination, blend, compound, amalgam, medley, potpourri, incorporation, hodgepodge
mix-up *n.* chaos, commotion, confusion, disorder
moan *v.* groan, wail, whine
mob *n.* throng, crowd, rabble, multitude, horde
mob *v.* attack, crowd, swarm, press, overwhelm
mobile *adj.* movable, loose, free
mock *adj.* imitation, counterfeit, sham, fake, fraudulent
mock *v.* deride, taunt, mimic, caricature, imitate
mockery *n.* disparagement, ridicule
mode *n.* manner, fashion
model *n.* **EXAMPLE:** prototype, ideal; **PATTERN:** design, standard; **POSER:** sitter, mannequin, nude
model *v.* **FORM:** shape, fashion; **SIT:** pose; **DEMONSTRATE:** show, wear, display

moderate *adj.* **MODEST:** temperate, calm, reserved; **INEXPENSIVE:** cheap, economical; **TOLERANT:** restrained, cautious; **PLEASANT:** temperate, mild

moderate *v.* abate, decline, decrease, diminish, calm

moderation *n.* restraint, temperance, balance

modern *adj.* **STYLISH:** chic, smart, fashionable; **CONTEMPORARY:** new, current, renovated, improved

modest *adj.* **HUMBLE:** unassuming, meek, diffident; **UNPRETENTIOUS:** plain, seemly, tasteful, unadorned, unaffected; **MODERATE:** reasonable, inexpensive, economical; **PROPER:** pure, chaste, seemly, decent; **LOWLY:** simple, unaffected

modify *v.* change, vary, alter

moist *adj.* wet, humid, dank, moistened, damp

mold *n.* **FORM:** matrix, shape, frame, pattern, die, cast; **GROWTH:** rust, parasite, fungus, lichen, decay

molest *v.* disturb, bother, annoy, irritate, badger

mollify *v.* assuage, pacify

molten *adj.* melted, liquefied

moment *n.* **TIME:** instant, jiffy, twinkling; **IMPORTANCE:** significance, note, consequence

momentary *adj.* fleeting, passing, transient, cursory

momentum *n.* impetus, impulse, force, drive, energy

monetary *adj.* pecuniary, financial, fiscal

money *n.* currency, cash, notes, specie, funds

monologue *n.* speech, talk, discourse, address

monopolize *v.* dominate, engross, corner

monopoly *n.* trust, syndicate, cartel

monotonous *adj.* tiresome, tedious, wearying, dull

monster *n.* **BRUTE:** criminal, rascal, savage; **MONSTROSITY:** chimera, werewolf; **FREAK:** abnormality

monstrous *adj.* **HUGE:** stupendous, prodigious, enormous, large; **UNNATURAL:** abnormal, unusual

monument *n.* memorial, shrine, statue, monolith

monumental *adj.* lofty, impressive, majestic, grand

mood *n.* state, condition, temper, humor, disposition

moody *adj.* downcast, pensive, unhappy, sad

moot *adj.* disputable, disputed, arguable, controversial

mope *v.* fret, pine, sorrow, brood, sulk

moral *adj.* virtuous, proper, scrupulous, honorable, aboveboard, principled, chaste, noble

morale *n.* assurance, resolve, spirit, confidence

morality *n.* righteousness, uprightness, virtue

morals *n.* ethics, ideals, standards, mores, principles

moratorium *n.* delay, halt, suspension

morbid *adj.* **DISEASED:** sickly, unhealthy, ailing; **PATHOLOGICAL:** gloomy, melancholic, depressed

morning *n.* dawn, morn, daybreak, cockcrow, sun–up

morose *adj.* surly, downcast, gloomy

morsel *n.* piece, bite, chunk, bit, part

mortal *adj.* **FATAL:** malignant, lethal, deadly; **TEMPORAL:** human, transient, perishable, temporary

mostly *adv.* **FREQUENTLY:** often, regularly; **LARGELY:** chiefly, essentially, principally

motel *n.* hotel, cabin, inn, resort

motherly *adj.* maternal, devoted, protective, loving
motif *n.* theme, melody
motion *n.* **MOVEMENT:** change, act, action, passage; **PROPOSAL:** suggestion, proposition, plan
motivate *v.* inspire, stimulate, incite, spur, goad
motive *n.* cause, purpose, idea, reason
motto *n.* maxim, adage, saw, aphorism, sentiment, slogan, catchword, axiom, proverb, saying
mound *n.* pile, heap, knoll, hill
mount *v.* **RISE:** ascend; **CLIMB:** scale, clamber
mountainous *adj.* steep, lofty, craggy, rugged
mourn *v.* grieve, sorrow, bemoan, languish, pine
mournful *adj.* sorrowful, unhappy, sad, saddened, sorry
movable *adj.* portable, mobile, detachable, free
move *v.* **EXCITE:** arouse, stir, stimulate; **PROPEL:** impel, actuate; **PROPOSE:** introduce, submit; **ADVANCE:** go, walk, run, travel, progress, proceed, traverse
movement *n.* **CHANGE:** migration, evolution, transition, progression; **TREND:** drift, tendency, inclination
mow *v.* cut, scythe, reap, harvest
mud *n.* muck, mire, slush, silt, ooze
muddle *v.* confuse, disarrange, mix, jumble, snarl, befuddle, entangle
muddy *adj.* **MURKY:** dull, cloudy, obscure, indistinct; **SWAMPY:** slushy, soggy, sodden, boggy
muffle *v.* deaden, mute, stifle, decrease, soften
muffler *n.* scarf, neckpiece, choker
mug *n.* vessel, stein, flagon, cup
muggy *adj.* damp, humid, moist

multitude *n.* throng, mob, crowd, gathering, people

mumble *v.* mutter, utter, murmur

munch *v.* chew, masticate, crunch, bite, eat

mundane *adj.* normal, ordinary, common, mediocre, everyday

municipality *n.* community, district, village, town

murder *n.* homicide, carnage, slaying, butchery

murder *v.* kill, slay, assassinate, butcher

murky *adj.* gloomy, dark, dim, dusky, dingy, dirty

muscular *adj.* brawny, powerful, husky, strong

museum *n.* collection, archives, treasury, depository

music *n.* melody, harmony, tune, air, strain

musical *adj.* tuneful, sweet, pleasing, lyrical

musty *adj.* moldy, sour, stale, crumbling

mutation *n.* change, modification, deviation

mute *adj.* speechless, silent, bewildered, unspoken

mutilate *v.* maim, damage, injure, deface, disfigure

mutiny *n.* insurrection, revolt, resistance, revolution

mutter *v.* mumble, murmur, grumble, complain

mutual *adj.* reciprocal, common, joint, shared

muzzle *v.* gag, muffle, silence, suppress, hush, quiet

myriad *n.* variable, innumerable, multiple

mysterious *adj.* **PUZZLING:** enigmatic, strange, unnatural; **SECRET:** veiled, obscure, hidden, ambiguous

mystical *adj.* occult, spiritual, mysterious, secret

mystify *v.* puzzle, perplex, hoodwink, deceive

myth *n.* legend, fable, lore, saga, parable, tale, story

mythological *adj.* whimsical, fantastic, imaginary

nab *v.* grab, take, snatch, seize

nag *v.* scold, vex, annoy, pester, bother

naïve *adj.* unaffected, artless, innocent, unsophisticated, gullible, credulous, trusting, inexperienced

naïveté *n.* inexperience, innocence

naked *adj.* uncovered, unclad, bare, exposed

name *n.* **REPUTATION:** renown, fame; **TITLE:** designation, appellation; **STAR:** hero, lion, celebrity

name *v.* appoint, nominate, select, delegate, designate

nameless *adj.* undistinguished, obscure, unknown

namely *adv.* specifically, particularly

nap *n.* **REST:** sleep, siesta, doze; **PILE:** shag, texture

narrate *v.* tell, recite, describe, reveal, report

narrow *adj.* **CRAMPED:** close, confined; **DOGMATIC:** intolerant, prejudiced; **CLOSE:** precarious, dangerous

nasty *adj.* **OFFENSIVE:** foul, gross, vulgar; **INDECENT:** immodest, smutty, lewd; **UNKIND:** sarcastic, mean

nation *n.* **PEOPLE:** populace, community, society; **STATE:** realm, country, domain

nationalism *n.* chauvinism, jingoism, loyalty

native *adj.* **NATURAL:** innate, inborn, hereditary; **INDIGENOUS:** aboriginal, primeval, domestic, local

natty *adj.* trim, spruce

natural *adj.* **INTRINSIC:** original, fundamental, inherited, native; **TYPICAL:** characteristic, usual, customary; **UNSTUDIED:** ingenuous, artless, spontaneous; **REAL:** actual, tangible, physical

naughty *adj.* bad, mischievous, wayward, roguish

nausea *n.* sickness, queasiness, vomiting, illness

nauseate *v.* sicken, repulse, bother, disgust, disturb

nauseous *adj.* ill, queasy, squeamish

navigable *adj.* passable, open, safe

near, nearby *adj., adv.* BORDERING: adjacent, adjoining, neighboring; EXPECTED: approaching, coming

neat *adj.* TIDY: trim, prim, spruce, dapper, orderly, precise; CLEVER: dexterous, skillful, agile

nebulous *adj.* vague, cloudy, hazy

necessary *adj.* essential, important, requisite, required, imperative, compulsory, mandatory

necessitate *v.* compel, constrain, oblige, force

necessity *n.* requirement, need, requisite

nectar *n.* drink, juice, fluid

need *n.* POVERTY: indigence, penury; LACK: shortage, inadequacy; REQUIREMENT: necessity, requirement

needy *adj.* destitute, indigent, penniless, poor

nefarious *adj.* vile, wicked

negate *v.* repeal, retract, neutralize, cancel, nullify

negative *n.* REFUSAL: contradiction, disavowal, refutation, denial; PICTURE: film, image, plate

neglect *v.* SLIGHT: disregard, disdain, affront, ignore, spurn; EVADE: defer, procrastinate, postpone

negligent *adj.* careless, indifferent, inattentive

negotiate *v.* bargain, mediate, conciliate, arbitrate

negotiation *n.* compromise, intervention, mediation

neighborhood *n.* vicinity, locality

neophyte *n.* convert, novice, apprentice

nerve *n.* **COURAGE:** resolution, mettle, boldness; **IMPUDENCE:** temerity, audacity, effrontery, rudeness

nervous *adj.* **EXCITABLE:** impatient, restless, uneasy, unstable; **EXCITED:** fidgety, jittery, agitated, bothered

nestle *v.* snuggle, cuddle, huddle

neurosis *n.* compulsion, nervousness, obsession

neurotic *adj.* disturbed, unstable, troubled

neutral *adj.* **UNBIASED:** impartial; **DULL:** drab, vague

new *adj.* **RECENT:** current, late; **MODERN:** contemporary, fashionable; **NOVEL:** unique, original, unusual; **INEXPERIENCED:** unseasoned, unskilled, incompetent

newcomer *n.* outsider, alien, stranger

news *n.* information, tidings, report, account

next *adj., adv.* **FOLLOWING:** succeeding, subsequent; **ADJACENT:** beside, adjoining, neighboring, touching

nibble *v.* nip, gnaw, snack, bite, eat

nice *adj.* pleasant, likable, agreeable, amiable, pleasing

niche *n.* cubbyhole, recess, cranny, corner,

nick *v.* indent, notch, slit, cut, dent

night *n.* evening, nightfall, twilight, bedtime

nimble *adj.* **AGILE:** light, quick, spry, active, graceful; **ALERT:** bright, clever, intelligent

noble *adj.* **EXALTED:** courtly, lordly, dignified, distinguished; **MERITORIOUS:** virtuous, refined, chivalrous; **TITLED:** aristocratic, patrician; **GRAND:** stately, impressive, imposing

nobody *n.* nonentity, upstart, cipher

nod *v.* **SIGNAL:** bow, acknowledge; **NAP:** drowse, sleep

noise *n.* sound, clamor, racket, fracas, din, uproar

noisome *adj.* unhealthy, disgusting, offensive, rank

noisy *adj.* clamorous, vociferous, boisterous, loud

nomad *n.* wanderer, migrant, vagabond, traveler

nominate *v.* name, appoint, propose, designate

nonchalant *adj.* **CASUAL:** unconcerned, impassive, detached, indifferent; **CARELESS:** negligent, trifling

nonconformist *n.* radical, rebel, eccentric, maverick

nonprofit *adj.* charitable, altruistic, humane

nonsense *n.* **INANITY:** trash, senselessness, buncombe; **FUN:** jest, absurdity

nonviolent *adj.* passive, calm, quiet

nook *n.* niche, cubbyhole, cranny, hole

noose *n.* loop, hitch, lasso, rope

normal *adj.* **USUAL:** ordinary, typical, common **REGULAR:** routine, orderly, methodical; **SANE:** lucid, rational, reasonable; **HEALTHY:** whole, sound

nostalgia *n.* longing, homesickness, wistfulness

nosy *adj.* snoopy, curious, inquisitive, interested

notable *adj.* remarkable, distinguished, striking, important, celebrated

notch *n.* nick, indent, cut, dent, groove

note *n.* memo, reminder, memorandum

note *v.* **NOTICE:** perceive, see; **RECORD:** transcribe

noted *adj.* well-known, celebrated, notorious, famous

notice *n.* warning, notification, announcement
noticeable *adj.* appreciable, conspicuous, obvious
notion *n.* whim, fancy, idea, assumption
notorious *adj.* infamous, known, disreputable
notwithstanding *adv.* despite, although, but
nourish *v.* feed, encourage, sustain
nourishing *adj.* healthy, nutritious
novel *adj.* new, strange, odd, unique, unusual
novelist *n.* writer, narrator, author
novelty *n.* fad, innovation, creation
novice *n.* beginner, neophyte, amateur
now *adv.* momentarily, promptly, instantly
noxious *adj.* injurious, harmful
nuance *n.* subtlety, distinction, difference
nucleus *n.* essence, core, kernel, center, hub, focus
nudge *v.* poke, bump, tap, push, touch
nugget *n.* lump, ingot, chunk, rock
nuisance *n.* BOTHER: annoyance, vexation, trouble; CRIME: breach, infraction, affront
null *adj.* void, invalid, vain, unsanctioned
numb *adj.* deadened, unfeeling, senseless
numb *v.* deaden, stupefy, paralyze, stun, dull
numerous *adj.* many, copious, diverse, infinite
nuptials *n.* wedding, marriage, matrimony
nurse *v.* tend, minister, aid, treat
nurture *v.* nourish, feed, sustain, cherish, support
nutriment *n.* food, nourishment, provisions, victuals
nutritious *adj.* nourishing, wholesome, healthful
nuzzle *v.* caress, cuddle, snuggle, nestle

oasis *n.* refuge, retreat

oath *n.* **PROMISE:** vow, pledge; **PROFANITY:** curse, swearword, blasphemy

obdurate *n.* stubborn, hardhearted

obedient *adj.* **DUTIFUL:** loyal, devoted, deferential, faithful; **DOCILE:** submissive, compliant

obese *adj.* fat, corpulent, plump, stout

obey *v.* yield, conform, submit, serve comply

object *n.* **THING:** article, gadget; **GOAL:** aim, objective

object *v.* disapprove, protest, complain, dispute

objective *adj.* impartial, impersonal

objective *n.* goal, aim, target, mission, destination

obligate *v.* bind, restrict, constrain, force

obligatory *adj.* required, essential, binding, necessary

oblige *v.* **ACCOMMODATE:** assist, aid, contribute, help; **REQUIRE:** constrain, bind, force, compel, coerce

obliging *adj.* amiable, accommodating, kind, helpful

oblivion *n.* obscurity, void, nothing, emptiness

oblivious *adj.* distracted, preoccupied, absorbed

obnoxious *adj.* offensive, annoying, disagreeable, displeasing, repulsive

obscene *adj.* indecent, lewd, wanton, lascivious

obscure *adj.* vague, indistinct, unclear, hazy, arcane

obscure *v.* **DIM:** cloud, screen; **CONCEAL:** cover, veil

observable *adj.* perceptible, noticeable, discernible

observance *n.* **CUSTOM:** ritual, practice, rite; **AWARENESS:** observation, notice

observant *adj.* alert, discerning, perceptive, bright

observe *v.* **WATCH:** scrutinize, see, notice; **COMMEMORATE:** dedicate, solemnize; **COMMENT:** remark, note, mention; **OBEY:** comply, discharge, follow

obsessed *adj.* haunted, beset, controlled, troubled

obsession *n.* fixation, fascination, passion, mania, preoccupation, craze

obsessive *adj.* compulsive, preoccupied

obsolete *adj.* antiquated, archaic, out–of–date

obstacle *n.* hindrance, restriction, obstruction, restraint

obstinate *adj.* stubborn, headstrong, opinionated

obstreperous *adj.* noisy, unruly

obstruct *v.* block, interfere, bar, hinder, prevent

obtain *v.* get, take, acquire, seize, procure

obtuse *adj.* blunt, ignorant, dull

obvious *adj.* apparent, perceptible, open, clear, intelligible, comprehensible, understandable

occasion *n.* event, occurrence, incident, happening

occasional *adj.* sporadic, random, infrequent

occult *adj.* hidden, mysterious, supernatural, secret

occupancy *n.* possession, occupation

occupation *n.* vocation, employment, job, profession

occupy *v.* **SEIZE:** conquer, invade; **FILL:**, pervade, permeate; **ENGAGE:** absorb, engross, involve, fascinate

occur *v.* happen, transpire, befall

oceanic *adj.* marine, aquatic, maritime, nautical

odd *adj.* **UNUSUAL:** unique, strange; **SINGLE:** sole, unpaired, unmatched, lone

odious *adj.* hateful, offensive, repulsive, despicable, repellent

odor *n.* smell, perfume, fragrance, bouquet

offal *n.* refuse, rubbish

offend *v.* displease, annoy, affront, outrage, bother

offense *n.* MISDEED: transgression, sin; RESENTMENT: pique, indignation, anger; ATTACK: assault, aggression

offensive *adj.* AGGRESSIVE: assaulting, attacking, invading; REVOLTING: disgusting, repulsive, detestable

offer *v.* present, proffer, tender, propose, submit

offering *n.* contribution, donation, present, gift

offhand *adj.* impromptu, informal, improvised

officer *n.* executive, manager, director, president

official *adj.* FORMAL: proper, accepted; AUTHORIZED: sanctioned, endorsed; RELIABLE: authentic, genuine

official *n.* UMPIRE: referee, judge, linesman; ADMINISTRATOR: comptroller, director, executive;

offspring *n.* child, progeny, issue, descendant, heir

ointment *n.* salve, unguent, lotion, cream, balm

old *adj.* AGED: venerable, seasoned, enfeebled; WORN: thin, faded; ANCIENT: archaic, prehistoric, antique

ombudsman *n.* investigator, mediator

omen *n.* warning, portent, augury, indication, sign

ominous *adj.* threatening, dismal, forbidding, menacing, portentious

omission *n.* exclusion, lack, need, want

omit *v.* exclude, ignore, slight, overlook, disregard

omnipotent *adj.* all-powerful, almighty

omnipresent *adj.* universal, pervasive

once *adj., adv.* formerly, previously

oncoming *adj.* impending, imminent, approaching

only *adj.* **SOLELY:** exclusively, entirely, totally; **MERELY:** simply, barely, hardly; **SOLE:** single, isolated, unique

onset *n.* beginning, opening, start, origin

ooze *v.* leak, seep, exude, flow

opaque *adj.* dim, dusky, darkened, murky, gloomy

open *adj.* **CLEAR:** divulged, revealed, unobstructed; **UNRESTRICTED:** free, public; **UNGUARDED:** accessible; **UNDECIDED:** debatable, questionable; **FRANK:** plain, candid, straightforward

open *v.* **BEGIN:** inaugurate, initiate; **UNLOCK:** undo, unbolt; **BREACH:** penetrate, pierce; **EXPOSE:** reveal

openly *adv.* **FRANKLY:** candidly, honestly; **SHAMELESSLY:** immodestly, flagrantly, wantonly

operate *v.* **FUNCTION:** work, serve, run, percolate; **MANAGE:** manipulate, conduct, administer

operation *n.* **ACTION:** act, deed, undertaking, work; **METHOD:** process, formula, procedure

operative *adj.* effective, functioning

opinion *n.* belief, view, sentiment, conception

opinionated *adj.* obstinate, bigoted, stubborn, unyielding, prejudiced

opponent *n.* rival, competitor, adversary, antagonist

opportunity *n.* chance, circumstance

oppose *v.* **CONTRADICT:** dispute, defy, confront, resist; **FIGHT:** compete, encounter, assail, storm, clash

opposite *n.* opposition, antithesis, counterpart

opposition *n.* **DISLIKE:** antagonism, defiance, abhorrence, antipathy; **CONFLICT;** hostility, resistance;

oppress *v.* harass, maltreat, abuse, bother

oppression *n.* tyranny, domination, persecution

opprobrium *n.* disgrace, shame

optimal *adj.* favorable, desirable, optimum

optimism *n.* faith, cheerfulness, confidence, enthusiasm, expectation, certainty

option *n.* choice, selection, alternative

optional *adj.* discretionary, elective, voluntary

opulence *n.* riches, wealth

oracle *n.* prophet, seer, sage, fortuneteller

oral *adj.* spoken, vocal, verbal, uttered, voiced

orbit *v.* revolve, encircle, encompass

ordain *v.* **ESTABLISH:** install, appoint; **DESTINE:** foreordain, intend; **CONSECRATE:** invest, bless

ordeal *n.* trial, test, distress, difficulty

order *n.* **ARRANGEMENT:** plan, method, system; **ORGANIZATION:** fraternity, club, society; **COMMAND:** stipulation, mandate, injunction; **CLASS:** kind, hierarchy; **SEQUENCE:** progression, succession, series

order *v.* **ARRANGE:** classify, organize; **COMMAND:** direct, instruct, require; **BUY:** secure, reserve, request

orderly *adj.* **NEAT:** tidy, arranged; **METHODICAL:** systematic, thorough, precise, careful

orderly *n.* aide, assistant

ordinance *n.* law, direction, mandate

ordinarily *adv.* usually, generally, habitually

ordinary *adj.* USUAL: normal, common; AVERAGE: mediocre, accepted, typical, characteristic

ordination *n.* investment, investiture, induction

organization *n.* SYSTEM: arrangement, classification; ASSOCIATION: federation, institute, alliance

organize *v.* ARRANGE: systematize, coordinate, classify; ESTABLISH: build, found, plan, formulate

orientation *n.* familiarization, introduction

origin *n.* birth, start, foundation, source, beginning, inception, genesis

original *adj.* FIRST: fundamental, primary; CREATIVE: imaginative, inventive; GENUINE: authentic, real, actual

originate *v.* introduce, found, start, begin

ornament *n.* decoration, embellishment, adornment, beautification

ornate *adj.* showy, gaudy, adorned, embellished

orphan *n.* foundling, waif, stray

ostensible *adj.* professed, apparent

other *adj.* separate, distinct, opposite, extra

oust *v.* eject, expel, discharge, evict, dislodge

out *n.* escape, excuse, explanation

outbreak *n.* ERUPTION: explosion, outburst, commotion, tumult; VIOLENCE: mutiny, revolution

outburst *n.* discharge, eruption, outbreak

outcast *n.* exile, fugitive, pariah, refugee

outcome *n.* upshot, consequence, result

outcry *n.* complaint, clamor, objection

outdated *adj.* outmoded, antiquated, old

outdo *v.* surpass, best, beat, exceed

outfit *v.* supply, equip, provide

outflank *v.* surround, outmaneuver, defeat

outgrowth *adj.* end, result, outcome, effect, result

outing *n.* excursion, airing, drive, vacation

outlandish *adj.* **STRANGE:** unusual, quaint, foreign; **BARBARIC:** rude

outlast *v.* outlive, outwear, endure, survive

outlaw *v.* forbid, ban, banish, condemn

outline *n.* **CONTOUR:** boundary, frame; **PLAN:** framework, draft; **SILHOUETTE:** profile, shape, formation

outlook *n.* **VIEWPOINT:** scope, vision; **PROSPECT:** likelihood, possibility, opportunity, probability

outlying *adj.* exterior, frontier, distant

outnumbered *v.* exceeded, bested, overcome, beaten

outrage *v.* offend, wrong, affront, insult, abuse

outrageous *adj.* shameless, disgraceful, scandalous, flagrant, contemptible, ignoble, atrocious

outright *adj.* unmitigated, unconditional, obvious

outside *adj.* outermost, external, outer

outsider *n.* foreigner, stranger, refugee, alien

outskirts *n.* suburbs, limits, boundary, edge

outspoken *adj.* blunt, candid, artless, frank

outstanding *adj.* distinguished, conspicuous, notable

outwit *v.* trick, bewilder, confuse, deceive

ovation *n.* outburst, applause

over *adj.* **ABOVE:** overhead, higher; **AGAIN:** afresh; **BEYOND:** past, farther; **DONE:** accomplished, finished

overbearing *adj.* domineering, tyrannical, dictatorial

overcast *adj.* cloudy, gloomy, dark
overcome *v.* conquer, overwhelm, best, vanquish
overconfident *n.* reckless, impudent, heedless, rash
overdo *v.* MAGNIFY: amplify, overreach, exaggerate, enhance; WEARY: tire, fatigue, exhaust, overtax
overdue *adj.* late, delayed, belated, tardy
overestimate *v.* overvalue, overrate, exaggerate
overflow *v.* SPILL OVER: waste, cascade, spout, gush, surge; FLOOD: inundate
overhaul *v.* recondition, modernize, fix, renew, repair
overpower *v.* overwhelm, master, subjugate, defeat
overrate *v.* overvalue, magnify, exaggerate
overrule *v.* invalidate, override, cancel, revoke, reject
overrun *v.* DEFEAT: overwhelm, invade, occupy; INFEST: ravage, invade, overwhelm
oversee *v.* superintend, supervise, manage
oversight *n.* failure, overlooking, mistake, error
overt *adj.* apparent, open
overtake *v.* catch, exceed, surpass, reach
overthrow *v.* upset, overcome, overrun, overpower
overture *n.* PRELUDE: prologue, introduction, preface; SUGGESTION: advance, tender, negotiations;
overturn *v.* subvert, ruin, reverse, overthrow, upset
overwhelm *v.* DEFEAT: overcome, overthrow, conquer; ASTONISH: bewilder, confound, confuse, surprise
overwrought *adj.* excited, overexcited
owed *adj.* owing, due, indebted, unpaid
own *v.* ACKNOWLEDGE: grant, admit, declare;

POSSESS: hold, have, enjoy, retain, keep

owner *n.* proprietor, landlord, landlady

ownership *n.* possession, claim, deed, title, control

pace *n.* step, gait, movement, speed

pacify *v.* calm, soothe, conciliate, appease, placate

package *n.* bundle, parcel, packet, box, carton

pact *n.* contract, agreement, bargain, treaty

pad *n.* **TABLET:** stationery, notebook; **STUFFING:** cushion, wadding, waste, filling

pad *v.* **STUFF:** pack, fill, **INCREASE:** inflate, increase

padding *n.* stuffing, wadding, waste, filling

paddle *v.* spank, thrash, rap, punish

padlock *n.* lock, latch, fastener, catch

pagan *adj.* heathen, unchristian, idolatrous

pagan *n.* heathen, gentile, unbeliever, infidel

page *n.* leaf, sheet, folio, side, surface, recto, verso

page *v.* call, summon

pageant *n.* parade, celebration, pomp

pail *n.* vessel, bucket, pot, receptacle, jug, container

pain *n.* **SUFFERING:** anguish, distress, misery, wretchedness, torment; **HURT:** ache, spasm, cramp, agony, sting, burn; **GRIEF:** despondency, worry, anxiety, depression, sadness

pain *v.* distress, hurt, grieve, trouble

painful *adj.* **SORE:** raw, throbbing, burning, hurtful, piercing, smarting, sensitive, tender

paint *v.* **PORTRAY:** sketch, picture, depict; **COAT:** brush, swab, daub, cover, spread

pair *n.* set, two, brace, couple

pair *v.* join, couple, combine, match, balance

palace *n.* manor, mansion, castle

pale *adj.* wan, pallid, sickly, anemic, cadaverous, haggard, deathlike, ghostly

palpitate *v.* tremble, quiver, pulsate

paltry *adj.* worthless, small, insignificant, trifling

pamper *v.* overindulge, spoil, indulge, pet, humor, gratify, coddle, please

pamphlet *n.* booklet, leaflet, brochure, bulletin, circular, handbill, broadside, announcement

pan *n.* vessel, kettle, pail, bucket, container

pandemonium *n.* noise, disorder, uproar, anarchy, riot, confusion

pane *n.* panel, window, glass

panel *n.* ornament, tablet, inset, decoration

pang *n.* pain, throb, sting, bite

panhandle *v.* solicit, ask, bum, beg

panic *n.* dread, alarm, fright, fear

panorama *n.* view, spectacle, scenery, prospect

pant *v.* gasp, desire, wheeze, throb, palpitate

pantomime *n.* sign, charade, mime

pantry *n.* storage, provisions, storeroom, larder, cupboard, closet, room

pants *n.* trousers, breeches, slacks, jeans, overalls, cords, shorts, corduroys, pantaloons, chaps, bloomers, rompers

paper *n.* **DOCUMENT:** record, abstract, affidavit, bill, certificate, contract, credentials, deed, diploma; **NEWSPAPER:** journal, daily; **ESSAY:** article, theme

par *n.* equality, standard, level, norm, model

parable *n.* fable, allegory, moral, story, tale

parade *n.* PROCESSION: spectacle, ceremony, demonstration, review, pageant, ritual

parade *v.* march, demonstrate, display, exhibit

paradox *n.* mystery, enigma, ambiguity, puzzle

paragon *n.* model, example, ideal, perfection, best

parallel *n.* match, correspond, correlate, equal

paraphernalia *n.* trappings, equipment, gear

parasite *n.* dependent, sponger, hanger–on, toady

parcel *n.* package, bundle, packet, carton

parch *v.* scorch, dry, shrivel, desiccate, dehydrate

pardon *v.* exonerate, clear, absolve, reprieve, acquit, liberate, discharge, free, release, forgive, condone, overlook, exculpate, excuse

pare *v.* cut, diminish, shave, skin

parentage *n.* birth, descent, parenthood

parental *adj.* paternal, maternal, familial, genetic

park *n.* plaza, square, lawn, green, promenade, tract, grounds, woodland, meadow

parochial *adj.* limited, restricted, narrow, provincial, insular, sectional, local, regional

parody *v.* mimic, copy, caricature, imitate, joke

parole *v.* release, discharge, pardon, liberate, free

parson *n.* clergyman, cleric, preacher, minister

part *n.* PORTION: piece, fragment, fraction, section, sector, segment, particle, component, share; ROLE: character, hero, heroine, constituent

part *v.* **DIVIDE:** separate, sever; **DEPART:** withdraw

partial *adj.* **INCOMPLETE:** unfinished; **PREJUDICED:** unfair, influenced, biased, inclined

partiality *n.* fondness, inclination, preference

participate *v.* compete, play, strive, engage

particle *n.* jot, scrap, atom, molecule, fragment, piece, shred, bit, part

particular *adj.* **SPECIFIC:** distinct, singular, appropriate, special; **ACCURATE:** precise, minute, exact

particularly *adj.* expressly, especially

partisan *n.* adherent, supporter, disciple, follower

partition *n.* **DIVISION:** apportionment, distribution, **BARRIER:** separation, wall, obstruction

partly *adj.* partially, somewhat

partner *n.* associate, co–worker, ally

partnership *n.* alliance, union, brotherhood, society

party *n.* **AFFAIR:** social, reception, gathering, function; **PERSON:** someone, somebody; **GROUP:** company, crowd, assembly; **ORGANIZATION:** bloc, faction

pass *v.* **ELAPSE:** transpire; **TRANSFER:** relinquish, give; **ENACT:** legislate, establish; **EXCEED:** excel, transcend; **PROCEED:** progress, advance; **THROW:** toss, fling

passable *adj.* open, navigable, accessible

passage *n.* **JOURNEY:** voyage, crossing, trek; **PASSAGEWAY:** entrance, hall; **READING:** excerpt, section, portion, paragraph, quote

passenger *n.* traveler, commuter

passion *n.* feeling, craving, desire, emotion

passionate *adj.* excitable, tempestuous, impassioned, fervent, moving, inspiring, dramatic, stirring, eloquent, spirited, intense

passive *adj.* complacent, inert, lifeless, idle

passport *n.* pass, permit, visa, identification

password *n.* countersign, watchword, identification

past *adj.* former, preceding, foregoing, earlier

past *n.* antiquity, history

paste *n.* adhesive, cement, glue, mucilage

paste *v.* fasten, affix, patch, stick

pastime *n.* amusement, recreation, sport, hobby

pastor *n.* priest, rector, clergyman, minister

pastry *n.* dessert, delicacy

pasture *n.* grass, grazing, meadow, field

pat *v.* tap, touch, stroke, pet, rub

patch *n.* piece, bit, scrap, spot

patch *v.* repair, darn, mend

path *n.* trail, way, track, byway

pathetic *adj.* sad, touching, affecting, moving, pitiful

pathos *n.* pity, sorrow, grief

patience *n.* forbearance, fortitude, endurance, perseverance, persistence

patient *adj.* submissive, forbearing, unruffled, imperturbable, passive, persevering, calm

patio *n.* porch, courtyard, square, yard

patriarch *n.* ruler, master, ancestor, chief

patriot *n.* statesman, nationalist, loyalist, chauvinist

patrol *v.* watch, walk, inspect, guard

patron *n.* protector, sponsor, benefactor, backer

patronize *v.* condescend, stoop, snub

pattern *n.* model, original, guide, copy

pause *n.* delay, respite, suspension, hiatus, interim, lapse, cessation, interval

pause *v.* **STOP:** halt, cease, interrupt, suspend; **REFLECT:** deliberate

pawn *v.* deposit, pledge, hock, sell

pay *n.* **PROCEEDS:** return, recompense, indemnity, reparation, settlement, reimbursement; **WAGES:** compensation, salary, remuneration, earnings

pay *v.* **COMPENSATE:** recompense, remunerate, repay, reimburse; **RETURN:** yield, profit, pay, dividends

payment *n.* **REIMBURSEMENT:** restitution, refund, reparation; **INSTALLMENT:** portion, part

peace *n.* **ARMISTICE:** pacification, conciliation, agreement; **CALM:** tranquillity, harmony, silence, stillness; **COMPOSURE:** contentment

peaceful *adj.* quiet, tranquil, serene, calm

peak *n.* summit, top, crown, zenith, height

peasant *n.* laborer, farmer, worker, workman

peculiar *adj.* **UNUSUAL:** wonderful, singular, outlandish, strange; **UNIQUE:** characteristic, eccentric

peddle *v.* hawk, vend, trade, sell

pedestal *n.* base, stand, foundation, support

pedestrian *adj.* common, ordinary

peek *n.* sight, glimpse, glance, look

peek *v.* glance, peep, glimpse

peel *n.* skin, rind, husk, bark, shell

peel *v.* strip, skin, pare, flay, uncover

peep *v.* **CHIRP:** cheep; **PEEK:** glimpse, glance

peer *n.* equal, match, rival, companion

peer *v.* gaze, inspect, scrutinize

peeve *v.* irritate, annoy, anger, bother

peevish *adj.* cross, fretful, angry
pen *n.* cage, coop, sty, enclosure
pen *v.* **ENCLOSE:** confine; **WRITE:** compose
penalize *v.* chasten, castigate, punish
penalty *n.* punishment, fine, discipline
penance *n.* repentance, atonement, reparation
penchant *n.* inclination, taste, bias
pencil *v.* write, sketch, mark,
pendant *n.* locket, lavaliere, decoration, jewelry
pending *adj.* continuing, awaiting, ominous
penetrable *adj.* permeable, open, accessible, porous
penetrate *v.* pierce, perforate, puncture
penetrating *adj.* keen, astute, shrewd, sharp, intelligent, perceptive
penitentiary *n.* prison, reformatory, pen, jail
pension *n.* annuity, payment, allowance, retirement
perceive *v.* **OBSERVE:** note, look, notice; **UNDERSTAND:** comprehend, sense, grasp
perceptible *adj.* discernible, recognizable, obvious
perception *n.* judgment, understanding, apprehension, discernment, insight
perceptive *adj.* alert, incisive, keen, observant
perch *v.* roost, land, rest, sit
peremptory *adj.* decisive, final, imperious, dictatorial
perfect *adj.* **COMPLETE:** absolute, whole; **FAULTLESS:** impeccable, immaculate, untainted, ideal, sublime, excellent; **EXACT:** precise, sharp, distinct, accurate
perfect *v.* finish, fulfill, realize, achieve, complete
perfectly *adj.* flawlessly, faultlessly, ideally

perforate *v.* bore, pierce, drill, slit, stab, penetrate
perforation *n.* break, aperture, slit, hole
perform *v.* **PRESENT:** enact, show, exhibit, display, dramatize, execute; **ACCOMPLISH:** do, achieve, fulfill, discharge, complete, effect, finish, realize;
performance *n.* exhibition, appearance, offering, representation, revue, play, concert, drama
perfume *n.* scent, fragrance, aroma, odor, essence
perhaps *adj.* maybe, possibly, conceivably, reasonably
perilous *adj.* precarious, unsafe, dangerous
perimeter *n.* boundary, margin, outline, border, edge
period *n.* **EPOCH:** era, age; **END:** limit, conclusion
periodical *adj.* rhythmic, regular, recurrent
periodical *n.* publication, magazine, newspaper
periphery *n.* circumference, perimeter, border
perish *v.* die, pass, depart
perjure *v.* prevaricate, falsify, lie
permanence *n.* continuity, durability, stability
permanent *adj.* fixed, enduring, abiding, continuing, lasting, imperishable, persevering, constant
permeate *v.* penetrate, pervade, saturate, fill
permissible *adj.* allowable, sanctioned, permitted
permission *n.* liberty, consent, license, authorization, approval, sanction, endorsement, affirmation
permit *n.* permission, warrant, license, grant
permit *v.* consent, sanction, tolerate, let, allow

perpetrate *v.* perform, commit, act, do

perpetual *adj.* **UNENDING:** continual, unceasing, constant, endless; **REPETITIOUS:** repeating, recurrent

perplex *v.* puzzle, confound, bewilder, confuse

perplexed *adj.* troubled, uncertain, bewildered

persecute *v.* oppress, harass, victimize, abuse

persecution *n.* torture, torment, teasing, provoking

perseverance *n.* grit, resolution, pluck, determination

persevere *v.* persist, remain, pursue, endure

persist *v.* persevere, pursue, strive, continue, endure

person *n.* individual, being, character, personage

personable *adj.* agreeable, friendly, pleasant, charming, sociable, amiable

personage *n.* someone, individual, person

personal *adj.* **PRIVATE:** secret, confidential; **INDIVIDUAL:** peculiar, particular, individual, special

personality *n.* **CHARACTER:** disposition, nature, temper, individuality; **CELEBRITY:** star, luminary

personify *v.* represent, symbolize, exemplify

personnel *n.* employees, workers, group, staff

perspective *n.* view, vista, aspect, attitude, outlook

persuade *v.* influence, induce, convince, cajole

persuasion *n.* **BELIEF:** creed, tenet, religion, faith, conviction; **INFLUENCE:** inducing, enticement

persuasive *adj.* convincing, influential, winning, enticing, compelling, potent, powerful, forceful, plausible

pertain *v.* belong, relate, refer, concern
pertinent *adj.* relevant, pertaining, related
perturb *v.* disturb, pester, worry, irritate, bother
pervade *v.* penetrate, spread, suffuse, permeate
perverse *adj.* deviant, wayward, delinquent, bad
perversion *n.* **DISTORTION:** deception, lie; **CORRUPTION:** depravity, wickedness, vice
pervert *v.* corrupt, ruin, vitiate, divert
pessimism *n.* unhappiness, gloom, sadness
pessimistic *adj.* **DISCOURAGING:** worrisome, troubling, dismal; **CYNICAL:** hopeless, gloomy, sad
pester *v.* annoy, harass, provoke, bother
pestilence *n.* disease, epidemic, sickness, illness
pet *n.* darling, lover, favorite, idol, adored
pet *v.* caress, fondle, cuddle, touch embrace
petition *n.* request, prayer, supplication, appeal
petrified *adj.* stone, hardened, mineralized, firm
petty *adj.* small, contemptible, insignificant, frivolous, trivial, unimportant
phantasm *n.* vision, illusion, specter, apparition, ghost
phenomenal *adj.* extraordinary, unique, remarkable
philanthropic *adj.* benevolent, humanitarian, kind
philosophic *adj.* thoughtful, reflective, cogitative, rational, profound, erudite, deep, learned
philosophy *n.* **STUDY:** wisdom, theory, explanation; **PRINCIPLE:** truth, axiom, conception, basis; **BELIEF:** outlook, view, position, opinion, viewpoint

phlegmatic *adj.* calm, sluggish, indifferent
phobia *n.* avoidance, aversion, hatred, resentment
phony *adj.* affected, imitation, artificial, false
photograph *n.* print, portrait, likeness, snapshot
photographic *adj.* accurate, detailed, exact, graphic
physical *adj.* material, corporeal, visible, tangible, palpable, substantial, real
physician *n.* healer, practitioner, surgeon, doctor
physique *n.* structure, build, constitution, body
pick *v.* **CHOOSE:** select, separate; **GATHER:** pluck, pull
picket *n.* **STAKE:** pole, post; **WATCHMAN:** guard, sentry
picket *v.* strike, blockade, boycott, protest
picture *n.* **REPRESENTATION:** photograph, image, portrait; **DESCRIPTION:** depiction, portrayal
picture *v.* **DEPICT:** sketch, portray, draw, paint, represent, describe; **IMAGINE:** create, conceive
picturesque *adj.* charming, pictorial, scenic, graphic, striking, quaint
piece *n.* part, portion, share, section
pierce *v.* penetrate, stab
piety *n.* reverence, devotion, veneration
pigment *n.* coloring, paint, dye, color
pile *n.* heap, collection, mass, quantity
pile *v.* amass, stack, gather, accumulate, store
pilgrim *n.* traveler, wayfarer, wanderer, sojourner
pill *n.* tablet, capsule, pellet, medicine, drug
pillage *v.* plunder, loot, rob, destroy, steal
pillar *n.* **COLUMN:** pedestal, mast, shaft, post; **SUPPORT:** mainstay, prop

pillow *n.* cushion, pad, support, headrest

pilot *v.* guide, conduct, manage, lead

pin *v.* close, clasp, bind, fasten

pinnacle *n.* apex, zenith, crest, summit, climax

pious *adj.* reverent, devout, divine, holy, religious

pipe *n.* tube, conduit, culvert, duct

piracy *n.* robbery, theft, pillage, holdup

pirate *n.* plunderer, marauder, privateer, buccaneer

pit *n.* hole, abyss, cavity, depression

pitch *n.* **SLOPE:** slant, incline, angle, grade; **THROW:** toss, hurl, cast; **FREQUENCY:** tone, sound

pitfall *n.* snare, mesh, deadfall, trap

pith *n.* center, essence, heart, core

pitiful *adj.* sorry, mean, despicable, miserable, distressed, pathetic, pitiable, depressing

pity *n.* compassion, charity, tenderness, kindliness, benevolence, clemency, humanity, sympathy

pity *v.* **COMMISERATE:** sympathize, console, grieve, weep, comfort; **FORGIVE:** pardon, reprieve, spare

pivot *v.* turn, whirl, swivel, rotate

place *n.* **POSITION:** point, spot; **LOCALITY:** locus, site, area, region; **RANK:** status, position

place *v.* **PUT:** locate, deposit; **ARRANGE:** fix, order

placement *n.* situation, position, arrangement

plague *n.* pestilence, illness, epidemic

plague *v.* afflict, vex, disturb, trouble, irk, bother

plain *adj.* **OBVIOUS:** open, manifest, clear, understandable; **SIMPLE:** unadorned, unpretentious, modest; **ORDINARY:** everyday, commonplace;

BLUNT: outspoken, candid, impolite, rude

plan *n.* **DRAFT:** diagram, design, schematic, drawing; **SCHEME:** project, idea, undertaking, plot, conspiracy, strategy; **ARRANGEMENT:** layout, disposition, order,

plan *v.* **SCHEME:** plot, devise, contrive, intrigue, conspire, calculate; **OUTLINE:** draft, sketch, map; **INTEND:** propose, think, expect, contemplate

plane *n.* level, horizontal, flat

plane *v.* smooth, finish, level, flatten

planned *adj.* projected, budgeted, programmed

plantation *n.* farm, acreage, estate, ranch

plateau *n.* tableland, mesa, elevation, hill

platform *n.* **STAGE:** dais, rostrum, stand, terrace; **PROGRAM:** principles, policies

plausible *adj.* convincing, probable, credible, likely

play *n.* **AMUSEMENT:** enjoyment, diversion; **RECREATION:** games, sports; **THEATER:** drama, musical

play *v.* revel, carouse, gambol, cavort, participate

player *n.* athlete, contestant, actor, performer

playful *adj.* joking, whimsical, comical, funny

playmate *n.* comrade, neighbor, companion, friend

playwright *n.* writer, author, tragedian

plea *n.* appeal, request, supplication, pleading

plead *v.* **BEG:** implore, beseech, solicit, ask; **ARGUE:** present, allege, cite, declare

pleasant *adj.* affable, agreeable, obliging, charming, gracious, amiable, polite, civil, cordial, sociable

please *v.* gratify, delight, satisfy

pleasing *adj.* charming, agreeable, delightful, pleasant

pleasure *n.* enjoyment, delight, happiness, amusement, preference, desire

pledge *n.* security, surety, guarantee, agreement

pledge *v.* promise, swear, vow, vouch

plentiful *adj.* bountiful, prolific, profuse, lavish, extravagant, copious, abundant, abounding

plenty *n.* abundance, lavishness, deluge, torrent, bounty, profusion, flood

pliable, pliant *adj.* flexible, limber, supple, plastic

plight *n.* condition, dilemma, state

plod *v.* trudge, hike, walk

plot *v.* **INTRIGUE:** frame, contrive, scheme, conspire; **PLAN:** sketch, outline, draft

plump *adj.* obese, stout, fleshy, fat

plunder *v.* seize, burn, steal, raid, ravage

plunge *v.* cast, fall, rush, dive, jump

plus *adj.* increase, additionally, surplus, extra

poach *v.* steal, filch, pilfer, smuggle

pocket *n.* **CAVITY:** hollow; **POUCH:** poke, sac

pocket *v.* take, conceal, hide, enclose, steal

poetic *adj.* lyrical, romantic, imaginative

poetry *n.* verse, rhythm, rhyme, poesy

poignant *adj.* penetrating, moving, touching

point *n.* **POSITION:** location, locality; **PURPOSE:** aim, object, intent; **MEANING:** force, drift, import

point *v.* **INDICATE:** show, name, denote; **DIRECT:** guide, steer, influence, lead

pointer *n.* **INDICATOR:** dial, gauge; **HINT:** clue, tip

pointless *adj.* **DULL:** prosaic, trivial, unnecessary; **INEFFECTIVE:** useless, impotent, incompetent, weak

poise *n.* carriage, bearing, grace, composure, dignity
poisonous *adj.* noxious, venomous, toxic, harmful
poke *v.* jab, punch, crowd, push
policy *n.* principle, doctrine, scheme, design
polish *v.* smooth, burnish, finish, shine
polite *adj.* polished, mannerly, amiable, gracious, cordial, diplomatic, civil, sociable, respectful
politeness *n.* refinement, culture, civility, courtesy
poll *v.* sample, canvass, question, register, enroll, list
pollute *v.* soil, defile, stain, contaminate, corrupt
pollution *n.* dirt, grime, smog, sewage, garbage, waste, exhaust, pesticides, smoke
poltergeist *n.* ghost, spirit, apparition, specter, spook
pomp *n.* pageantry, magnificence, splendor
pompous *adj.* pretentious, haughty, arrogant, proud
ponder *v.* meditate, think, deliberate, consider
ponderous *adj.* heavy, weighty, dull, lifeless
pool *n.* **WATER:** puddle; **STAKES:** ante, pot, kitty
pool *v.* merge, unite, consolidate, combine, blend, join
poor *adj.* **INSOLVENT:** indigent, penniless, destitute, needy, starved, beggared, broke, **WEAK:** puny, feeble, infirm; **INFERIOR:** mediocre, trashy, shoddy, deficient, cheap, flimsy
pop *n.* **SODA:** beverage, seltzer, cola; **NOISE:** report, burst, shot, crack, detonation
poppycock *n.* drivel, nonsense, gibberish
populace *n.* people, multitudes, masses, people

popular *adj.* liked, favorite, beloved, celebrated, admired, famous, widespread
popularity *n.* acceptance, notoriety, prevalence
populated *adj.* inhabited, occupied, peopled, urban
population *n.* inhabitants, citizenry, populace, society
porous *adj.* absorbent, pervious, permeable
port *n.* harbor, haven, refuge, anchorage, dock
portable *adj.* movable, transportable, transferable
portal *n.* entrance, archway, gateway
portend *v.* foretell, predict, herald
porter *n.* doorkeeper, custodian, caretaker
portfolio *n.* **CASE:** briefcase, folder; **ASSETS:** holdings, stocks, bonds
portion *n.* **PART:** scrap, fragment, piece; **ALLOTMENT:** share, quota
portrait *n.* likeness, painting, picture
portray *v.* draw, describe, depict, characterize
portrayal *n.* description, replica, likeness
pose *n.* position, attitude, pretense, affectation
pose *v.* **MODEL:** sit; **PRETEND:** profess, act, feign
posh *adj.* rich, smart, comfortable
position *n.* **LOCATION:** whereabouts, bearings; **OPINION:** view, belief; **PROFESSION:** job, office, occupation; **STATION:** status, rank; **POSTURE:** carriage, bearing
positive *adj.* decisive, emphatic, assertive, resolute, certain, confident, sure
possess *v.* have, hold, own, occupy, control
possessions *n.* belongings, effects, estate, property
possessor *n.* owner, holder, proprietor, occupant

possibility *n.* plausibility, feasibility, chance, hazard, hope, prospect

possible *adj.* likely, conceivable, imaginable

possibly *adv.* likely, maybe, perhaps, potentially

post *n.* column, pillar, pedestal, upright, mast

poster *n.* advertisement, sign, card, note

posterior *adj.* **SUBSEQUENT:** coming, after, succeeding, next, following, later; **BEHIND:** back

posterity *n.* eternity, descendants, children, offspring

postpone *v.* defer, table, delay, suspend, retard, withhold, shelve, adjourn, pause

postscript *n.* appendix, addition, supplement

posture *n.* **STANCE:** pose, carriage, aspect, presence; **ATTITUDE:** feeling, sentiment, disposition

pot *n.* **KITTY:** jackpot, ante; **CONTAINER:** vessel, kettle, pan, crock, receptacle, urn, bowl

potable *adj.* clean, fresh, unpolluted

potency *n.* **STRENGTH:** power, energy, vigor; **AUTHORITY:** influence, control, dominion, command

potential *adj.* possible, latent, implied, likely

pouch *n.* bag, sack, receptacle, container

pounce *v.* seize, spring, attack, bound, jump

pound *v.* beat, crush, pulverize, strike, hit

pour *v.* **FLOW:** discharge, emit, issue, drain, rush; **EMPTY:** spill, splash; **RAIN:** stream, flood, drench

poverty *n.* **DESTITUTION:** indigence, want, privation, insolvency; **LACK:** shortage, inadequacy, scarcity

power *n.* **STRENGTH:** vigor, stamina; **AUTHORITY:** jurisdiction, dominion, dominance, control, sway, sovereignty, supremacy; **FORCE:** compulsion, coercion, duress; **ENERGY:** potential, dynamism

powerful *adj.* mighty, omnipotent, influential, potent, forceful, compelling

powerless *adj.* helpless, feeble, weak, impotent, infirm

practical *adj.* useful, feasible, workable, rational, utilitarian, serviceable, effective

practically *adv.* virtually, nearly, almost

practice *n.* **CUSTOM:** usage; **METHOD:** mode, manner, fashion; **REPETITION:** exercise, rehearsal

practice *v.* drill, train, exercise, rehearse

practiced *adj.* skilled, able, experienced

pragmatic *adj.* logical, sensible, practical, realistic

praise *v.* commend, applaud, acclaim, endorse, eulogize, compliment, celebrate, honor, glorify, extol

prance *v.* strut, caper, cavort, frisk, gambol, dance

prank *n.* trick, antic, game, escapade, caper, joke

pray *v.* ask, petition, plead, beseech, beg, implore

prayer *n.* appeal, request, petition, plea, entreaty,

preach *v.* lecture, teach, sermonize, discourse, exhort, moralize, talk, harangue, inform, address

preacher *n.* missionary, parson, evangelist, minister

preamble *n.* preface, prelude, introduction

precarious *adj.* uncertain, unsafe, risky, doubtful, dubious, dangerous, unstable

precaution *n.* care, prudence, anticipation, forethought, regard, foresight

precede *v.* lead, antedate, preface, introduce, herald

precedence *n.* preference, priority

preceding *adj.* foregoing, former, previous, earlier

precious *adj.* **BELOVED:** cherished, prized; **VALUABLE:** costly, expensive; **REFINED:** delicate, dainty

precipice *n.* cliff, crag, bluff, hill, mountain

precipitate *v.* cause, accelerate, press, hasten, speed

precipitous *adj.* sheer, steep, sharp, abrupt

precise *adj.* exact, accurate, careful

precision *n.* exactness, correctness, accuracy

preconception *n.* prejudice, bias, assumption

predecessor *n.* forerunner, antecedent, ancestor

predicament *n.* difficulty, strait, plight, scrape, circumstance, mess, pinch, crisis

predict *v.* foretell, prophesy, prognosticate, divine

predominance *n.* dominance, supremacy, control

predominant *adj.* **SUPREME:** almighty, powerful; **FIRST:** transcendent, surpassing, superlative, principal

preeminent *adj.* distinguished, eminent, outstanding

preface *v.* introduce, commence, precede, begin

preference *n.* choice, election, option, selection, pick

preferred *adj.* chosen, selected, favored

prehistoric *adj.* ancient, primitive, antiquated, old

prejudice *n.* bias, inclination, partiality

prejudiced *adj.* predisposed, opinionated, partisan, narrow, intolerant, parochial, provincial

preliminary *adj.* preparatory, preceding, introductory

prelude *n.* introduction, preamble, prologue, preface

premature *adj.* rash, precipitate, untimely, early

premise *n.* supposition, assumption, proposition

premium *adj.* excellent, select, prime, superior

premium *n.* reward, prize, remuneration, bonus

premonition *n.* foreboding, portent, sign, warning

preoccupied *adj.* distracted, absorbed, engrossed, disturbed, troubled,

preparation *n.* **READYING:** rehearsal, anticipation, build–up; **PREPAREDNESS:** readiness, fitness, training, education; **MIXTURE:** compound, medicine, poultice

prepare *v.* **READY:** fix, fabricate, devise, anticipate, plan, arrange, make; **OUTFIT:** equip; **COOK:** concoct

prepossessing *adj.* winning, captivating, charming

prerequisite *n.* requirement, necessity, essential

prerogative *n.* privilege, advantage, exemption, right

prescription *n.* remedy, formula, medicine

presence *n.* **ATTENDANCE:** occupancy, residence, inhabitancy; **PROXIMITY:** nearness, closeness; **DEMEANOR:** appearance, behavior, carriage

present *adj.* now, existing, contemporary, immediate, instant, today, nowadays, already, current

present *n.* gift, grant, donation, offering

present *v.* **EXHIBIT:** do, act, perform; **BESTOW:** give, grant, confer donate, proffer, offer

presentable *adj.* proper, satisfactory, attractive

presently, *adv.* soon, directly, shortly, immediately

preservation *n.* protection, conservation, keeping, storage, curing, refrigeration

preserve *v.* **GUARD:** protect, shield; **KEEP:** process, cure

preside *v.* superintend, direct, lead, manage

press *n.* haste, urgency, rush, confusion, strain

pressing *adj.* important, urgent, demanding

pressure *n.* **TENSION:** burden, stress, squeeze; **PERSUASION:** compulsion, coercion

pressure *v.* press, compel, constrain, urge, persuade

prestige *n.* influence, reputation, esteem

presume *v.* believe, consider, suppose, assume

presumption *n.* **ASSUMPTION:** conjecture, supposition; **IMPUDENCE:** audacity, arrogance, effrontery

pretend *v.* feign, affect, imitate, simulate, represent

pretense *n.* simulation, fabrication, imitation; deception, affectation, subterfuge, pretext

pretentious *adj.* presumptuous, arrogant, pompous

pretty *adj.* **PLEASANT:** delightful, cheerful, pleasing; **ATTRACTIVE:** comely, lovely, beautiful;

prevalent *adj.* prevailing, widespread, common

prevent *v.* preclude, block, stop, thwart, halt, impede, check, frustrate, obstruct, inhibit, restrain

previous *adj.* former, antecedent, prior, preceding

prey *v.* hunt, spoil, pillage, loot, victimize

price *n.* expense, cost, worth, payment

price *v.* appraise, assess, rate, value

priceless *adj.* invaluable, inestimable, valuable

prick *v.* pierce, stick, cut, hurt, puncture

prickly *adj.* thorny, pointed, spiny, sharp

pride *n.* egotism, haughtiness, disdain, condescension

prim *adj.* exact, stiff, formal, demure, decorous, polite

primary *adj.* **EARLIEST:** primitive, first, original; **FUNDAMENTAL:** elemental, basic; **PRINCIPAL:** chief, prime, main

primitive *adj.* **SIMPLE:** rough, rude, fundamental; **ANCIENT:** primeval, old, beginning, uncivilized

primp *v.* dress, prepare, paint, powder

princely *adj.* lavish, sumptuous, luxurious, expensive, handsome, rich

principal *adj.* chief, leading, first, main, foremost, preeminent, dominant, prevailing

principle *n.* **FUNDAMENTAL:** law, origin, source, postulate; **BELIEF:** opinion, teaching, faith

prior *adj.* before, antecedent, foregoing, preceding

priority *n.* preference, precedence, advantage

prisoner *n.* captive, convict, detainee, hostage

privacy *n.* seclusion, solitude, isolation, aloofness, separation, concealment, secrecy

private *adj.* personal, separate, secluded, clandestine

privilege *n.* right, perquisite, prerogative, concession

prize *n.* reward, premium, bonus, booty, plunder, loot, award, medal, trophy, crown

probable *adj.* likely, seeming, presumable, feasible

problem *n.* **DIFFICULTY:** dilemma, quandary, obstacle; **QUESTION:** query, intricacy, enigma, puzzle

procedure *n.* fashion, mode, method, system, order

proceed *v.* progress, continue, advance

proceeding *n.* performance, undertaking, venture, happening, operation, procedure, exercise

proceeds *n.* gain, interest, yield, return

process *n.* means, manner, method

process *v.* treat, ready, concoct, prepare

prod *v.* provoke, crowd, shove, push

produce *v.* **CREATE:** originate, devise, conceive, design, compose, invent; **MAKE:** assemble, construct, manufacture; **CAUSE:** effect, occasion

product *n.* result, output, outcome

productive *adj.* rich, fruitful, prolific, fertile

profanity *n.* irreverence, abuse, cursing, swearing

profession *n.* **CAREER:** occupation, calling, avocation, vocation; **DECLARATION:** avowal, vow, oath

professional *adj.* skillful, expert, adept, able, qualified

professor *n.* teacher, educator, instructor, lecturer

proficiency *n.* skill, knowledge, ability

proficient *adj.* adept, expert, skilled, able

profit *n.* gain, return, proceeds

profitable *adj.* lucrative, beneficial, advantageous

profound *adj.* **SCHOLARLY:** learned, sagacious, intellectual; **HEARTFELT:** great, intense

program *n.* **SCHEDULE:** agenda, curriculum, calendar, plan, outline; **ENTERTAINMENT:** performance, show

progress *n.* headway, impetus, improvement, advancement, development, growth

progressive *adj.* tolerant, lenient, open-minded

prohibit *v.* forbid, interdict, obstruct, prevent, ban

project *n.* plan, scheme, outline, design

projection *n.* **BULGE:** prominence, protuberance; **FORECAST:** prognostication, prediction, guess

prolong *v.* lengthen, extend, increase

prominent *adj.* **FAMOUS:** notable, distinguished, leading; **CONSPICUOUS:** striking, noticeable

promiscuous *adj.* indiscriminate, unrestricted, lewd

promise *n.* agreement, pact, covenant, contract

promise *v.* pledge, declare, vow, swear, profess, guarantee, warrant, insure, underwrite, subscribe

promising *adj.* likely, encouraging, hopeful

promote *v.* further, encourage, help, aid, assist, support, back, champion, advocate, bolster, nourish, nurture, subsidize, boost, advance

prompt *adj.* timely, precise, punctual

prompt *v.* instigate, arouse, inspire, incite, urge

prone *adj.* disposed, inclined, predisposed, likely

pronounced *adj.* noticeable, clear, definite, obvious

pronouncement *n.* report, declaration, statement

proof *n.* verification, confirmation, corroboration, substantiation, testimony

propensity *n.* talent, capacity, ability

proper *adj.* decent, conventional, decorous, prudish, prim

property *n.* possessions, belongings, assets, holdings

prophecy *n.* prediction, forecast, prognostication

prophesy *v.* foretell, predict, divine

prophet *n.* seer, oracle, soothsayer, astrologer

propitious *adj.* auspicious, encouraging, promising

proponent *n.* defender, advocate, champion

proposal *n.* **OFFER:** overture, proposition, suggestion, **PLAN:** scheme, program, prospectus

propose *v.* offer, recommend, submit, volunteer
proposition *n.* offer, scheme, project, plan
propriety *n.* accordance, compatibility, congruity, modesty, dignity, pleasantness
prospect *n.* expectation, promise, outlook, possibility
prospective *adj.* proposed, promised, planned
prosper *v.* flourish, thrive, flower, succeed
protect *v.* shelter, shield, guard, preserve, defend
protection *n.* shield, screen, shelter, defense, security
protector *n.* champion, defender, patron, sponsor, benefactor, supporter, advocate
protest *n.* rally, demonstration, dissent
protest *v.* object, demur, disagree, oppose
proud *adj.* **DIGNIFIED:** stately, lordly; **EGOTISTICAL:** vain, haughty, arrogant
prove *v.* demonstrate, substantiate, authenticate, corroborate, validate, confirm
provide *v.* furnish, equip, outfit, stock, supply
provincial *adj.* narrow, backward, rude, unpolished
provision *v.* requirement, stipulation, prerequisite
provisional *adj.* transient, passing, temporary
provoke *v.* **VEX:** irritate, aggravate, bother; **INCITE:** stir, rouse, arouse; **CAUSE:** make, produce, begin
prowl *v.* slink, lurk, rove, sneak
proxy *n.* agent, broker, representative, delegate
prudent *adj.* **CAREFUL:** cautious, circumspect, wary, discreet; **PRACTICAL:** sensible, wise, discerning
pry *v.* snoop, spy, nose, inquire, meddle
pseudo *adj.* imitation, quasi, sham, false

publication *n.* broadcasting, announcement, advisement, disclosure

publicize *n.* announce, broadcast, promulgate

publish *v.* **DISTRIBUTE:** print, issue; **ADVERTISE:** announce, promulgate, proclaim

pull *n.* **TOW:** drag, haul; **INFLUENCE:** power, authority

pulpy *adj.* soft, smooth, thick, fleshy

pulse *n.* beating, pulsation, vibration

pun *n.* witticism, quip, joke

punch *v.* **HIT:** thrust, blow, strike, knock; **PERFORATE:** pierce, puncture, bore, penetrate, prick

punctual *adj.* prompt, precise, exact, meticulous

puncture *v.* pierce, prick, perforate, penetrate

punish *v.* correct, discipline, chasten, reprove, penalize, fine, incarcerate, chastise

puny *adj.* small, feeble, inferior, diminutive, weak

purchase *v.* obtain, acquire, buy

pure *adj.* **CLEAN:** immaculate, germ–free, sterilized, sanitary, refined; **UNMIXED:** unadulterated, undiluted, simple, clear; **CHASTE:** virginal, celibate; **ABSOLUTE:** sheer, utter, complete

purge *v.* cleanse, evacuate, eliminate

purpose *n.* aim, intention, end, goal, mission, objective, expectation, intent, aspiration

pursue *v.* chase, seek, hound, track, stalk

push *n.* shove, drive, exertion, straining, inducement, impact, blow, pressure

push *v.* **PRESS:** thrust, shove, ram, jostle, elbow; **PROMOTE:** advance, launch, start, sell

put *v.* **PLACE:** set, plant, lodge, situate, deposit

putrid *adj.* rotten, corrupt, putrefied, decayed

puzzle *v.* **PERPLEX:** obscure, bewilder, complicate, confuse; **WONDER:** marvel, surprise, astonish

puzzling *adj.* obscure, uncertain, ambiguous, mystifying, difficult, perplexing, abstruse, hard

quaint *adj.* strange, odd, fanciful, cute, whimsical

quake *v.* tremble, shrink, cower, shake

qualified *adj.* **LIMITED:** conditional, confined, restricted; **COMPETENT:** adequate, equipped, able

quality *n.* **ATTRIBUTE:** trait, endowment, condition, property; **CHARACTER:** nature, essence; **GRADE:** class, merit, worth, excellence, variety, rank

qualm *n.* scruple, doubt, uncertainty

quantity *n.* amount, number, measure

quarrel *v.* dispute, wrangle, clash, contend, squabble, disagree, bicker, contest, argue, feud, oppose

quarrelsome *adj.* factious, irritable, pugnacious, contentious, cantankerous

queasy *adj.* squeamish, sick, uneasy, uncomfortable

queer *adj.* odd, peculiar, strange, curious

question *v.* **ASK:** inquire, interrogate, petition, solicit, quiz, probe, investigate; **DOUBT:** challenge, dispute

questionable *adj.* **CONTROVERSIAL:** vague, unsettled, debatable, ambiguous, indefinite; **DUBIOUS:** disreputable, notorious, suspicious

quick *adj.* **RAPID:** swift, fleet, fast; **IMMEDIATE:** instantaneous, prompt; **HASTY:** impetuous, quick–tempered, rash; **ALERT:** ready, sharp, vigorous, active

quicken *v.* **HASTEN:** speed, hurry, accelerate, move, **EXPEDITE:** urge, promote

quiet *adj.* silent, calm, peaceful, hushed, reserved, muffled, reticent, noiseless, still

quiet *n.* calm, tranquillity, relaxation, peace, repose; silence, hush, stillness

quip *n.* retort, remark, jest, repartee, banter

quirk *n.* whim, caprice, fancy, peculiarity

quit *v.* **ABANDON:** surrender, renounce, relinquish; **CEASE:** discontinue, halt, desist, stop; **LEAVE:** go, depart, vacate, resign

quiver *v.* vibrate, shudder, tremble

quiz *v.* question, examine, test, query

quote *v.* **EXCERPT:** extract, say, repeat; **PRICE:** request, demand, value

rabid *adj.* **FANATICAL:** obsessed, zealous; **INSANE:** raging, deranged, mad

race *v.* hurry, run, tear, bustle, fly, dash, sprint

racket *n.* **UPROAR:** clatter, disturbance, din; **CONSPIRACY:** scheme, corruption, crime, theft

racketeer *n.* criminal, extortionist, trickster

radial *adj.* branched, outspread, spreading

radiant *adj.* shining, luminous, radiating, bright

radiate *v.* spread, diffuse, disperse, disseminate

radiation *n.* fallout, pollution, radioactivity, heat

radical *adj.* **EXTREME:** progressive, militant, seditious, riotous, rebellious, revolutionary, heretical; **FUNDAMENTAL:** original, primitive, native, organic

raffle *n.* lottery, sweepstakes, pool

raft *n.* flatboat, barge, float, catamaran, boat

rag *n.* cloth, remnant, wiper, shred

rage *n.* **FURY:** frenzy, tantrum, uproar, storm, outburst; **FAD:** fashion, style, mode, vogue, craze, mania

rage *v.* rave, splutter, scream, rant, bluster, storm

ragged *adj.* tattered, frayed, threadbare, frazzled

raid *n.* attack, invasion, foray, assault

rain *v.* pour, drizzle, shower, sprinkle, mist

raise *v.* **LIFT:** elevate, hoist, boost; **REAR:** breed, cultivate, produce; **ERECT:** construct, build

rake *n.* **RASCAL:** lecher, drunkard, scoundrel

rally *n.* gathering, meeting, session

ram *v.* butt, bump, collide, thrust, drive

ramble *v.* **SAUNTER:** stroll, roam, wander; **DRIFT:** stray, diverge, meander, digress

ramp *n.* incline, slope, grade, hill, inclination

rampant *adj.* raging, violent, turbulent, tumultuous, unruly

rancid *adj.* unpleasant, tainted, stale, rotten

random *adj.* aimless, haphazard, casual, unpredictable

range *n.* **SCOPE:** extent, area, expanse; **MOUNTAINS:** highlands; **DISTANCE:** reach, span, projection

range *v.* **VARY:** differ, fluctuate, diverge; **TRAVERSE:** wander, ramble, explore, traverse

rank *adj.* foul, smelly, fetid, putrid, stinking, rancid, offensive, noxious, gamy, disgusting, malodorous

rank *n.* **ROW:** column, file, string, line; **EMINENCE:** position, distinction, standing, status, ancestry

rank *v.* **ARRANGE:** assign, order; **EVALUATE:** judge, fix, valuate, classify

ransack *v.* **SEARCH:** rummage, scour, seek; **LOOT:** pillage, plunder, ravish, strip, rifle

rant *v.* rave, fume, rail, rage, yell
rap *n.* knock, thump, slap, blow
rapid *adj.* accelerated, swift, speedy, hurried
rapt *adj.* awed, transported, entranced, enchanted
rapture *n.* delight, ecstasy, pleasure, satisfaction
rare *adj.* **UNCOMMON:** exceptional, singular, extraordinary, unusual; **SCARCE:** expensive, precious; **CHOICE:** select, superlative, excellent
rascal *n.* scoundrel, rogue, rake, knave, shyster, cad, scalawag, reprobate, miscreant
rash *adj.* hasty, impetuous, impulsive, foolish, heedless, foolhardy, brash
rate *v.* rank, judge, evaluate, grade
ratify *v.* substantiate, endorse, approve, sanction
rating *n.* grade, class, degree, rank
ration *n.* allowance, allotment, portion, quota, share
rational *adj.* **LOGICAL:** stable, thoughtful, sensible, impartial, objective, sober; **REASONABLE:** intelligent, sensible, wise; **SANE:** normal, lucid, responsible
rattle *v.* disconcert, bother, unnerve, confuse, disturb, embarrass
raucous *adj.* hoarse, harsh, loud, gruff, rough
ravage *v.* pillage, devastate, despoil, plunder, sack
rave *v.* **TALK:** babble, gabble, jabber; **RAGE:** storm, splutter, rail, rant
ravel *v.* untwist, disentangle, unsnarl, free, loosen
ravenous *adj.* voracious, starved, hungry
ravine *n.* hollow, gully, gorge, cànyon, gulch, valley, gap, chasm, abyss, break, crevice, crevasse

raw *adj.* **UNFINISHED:** natural, crude, rough; **UNTRAINED:** immature; **COLD:** biting, windy, bleak

reach *n.* compass, range, scope, grasp, stretch, extension, orbit, horizon, gamut, ability, limit, extent

reach *v.* **EXTEND:** span, encompass, overtake; stretch, strain, seize; **ARRIVE:** gain, enter

react *v.* respond, reciprocate, behave, answer

reaction *n.* response, rejoinder, repercussion

read *v* **UNDERSTAND:** comprehend, perceive, apprehend, grasp, learn; **INTERPRET:** decipher, explain, expound, construe

readable *adj.* **LEGIBLE:** distinct, comprehensible, decipherable; **INTERESTING:** absorbing, fascinating, engrossing, entertaining, engaging, stimulating

readily *adv.* quickly, promptly, eagerly, willingly

reading *n.* **EXCERPT:** passage, quotation; **INTERPRETATION:** translation, commentary

ready *adj.* **PREPARED:** alert, handy, expectant; **ENTHUSIASTIC:** eager, willing, ardent, zealous

real *adj.* **GENUINE:** authentic, original; **EXISTING:** actual, substantive, tangible

realism *n.* authenticity, naturalness, actuality, reality

realization *n.* understanding, comprehension, consciousness, awareness

realize *v.* **FULFILL:** complete, accomplish; **UNDERSTAND:** recognize, apprehend, discern; **OBTAIN:** receive get

realm *n.* kingdom, province, domain

rear *n.* back, hindmost, tail, posterior, rump, butt

reason *n.* **JUDGMENT:** intelligence, sanity; **LOGIC:** rationalism, analysis; **MOTIVE:** rationale, intent, aim; **MIND:** brain, mentality, intellect

reason *v.* **THINK:** reflect, deliberate, contemplate; **ASSUME:** suppose, gather, conclude; **DISCUSS:** persuade, argue, contend, debate

reasonable *adj.* **RATIONAL:** sane, conscious, sensible, unbiased; **JUST:** fair, right, honest; **LIKELY:** feasible, sound, plausible; **MODERATE:** inexpensive, fair, cheap

reassure *v.* console, comfort, encourage, guarantee

rebel *n.* revolutionary, agitator, insurgent, seditionist, malcontent, dissenter, renegade, radical

rebel *v.* rise, revolt, resist, mutiny, riot, oppose

rebellion *n.* insurrection, revolt, revolution

rebound *v.* recoil, reflect, ricochet, bounce

rebuke *v.* chide, reprove, reprimand

recede *v.* retreat, ebb, abate, decline, lessen, decrease

receipt *n.* **ACQUISITION:** receiving, acceptance, arrival; **VOUCHER:** acknowledgment, notice

receive *v.* **ACCEPT:** inherit, acquire, obtain, secure; **EXPERIENCE:** undergo, suffer; **WELCOME:** accommodate, accept, greet

recent *adj.* modern, fresh, novel, contemporary, late

receptacle *n.* repository, holder, container

reception *n.* gathering, party, soiree, entertainment

receptive *adj.* alert, sensitive, perceptive, observant

recess *n.* **ALCOVE:** nook, cell, cubicle; **SUSPENSION:** intermission, interlude

recipe *n.* formula, compound, instructions, directions

recite *v.* dramatize, enact, interpret, soliloquize, narrate, recount, portray
reckless *adj.* heedless, thoughtless, rash
reckon *v.* consider, evaluate, estimate
reclaim *v.* recover, redeem, regain, mend
recognition *n.* acknowledgment, verification, appreciation, esteem, regard, honor
recognize *v.* **RECALL:** distinguish, place, remember, perceive; **ACKNOWLEDGE:** appreciate, realize
recoil *v.* shrink, retreat, bounce, spring
recommend *v.* commend, endorse, suggest, prescribe, advise
reconcile *v.* **ADJUST:** adapt, arrange, regulate; **HARMONIZE:** pacify, mitigate, mediate, intercede
reconciliation *n.* conciliation, adjustment, agreement
record *n.* document, manuscript, account, history, disk
record *v.* write, transcribe, catalogue, tabulate, chronicle
recover *v.* **SALVAGE:** redeem, rescue, reclaim; **RALLY:** convalesce, heal, mend, revive, recuperate
recreation *n.* pastime, amusement
recuperate *v.* recover, convalesce, heal
recur *v.* return, reappear, happen, repeat
redecorate *v.* refurbish, refresh, restore, recondition, remodel, renovate, revamp
redeem *v.* **RECOVER:** repay, purchase, atone, compensate; **SAVE:** liberate, free, deliver, rescue
redemption *n.* regeneration, salvation, rebirth, rescue
redress *n.* compensation, reparation
reduce *v.* **LESSEN:** dilute, diminish, decrease, lower; **DEFEAT:** conquer, overcome, subdue; **HUMBLE:** degrade, demote, abase, humiliate

redundant *adj.* superfluous, wordy, verbose, dull
refine *v.* purify, filter, strain, clean, improve, better, clarify
refined *adj.* genteel, cultivated, elegant, gracious, mannerly, courteous, polite
refinement *n.* **CULTURE:** sophistication, breeding, enlightenment, scholarship; **POLITENESS:** polish, manners, tact, civility, affability
reflect *v.* ponder, contemplate, concentrate, weigh, consider, think
reflection *n.* thought, consideration, contemplation, deliberation, meditation
reform *n.* reformation, betterment, improvement
reform *v.* revise, redeem, rectify, rehabilitate, remedy, restore, rebuild, reclaim, regenerate, amend, correct
refrain *v.* avoid, cease, forbear, abstain
refresh *v.* invigorate, renew, replenish, restore
refuge *n.* shelter, sanctuary, retreat, haven
refugee *n.* exile, expatriate, fugitive, foundling, alien, outcast
refund *n.* return, reimbursement, compensation, remuneration, repayment, rebate
refuse *n.* rubbish, leavings, remains, residue, trash
refuse *v.* reject, decline, rebuff, spurn, deny
refute *v.* disprove, answer, deny
regain *v.* recapture, retrieve, reacquire, recover
regard *n.* **LOOK:** gaze, glance; **OPINION:** estimation, appreciation, affection, admiration
regard *v.* **OBSERVE:** notice, mark; **CONSIDER;** view, think; **RESPECT:** esteem, value, admire
region *n.* territory, area, realm, locale, domain, sphere

regress *v.* backslide, relapse, revert, retreat, sink
regret *n.* **REMORSE:** repentance, misgiving, qualm; **GRIEF:** pain, anxiety, sorrow
regret *v.* mourn, lament, rue, repent, grieve, sorrow
regular *adj.* **ORDERLY:** methodical, precise, systematic, organized, consistent, rhythmic, periodic, measured; **CUSTOMARY:** conventional, usual;
regularly *adv.* customarily, habitually, usually, commonly, ordinarily, normally
regulate *v.* **CONTROL:** rule, legislate, direct, govern; **ADJUST:** standardize, adapt, rectify, correct
regulation *n.* rule, law, statute, ordinance
rehabilitate *v.* restore, reinstate, reestablish
reinforce *v.* buttress, strengthen, support
reject *v.* **REFUSE:** repudiate, renounce, deny; **DISCARD:** expel
rejoice *v.* exult, enjoy, revel, celebrate
rejoinder *n.* answer, reply, rebuttal, refutation
rejuvenate *v.* reinvigorate, refresh
relapse *v.* backslide, revert, regress, deteriorate, degenerate
relate *v.* **TELL:** recount, recite, retell, describe, report; **CONNECT:** associate, correlate, compare
related *adj.* associated, linked, affiliated, akin, parallel, correlated, similar
relax *v.* slacken, repose, recline, unbend, rest
relaxed *adj.* untroubled, carefree, comfortable
relay *n.* communicate, transmit, carry, deliver, send
release *v.* liberate, acquit, loose, free
relent *v.* soften, comply, relax, yield
relentless *adj.* unmerciful, vindictive, hard, ruthless

relevance *n.* connection, pertinence, importance

relevant *adj.* pertinent, pertaining, applicable, related, concerning, connected

reliable *adj.* unimpeachable, trustworthy, reputable, irrefutable, incontestable, dependable

reliance *n.* confidence, hope, faith, trust, dependence

relic *n.* vestige, trace, heirloom, antique, keepsake, memento, curiosity, token

relief *n.* **SOFTENING:** alleviation, comforting; **AID:** assistance, support, help, succor; **RELAXATION:** comfort, contentment, restfulness

relieve *v.* **REPLACE:** discharge, dismiss; **LESSEN:** ease, alleviate, allay, lighten, mitigate

religion *n.* **FAITH:** belief, persuasion, theology, doctrine, communion, piety

religious *adj.* **DEVOUT:** pious, sanctimonious, reverential; **SCRUPULOUS:** methodical, thorough

reluctance *n.* unwillingness, disinclination, qualm, hesitation, doubt

remain *v.* **STAY:** inhabit, stop, settle; **ENDURE:** prevail, continue; **SURVIVE:** outlive, outlast

remainder *n.* residue, remains, remnant, dregs, surplus, leavings, excess, scrap, fragment, salvage

remark *v.* say, state, speak, mention

remarkable *adj.* exceptional, extraordinary, unusual

remedy *v.* help, aid, heal, counteract, repair, cure

remember *v.* **RECALL:** recollect, reminisce; **MEMORIZE:** learn, master, retain

remembrance *n.* **GIFT:** reward, token; **MEMORY:** recollection, recognition, reminder

remind *v.* hint, mention, prompt, prod, stress, emphasize, note, warn

remit *v.* transmit, pay, tender, forward

remnant *n.* remainder, residue, dregs, leavings

remodel *v.* renovate, refurbish, redecorate, modernize

remorse *n.* anguish, guilt, compunction, contrition, regret

remote *adj.* DISTANT: removed, secluded, isolated; ANCIENT: aged, old; SEPARATED: unrelated, irrelevant

removal *n.* dismissal, discharge, expulsion, exile, deportation, banishment, elimination, ejection

rend *v.* tear, burst, rip, sever, sunder, break

rendition *n.* interpretation, translation, version

renew *v.* refresh, regenerate, rehabilitate, restore, freshen

renounce *v.* disown, disavow, deny

renovate *v.* remake, rehabilitate, renew

rent *n.* LEASE: lend, sublet; HIRE: charter, engage

reorganize *v.* renovate, regenerate, reconstruct

repair *v.* restore, fix, correct, refurbish, mend

reparation *n.* amends, compensation, indemnity, retribution

repay *v.* REIMBURSE: recompense, refund, indemnify, compensate; RETALIATE: reciprocate, revenge

repeal *v.* revoke, abrogate, annul, abolish, cancel

repeat *v.* iterate, echo, recite, recapitulate

repel *v.* REBUFF: resist, oppose, repulse; OFFEND: revolt, disgust; REJECT: disown, dismiss, refuse

repentance *n.* sorrow, remorse, self–reproach, regret

repentant *adj.* penitent, regretful, contrite, sorry

repetition *n.* recurrence, duplication, renewal, reiteration, wordiness

repetitious *adj.* boring, wordy, repeating, dull

replace *v.* substitute, supplant, restore, reinstate

replenish *v.* refill, restock, renew

replica *n.* copy, likeness, model, duplicate, imitation

reply *v.* answer, retort, rejoin, return

report *v.* narrate, recount, inform, advise, relate, tell

reporter *n.* journalist, newsman, correspondent

represent *v.* **DEPICT:** render, portray, enact, symbolize, describe; **IMITATE:** substitute, impersonate

representative *n.* emissary, deputy, agent, delegate, congressman, deputy, diplomat

repress *v.* check, restrain, control, curb, hinder

reprieve *n.* delay, respite, suspension

reprimand *v.* reprove, rebuke, chide, reproach, denounce, criticize, scold

reproach *v.* censure, upbraid, condemn, scold, blame

reproduce *v.* **COPY:** duplicate; **REPEAT:** recreate, re–enact, relive, mirror, echo; **MULTIPLY:** procreate, breed, propagate

repudiate *v.* reject, retract, repeal, revoke, abandon

repulse *v.* resist, repel, rebuff, spurn, snub

repulsive *adj.* offensive, disgusting: odious, forbidding

reputable *adj.* distinguished, celebrated, honorable, trustworthy, honest, worthy, brave, noble

reputation *n.* character, honor, standing, prestige, prominence, eminence, notoriety

request *v.* ask, solicit, beseech, entreat, sue, beg

require *v.* **NEED:** want; **DEMAND:** exact, expect

requirement *n.* **NEED:** necessity, demand; **PREREQUISITE:** condition, stipulation, provision, qualification;

rescue *v.* **SAVE:** recover, redeem, salvage, retrieve; **FREE:** liberate, release

research *n.* analysis, experimentation, examination, study

resemblance *n.* likeness, correspondence, coincidence, similarity

resentment *n.* annoyance, irritation, anger

reserve *n.* **SECURITY:** savings, insurance, resources, provisions, assets, hoard; **CALM:** caution, restraint, reticence, inhibition, demureness

reserve *v.* retain, keep, possess, hold

reserved *adj.* **BOOKED:** saved, claimed, held; **WITHHELD:** preserved, conserved; **RESTRAINED:** composed, sedate, collected, serene, placid

reside *v.* dwell, live, stay, lodge, occupy

residence *n.* habitation, quarters, apartment, home

residue *n.* remainder, leavings, scraps

resign *v.* **RELINQUISH:** yield, surrender, capitulate, abandon, submit; **QUIT:** retire, leave

resigned *adj.* quiet, peaceable, docile, submissive, yielding, relinquishing, obedient, passive

resilient *adj.* rebounding, elastic, springy, flexible

resist *v.* oppose, endure, bear, persist, suffer, abide, persevere, last, repel

resolute *adj.* constant, determined, steadfast, firm

resolution *n.* **DETERMINATION:** fortitude, perseverance, resolve; **PROPOSAL:** recommendation, declaration

resolve *v.* decide, determine, conclude

resource *n.* reserve, support, stratagem, means

resourceful *adj.* ingenious, capable, active, intelligent

resources *n.* means, money, riches, assets, capital, property, reserve, wealth

respect *n.* regard, relation, esteem, honor, admiration

respectable *adj.* presentable, tolerable, passable, virtuous, honorable

respectful *adj.* deferential, courteous, reverent, attending, venerating, deferring, polite

respite *n.* delay, postponement, reprieve, pause, delay

respond *v.* reply, rejoin, acknowledge

response *n.* reply, rejoinder, acknowledgment, answer

responsibility *n.* **STABILITY:** loyalty, faithfulness, competence, honesty; **DUTY:** obligation, trust

responsible *adj.* **ACCOUNTABLE:** liable, obligated, bound, answerable, obliged, pledged; **ABLE:** reliable, capable, dependable, competent

rest *n.* **REPOSE:** quiet, slumber, relaxation, doze, nap, respite; **REMAINDER:** residue, surplus, balance, remnant; **CESSATION:** intermission, interval, inactivity, pause

restful *adj.* tranquil, calm, peaceful, quiet, serene, soothing, relaxing, refreshing

restless *adj.* fidgety, jumpy, nervous, uneasy, agitated, unsettled, restive, impatient, jittery

restore *v.* **RETURN:** replace; **RECREATE:** revive, recover, renew; **REBUILD:** reconstruct, rehabilitate, repair; **HEAL:** refresh, cure

restrain *v.* curb, bridle, rein, regulate, muzzle, inhibit, deter, hamper, restrict, gag, limit, contain, check

restraint *n.* **SELF-CONTROL:** reserve, reticence, forbearance, abstinence, abstention; **LIMITATION:** hindrance, restriction, impediment

restrict *v.* limit, circumscribe, contract, shorten

restricted *adj.* limited, confined, hampered, bridled, blocked, decreased, barred, diminished, reduced

result *n.* consequence, outcome, aftermath, upshot, settlement, determination, payoff, end

retain *v.* **HOLD:** grasp, clutch; **REMEMBER:** recall, recollect, recognize; **EMPLOY:** engage, maintain, hire

retaliate *v.* repay, requite, return, revenge

retard *v.* hinder, postpone, delay, impede

retire *v.* **LEAVE:** withdraw, part, retreat; **REST:** sleep; **RESIGN:** relinquish

retort *n.* reply, counter, response, answer

retort *v.* reply, rejoin, answer

retraction *n.* denial, revocation

retreat *n.* refuge, sanctuary, port, haven, resort

retreat *v.* withdraw, depart, backtrack, reverse, leave

retribution *n.* punishment, reprisal, retaliation

retrieve *v.* recover, regain, reclaim

return *n.* **HOMECOMING:** arrival, reappearance; **RESTORATION:** restitution, recompense; **PROCEEDS:** profit, income, results, gain, revenue, yield, interest

return *v.* **REAPPEAR:** recur, repeat, revive, rebound; **REINSTATE:** restore, replace; **ANSWER:** reply, respond, retort; **REPAY:** reimburse, recompense, refund; **YIELD:** interest, profit

reveal *v.* disclose, publish, betray, announce, declare

revenge *n.* retaliation, reprisal, retribution

revenue *n.* income, return, earnings, proceeds, yield, receipts, profits

reverence *n.* veneration, respect, admiration, regard, esteem, adoration, praise

reverse *n.* **OPPOSITE:** converse, contrary; **DEFEAT:** downfall, annihilation

review *v.* correct, criticize, revise, inspect, examine, analyze

revise *v.* improve, correct, reconsider, rewrite, edit

revival *n.* renewal, rebirth, resurrection, restoration, freshening, awakening

revive *v.* enliven, refresh, renew, resuscitate, invigorate; freshen, rouse, arouse, strengthen

revoke *v.* annul, reverse, recall, retract, cancel

revolt *n.* rebellion, uprising, mutiny, revolution

revolting *adj.* awful, loathsome, repulsive, offensive

revolutionary *adj.* **REBELLIOUS:** mutinous, insurgent, subversive; **NOVEL:** new, unusual, advanced, forward

revolve *v.* roll, spin, rotate, twirl, turn

reward *n.* **PAYMENT:** compensation, remuneration, pay, recompense; **PRIZE:** premium, bonus, award

rhythmic *adj.* measured, regular, balanced

rich *adj.* **WEALTHY:** moneyed, affluent; **SUMPTUOUS:** luxurious, magnificent, resplendent, lavish, ornate, splendid, elegant; **FERTILE:** lush, fruitful, luxuriant

riches *n.* wealth, fortune, possessions, money

rid *v.* clear, relieve, shed, free

riddle *n.* enigma, puzzle, dilemma, complexity

ride *n.* excursion, drive, trip, transportation, journey

rider *n.* addition, codicil, addendum, appendix, amendment, supplement

ridicule *v.* mock, gibe, scoff, sneer, taunt, mimic, deride, scorn, caricature, satirize

ridiculous *adj.* absurd, ludicrous, preposterous, funny, unusual

right *adj.* **CORRECT:** precise, accurate, exact, factual, true, valid; **JUST:** lawful, legitimate, honest, fair

right *n.* **PREROGATIVE:** immunity, exemption, license; **JUSTICE:** equity, fairness

right *v.* correct, repair, restore, remedy, rectify, mend

righteous *adj.* **VIRTUOUS:** just, honorable, exemplary, impartial, noble, trustworthy, ethical; **RELIGIOUS:** devout, pious, saintly, angelic, devoted, reverent, spiritual, holy

rightful *adj.* proper, just, honest, fair, legal

rigid *adj.* **STIFF:** unyielding, inflexible, solid, firm; **STRICT:** exact, rigorous, severe; **FIXED:** set, unmoving, definite, determined

rigorous *adj..* harsh, austere, uncompromising, severe

rim *n.* margin, edge, border, verge, brim, lip, brink

rind *n.* covering, skin, peel, hull, shell

ring *n.* **CIRCLE:** circlet, girdle, rim; **JEWELRY:** band, signet, bracelet; **GROUP:** party, bloc, faction, group, gang, band; **SOUND:** clangor, jangle

rinse *v.* cleanse, clean, flush, dip, soak, wash

riot *n.* uproar, tumult, confusion, disorder, disturbance, protest

rip *v.* divide, tear, cut, rend, split, cleave, rive, shred

ripe *adj.* matured, grown, developed

ripen *v.* develop, evolve, advance, grow
rise *v.* **ASCEND:** mount, climb, scale; **IMPROVE:** prosper, flourish, thrive; **HEIGHTEN:** enlarge, grow, extend, raise; **SWELL:** inflate, billow, bulge; **BEGIN:** spring, emanate, issue
risk *n.* **DANGER:** hazard, peril, jeopardy; **CHANCE:** contingency, prospect, uncertainty
risky *adj.* perilous, precarious, hazardous, dangerous
rite *n.* ceremony, observance, service, ritual, custom
rival *n.* competitor, antagonist, opponent
rivalry *n.* competition, contention, opposition, dispute
roam *v.* ramble, range, meander, saunter, traipse
rob *v.* burglarize, plunder, defraud, cheat, pilfer, purloin, filch, pillage, sack, loot
robbery *n.* burglary, larceny, thievery
robust *adj.* vigorous, husky, hale, hearty, sound
rock *v.* totter, sway, reel, quake, tremble
rogue *n.* knave, outlaw, miscreant, criminal
roll *n.* **ROTATION:** turn, revolution; **LIST:** register, index, record;
roll *v.* rotate, circle, turn, revolve, spin
romantic *adj.* poetic, fanciful, chivalrous, courtly
room *n.* **SPACE:** vastness, sweep, extent; **OPENING:** place, vacancy; **QUARTERS:** lodgings, apartment
roomer *n.* lodger, occupant, dweller, renter, tenant
rooted *adj.* grounded, based, fixed, firm
rosy *adj.* promising, optimistic, favorable, cheerful
rot *n.* **DECAY:** decomposition, corruption, disintegration, **NONSENSE:** trash, silliness, foolishness
rotate *v.* turn, twist, wheel, revolve, move

rotation *n.* turn, circumrotation, circle, revolution

rotten *adj.* **SPOILED:** putrefying, decaying, rancid; **UNSOUND:** defective, impaired, weak; **CORRUPT:** contaminated, polluted, tainted, defiled, dirty

rough *adj.* **UNEVEN:** irregular, bumpy, jagged, coarse; **SEVERE:** harsh, strict, stern; **CRUDE:** boorish, uncivil, rude, uncultivated; **TURBULENT:** stormy, tumultuous; **UNFINISHED:** incomplete, imperfect; **APPROXIMATE:** inexact, unprecise, uncertain

round *adj.* **SPHERICAL:** circular, globular, cylindrical; **CURVED:** arched, rounded, bowed, curled

rouse *v.* **WAKEN:** arouse, raise, awaken; **STIMULATE:** urge, stir, provoke, animate, excite

routine *adj.* usual, customary, conventional, habitual

rove *v.* walk, meander, wander, roam

row *n.* line, series, order, file

rowdy *adj.* noisy, rebellious, mischievous, unruly

royal *adj.* **REGAL:** imperial, sovereign, noble; **STATELY:** dignified, majestic, aristocratic, courtly, lordly, imposing, resplendent

rub *v.* stroke, smooth, scrape, scour, polish

rubbish *n.* waste, debris, litter, trash

rude *adj.* **BOORISH:** loutish, brutish, uncouth, vulgar, ribald; **HARSH:** gruff, abusive, brazen, audacious, hostile, rough, insensitive; **COARSE:** rough, unrefined, crude, unpolished; **PRIMITIVE:** ignorant, uncivilized, barbarous

ruffle *v.* **DISARRANGE:** rumple, tousle; **ANGER:** irritate, fret, bother, agitate

rugged *adj.* **ROUGH:** uneven, hilly, broken, mountainous;

STRONG: vigorous, hale, sturdy, hardy, healthy

ruin *v.* **DESTROY:** demolish, wreck, ravage; **BANKRUPT:** impoverish, beggar

rule *v.* govern, control, dictate, manage, regulate

rumor *n.* report, gossip, tidings, hearsay

rumple *v.* wrinkle, crumple, crush, fold

run *n.* **SPRINT:** pace, amble, gallop, canter, lope, trot, dart, rush, dash, flight, escape, race, scamper, tear, whisk; **SERIES:** continuity, succession, sequence; **COURSE:** way, route, field, track

run *v.* **FLOW:** pour, tumble, drop, melt; **RUSH:** hurry, scurry, scramble, scamper, dash, speed, scuttle; **FUNCTION:** move, work, go; **MANAGE:** control, govern; **CONTINUE:** last, persevere

rupture *v.* break, burst, crack, tear

rural *adj.* country, rustic, agrarian, suburban

rush *n.* haste, dash, charge, hurry

rut *n.* **GROOVE:** hollow, trench, furrow, track; **HABIT:** routine, custom, course, practice

ruthless *adj.* cruel, savage, brutal, merciless, fiendish, unmerciful, ferocious, vengeful, barbarous

sabotage *v.* subvert, undermine, attack, destroy

sacrifice *n.* **OFFERING:** tribute, atonement; **LOSS:** discount, deduction, reduction

sacrifice *v.* forfeit, forgo, relinquish, yield, renounce

sad *adj.* **UNHAPPY:** downcast, gloomy, sorrowful, glum, dispirited, depressed, melancholy, blue; **PITIABLE:** disheartening, discouraging, dreary, disquieting

safe *adj.* **SECURE:** protected, guarded,

shielded, sheltered; **INNOCENT:** innocuous, harmless; **RELIABLE:** trustworthy, dependable, competent

safe *n.* chest, strongbox, coffer, repository, vault, case

salary *n.* wages, recompense, pay

sale *n.* **COMMERCE:** traffic, barter, exchange, trade; **DEAL:** transaction, auction, purchase, disposal; **CLEARANCE:** bargain, reduction, unloading

salute *v.* greet, recognize, praise

salvage *v.* save, retrieve, recover, regain

salvation *n.* deliverance, liberation, emancipation, rescue, safeguard, assurance

same *adj.* equivalent, identical, corresponding, equal

sanction *v.* approve, confirm, authorize, countenance

sanctuary *n.* **CHURCH:** shrine, temple; **SHELTER:** refuge, asylum, haven

sane *adj.* rational, normal, lucid, sober, sound, balanced, sensible, reasonable, wise

sap *n.* **FLUID:** secretion, essence, liquid; **DUPE:** dolt, gull, simpleton, fool

sarcastic *adj.* scornful, mocking, ironical, satirical, taunting, derisive, sneering, snickering, cynical

satire *n.* irony, sarcasm, mockery, ridicule, caricature

satisfaction *n.* **GRATIFICATION:** fulfillment, achievement; **COMFORT:** pleasure, contentment, serenity

satisfy *v.* please, delight, amuse, entertain, gladden, gratify, indulge, humor, fascinate, fill

saturate *v.* soak, drench, steep, immerse

savage *adj.* **PRIMITIVE:** crude, simple; **CRUEL:** barbarous, inhuman, brutal; **WILD:** untamed, uncivilized, uncultured

save *v.* DELIVER: rescue, extricate, liberate, ransom, redeem; HOARD: collect, store, accumulate, gather; PRESERVE: conserve, keep

savor *v.* partake, enjoy, relish, appreciate, like

say *v.* utter, speak, state, announce, declare, assert

saying *n.* aphorism, maxim, proverb, adage

scaffold *n.* platform, gallows, framework, structure

scald *v.* burn, steam, char, blanch, parboil

scale *v.* MOUNT: climb, ascend, surmount; MEASURE: compare, balance, compute

scamper *v.* hasten, speed, hurry, run

scan *v.* examine, scrutinize, browse, consider, look

scandal *n.* gossip, slander, defamation

scanty *adj.* scarce, meager, small, inadequate, thin, skimpy, sparse, diminutive

scarcity *n.* deficiency, inadequacy, insufficiency, lack

scare *v.* panic, terrify, alarm, frighten

scatter *v.* DISPERSE: disband, spread; DIFFUSE: dispel, dissipate, distribute

scene *n.* spectacle, view, display

scenic *adj.* beautiful, spectacular, dramatic

scent *v.* smell, odor, fragrance

scheme *v.* plan, contrive, intrigue, devise

scholarly *adj.* erudite, studious, learned

schooling *n.* education, learning, nurture, discipline

scientific *adj.* LOGICAL: deductive, methodical, sound; ACCURATE: precise, exact, clear, objective;

scoff *v.* mock, deride, jeer, ridicule

scold *v.* chide, admonish, rebuke, censure, reprove, reprimand, criticize, chasten

scoot *v.* run, dart, speed, hasten, hurry

scope *n.* range, reach, field, extent

scorching *adj.* fiery, searing, sweltering, burning, hot

score *v.* **ORCHESTRATE:** arrange, adapt; **PROCURE:** get, secure

scorn *v.* refuse, despise, disdain

scornful *adj.* contemptuous, disdainful, haughty

scoundrel *n.* rogue, scamp, villain, rascal

scowl *v.* frown, glower, disapprove, grimace

scramble *v.* **MIX:** combine, blend, beat; **CLIMB:** clamber, push, struggle

scrap *n.* **TRASH:** junk, waste, cuttings, chips; **BIT:** fragment, particle, piece, morsel; **FIGHT:** quarrel, brawl, squabble

scrape *v.* rub, abrade, scour, rasp

scratch *v.* wound, hurt, cut, mark, scar

scrawl *v.* write, scribble, scratch, doodle

scrawny *adj.* lean, lanky, gaunt, thin

scream *v.* shriek, screech, squeal, cry

screen *v.* **HIDE:** veil, conceal, mask, shelter; **CHOOSE:** select, eliminate

scrub *v.* rub, cleanse, scour, clean, wash

scrupulous *adj.* exact, punctilious, exacting, careful

scrutinize *v.* examine, view, study, stare, watch

scrutiny *n.* analysis, inspection, examination

sealed *adj.* secured, fixed, firm, tight

seam *n.* joint, union, stitching, closure, suture

search *v.* seek, examine, rummage, hunt, quest

seasonal *adj.* periodically, biennial, annual, yearly

seasoned *adj.* **SPICY:** tangy, sharp, aromatic; **EXPERIENCED:** established, settled, mature, able

secede *v.* withdraw, retract, leave, retreat

seclude *v.* screen, conceal, cover, hide
seclusion *n.* solitude, aloofness, privacy, retirement
secondary *adj.* **MINOR:** inconsiderable, petty, small, trivial, unimportant; **DERIVED:** dependent, subsequent, subsidiary, subordinate
secrecy *n.* concealment, hiding, seclusion, privacy, mystery, dark, darkness, isolation, reticence, stealth
secret *adj.* unknown, mysterious, arcane, cryptic, occult, mystical, veiled, obscure, shrouded, hidden, concealed, clandestine, underhanded, stealthy
secretary *n.* **ASSISTANT:** clerk, typist, stenographer, correspondent; **OFFICER:** director, executive
secrete *v.* **HIDE:** conceal, cover, disguise; **EMIT:** discharge, produce, exude
secretive *adj.* reticent, taciturn, undercover, reserved
secure *adj.* **SAFE:** guarded, defended; **SELF–CONFIDENT:** assured, determined, confident
secure *v.* **FASTEN:** bind, tighten; **OBTAIN:** get, achieve, acquire, grasp
security *n.* guarantee, token, pawn, pledge, collateral, bail, warranty, agreement, covenant, hostage
sediment *n.* dregs, silt, grounds, residue
see *v.* **PERCEIVE:** observe, regard, view, gaze, detect, notice, contemplate; **UNDERSTAND:** comprehend, discern, recognize; **WITNESS:** observe, regard
seek *v.* search, delve, dig, ransack, look, sniff, prowl
seem *v.* appear, look, resemble, show
seep *v.* percolate, trickle, leak, flow, drain

segment *n.* part, portion, section, fragment, division
segregate *v.* separate, isolate, sever, divide
seize *v.* GRASP: take, catch, grab, clutch, snatch; CAPTURE: conquer, overwhelm, apprehend, arrest; UNDERSTAND: comprehend, perceive
seizure *n.* spasm, spell, convulsion
seldom *adv.* rarely, infrequently, occasionally, uncommonly, scarcely, hardly
select *v.* pick, decide, elect, choose
selective *adj.* discriminating, judicious, particular
self-conscious *n.* unsure, uncertain, shy, doubtful
self-control *n.* poise, restraint, reserve, discretion, stability, dignity, constraint
self-esteem *n.* pride, vanity, egotism
self-evident *n.* obvious, plain, visible, apparent
self-restraint *n.* patience, endurance, control
sell *v.* market, vend, barter, trade, exchange, bargain, peddle, retail, wholesale, contract, retail
seller *n.* dealer, salesman, tradesman, retailer, agent, vender, merchant, auctioneer, shopkeeper, peddler, trader, storekeeper, marketer
semblance *n.* resemblance, aspect, appearance
send *v.* DISPATCH: convey, ship, post, convey; BROADCAST: relay, transmit
senile *adj.* aged, infirm, feeble, old, sick
senior *adj.* older, elder, higher, superior
seniority *n.* standing, ranking, station
sensation *n.* consciousness, perception, feeling
sensational *adj.* FASCINATING: exciting, marvelous, incredible, impressive;

MELODRAMATIC: exaggerated, excessive, emotional
sense *n.* **SENSATION:** feeling, touch, sight, hearing, taste, smell; **REASONABLENESS:** judgment, discretion, fairness; **INTELLECT:** perception, reason, cleverness, thought; **INSIGHT:** tact, understanding, discernment
senseless *adj.* ridiculous, silly, foolish, illogical, stupid
sensible *adj.* reasonable, prudent, perceptive, careful, aware, capable, rational, intelligent
sensitive *adj.* **TENDER:** delicate, sore, painful; **TOUCHY:** tense, nervous, irritable, unstable
sensitivity *n.* awareness, delicacy, feelings, sympathy
sensuality *n.* appetite, ardor, desire, emotion
sensuous *adj.* passionate, physical, exciting, sensual
sentence *n.* judgment, decree, punishment, verdict
sentiment *n.* feeling, emotion, opinion, thought
sentimental *adj.* emotional, tender, romantic, idealistic, visionary, affected
sentry *n.* sentinel, protector, watchmen
separate *v.* **ISOLATE:** divide, seclude; **DEPART:** leave
separated *adj.* disconnected, severed, removed, disjointed, scattered
sequence *n.* **SUCCESSION:** order, continuity, progression, flow; **ARRANGEMENT:** distribution, classification; **SERIES:** chain, string, array
serene *adj.* calm, unruffled, tranquil, composed, sedate, placid
serious *adj.* **GRAVE:** solemn, pressing; **THOUGHTFUL:** earnest, somber, sincere

sermon *n.* discourse, lesson, lecture

serve *v.* help, aid, assist, attend

service *v.* maintain, sustain, repair

session *n.* sitting, assembly, gathering

set *adj.* **FIRM:** stable, settled, fixed, rigid; **DETERMINED:** steadfast, decided

set *n.* **COLLECTION:** assemblage, assortment; **GROUP:** clique, circle, faction

set *v.* **ESTABLISH:** anchor, fix, install; **JELL:** solidify, harden, congeal; **PLACE:** put, plant, situate

setting *n.* environment, surroundings, mounting, backdrop, frame, context

settle *v.* **PROVE:** establish, verify; **FINISH:** end, achieve; **LOCATE:** reside, dwell, colonize

settlement *n.* **AGREEMENT:** covenant, compact, contract; **COMPENSATION:** remuneration, reimbursement

sever *v.* separate, part, split, cleave, cut

several *adj.* some, sundry, various, numerous, many

severe *adj.* exacting, inflexible, harsh, oppressive, cruel, rigid, rigorous, difficult, oppressive, relentless

sew *v.* join, fasten, stitch, tack, bind, piece, baste

shabby *adj.* threadbare, worn, ragged, faded, seedy

shade *n.* **DARKNESS:** blackness, shadow; **TINT:** color, brilliance, saturation, hue; **VARIATION:** difference, hint, suggestion; **SCREEN:** shelter, covering, curtain

shake *n.* tremble, shiver, pulsation, movement

shaken *adj.* unnerved, upset, overcome, excited

shaky *adj.* **INFIRM:** trembling, unsteady, tottering, unstable; **UNRELIABLE:** uncertain, questionable

shallow *adj.* **SLIGHT:** inconsiderable, superficial; **SILLY:** trifling, inane, frivolous, petty, foolish

sham *adj.* pretended, false, misleading, untrue

shame *v.* humiliate, mortify, dishonor, disgrace

shameful *adj.* **IMMODEST:** immoral, debauched, degraded, indecent, lewd, vulgar; **DISHONORABLE:** scandalous, disreputable, outrageous, infamous

shameless *adj.* brazen, bold, forward, rude, lewd

shape *v.* **CAST:** mold, form; **DEVELOP:** grow, adapt, become

shape *n.* **FORM:** contour, configuration; **PATTERN:** frame, mold; **CONDITION:** fitness, health

share *v.* **DIVIDE:** allot, apportion; **PARTAKE:** participate, receive; **GIVE:** yield, bestow, accord

sharp *adj.* **EDGED:** honed, cutting, keen; **CLEVER:** astute, intelligent; **DISTINCT:** explicit, clear, definite; **INTENSE:** piercing, shrill; **STYLISH:** chic, fashionable

shatter *v.* break, sliver, split, burst

shears *n.* clippers, cutters, snips, scissors

sheath *n.* scabbard, case, covering

shed *n.* shelter, hut, outbuilding, lean–to, woodshed

shed *v.* drop, molt, slough, discard, exude, emit

sheer *adj.* **ABRUPT:** steep, precipitous, perpendicular; **THIN:** transparent, delicate, fine

shelter *n.* protection, refuge, haven, sanctuary

shelter *v.* cover, defend, screen, hide, conceal, harbor, protect, shield, safeguard, surround, enclose

shine *v.* **RADIATE:** glitter, sparkle, twinkle, glimmer, glow, blaze; **REFLECT:** glisten, gleam, mirror; **POLISH:** scour, brush, burnish, wax
ship *v.* transport, send, consign
shock *v.* **STARTLE:** astound, disturb; **OFFEND:** disgust, outrage, horrify, abash, dismay; **JAR:** rock, jolt
shocking *adj.* repulsive, revolting, offensive
shoddy *adj.* cheap, flimsy, tacky, inferior, poor
shore *n.* coast, beach, seaside, bank
short *adj.* **CONCISE:** brief, condensed; **ABRUPT:** curt, inconsiderate, rude, testy; **DEFICIENT:** inadequate substandard
shortage *n.* lack, deficiency, dearth
shove *v.* push, nudge, jostle, press
show *v.* display, explain, indicate, reveal, demonstrate
show *n.* **PRODUCTION:** play, ceremony; **DISPLAY:** appearance, plausibility, pretext
shower *n.* rainfall, sprinkle, drizzle, mist
shred *n.* strip, fragment, splinter, rag
shred *v.* cut, mince, grate, tear
shrew *n.* scold, nag, harridan
shrewd *adj.* cunning, sharp, keen, intelligent, perceptive, sly, canny, crafty, cagey
shriek *v.* scream, yell, shout, howl, squawk
shrill *adj.* piercing, sharp, harsh
shrine *n.* temple, altar, church, sanctuary
shrink *v.* **CONTRACT:** shrivel, constrict, lessen; **RECOIL:** cringe , wince, retreat, withdraw
shrivel *v.* wither, shrink, decrease
shudder *v.* tremble, shake, shiver, quiver
shun *v.* avoid, ignore, eschew, evade
shut *v.* close, bar, secure, fasten, enclose

shy *adj.* timid, reserved, distrustful, suspicious

sick *adj.* ill, diseased, infected, afflicted, queasy, nauseous, feeble, unhealthy

side *n.* **EDGE:** border; **FACTION:** team, party

siege *n.* attack, assault, onslaught, blockade

sieve *v.* strain, purify, filter

sift *v.* separate, strain, filter, screen

sigh *n.* moan, groan, gasp, cry

sight *n.* view, spectacle, scene, display, show, vision

sign *n.* **SYMPTOM:** indication, hint, clue, suggestion; **EMBLEM:** badge

sign *v.* **GESTURE:** indicate, signal; **ENDORSE:** confirm, acknowledge, initial, autograph

signal *v.* signify, motion, gesture, wave

significant *adj.* important, notable, momentous, symbolic, meaningful

signify *v.* mean, indicate, communicate, denote, imply, intimate, portend

silence *n.* serenity, hush, tranquillity, quiet

silence *v.* hush, still, quiet, muzzle, stifle, suppress

silent *adj.* quiet, hushed, still, reserved, dormant

silly *adj.* foolish, imprudent, ridiculous, absurd, inane, frivolous

similar *adj.* resembling, like, comparable, related

similitude *n.* resemblance, likeness

simple *adj.* unaffected plain clear, unadorned, uncomplicated, bare, innocent, artless

simplify *v.* clarify, explain, elucidate, interpret

simulate *v.* feign, fake, pretend, disguise, fabricate

simultaneous *adj.* concurrent, coexisting

sin *v.* transgress, misbehave, offend, trespass
sincere *adj.* honest, genuine, earnest, faithful
single *adj.* individual, lone
singular *adj.* unique, unusual, remarkable, individual
sinister *adj.* ominous, menacing, base, bad, evil
sink *v.* submerge, depress, fall, slump, lower, droop
sip *v.* drink, imbibe, taste, sample, savor
sit *v.* **PERCH:** seat, squat; **MEET** convene, assemble
site *n.* location, place, spot, position
situation *n.* circumstances, predicament, state, job, profession, trade, status, station, rank
size *n.* bulk, magnitude, extent, mass, dimensions
skeleton *n.* bones, framework, outline, structure
skeptic *n.* doubter, cynic, unbeliever, agnostic
skeptical *adj.* doubtful, cynical, incredulous
sketch *v.* draw, outline, design, plan, draft, picture
skid *v.* slip, slide, swerve, veer, glide
skill *n.* **DEXTERITY:** ability, expertise, competence, talent; **OCCUPATION:** craft, vocation, trade, job
skillful *adj.* adept, adroit, proficient, accomplished
skin *v.* strip, peel, husk, scale, scalp
skinny *adj.* thin, lean, bony, gaunt, emaciated
skirmish *n.* scuffle, scrimmage, engagement, combat
skirt *v.* circumvent, bypass, detour, sidestep
skittish *adj.* jumpy, nervous, fidgety, timid, bashful
skulk *v.* sneak, lurk, prowl

slab *n.* hunk, block, chunk

slack *adj.* lax, loose, lazy, indolent, sluggish, slow

slacken *v.* decrease, abate, diminish

slander *n.* gossip, libel, scandal, misrepresentation

slander *v.* malign, vilify, besmirch, disparage

slang *n.* jargon, lingo, dialect, colloquialism

slant *n.* slope, incline, grade, inclination, bent

slant *v.* **LEAN:** angle, tilt; **DISTORT:** misrepresent, color

slap *v.* smack, strike, hit, spank, cuff, buffet

slaughter *n.* slaying, bloodshed, carnage, massacre

slay *v.* kill, murder, butcher, destroy, annihilate

sleek *adj.* smooth, glossy, glassy, shiny, neat

sleep *v.* slumber, rest, doze, snooze, nod, nap

sleepy *adj.* drowsy, tired, sluggish

slender *adj.* thin, slim, slight, spare, fragile, flimsy

slight *adj.* **TRIVIAL:** trifling, insignificant, petty, unimportant, superficial; **DELICATE,** dainty, flimsy, slender, fragile, frail, insubstantial

slight *v.* disregard, insult, snub, neglect, overlook

slim *adj.* slender slight trifling, dainty, slender

slime *n.* mire, muck, mud, ooze

sling *v.* hurl, throw, chuck, pitch, launch

slink *v.* skulk, cower, creep, lurk, sneak, steal, prowl

slip *n.* error, mistake, blunder, indiscretion

slip *v.* slide, totter, stumble, fall

slipshod *adj.* slovenly, careless, sloppy, untidy

slit *v.* cut, gash, slash, rip, slice, split, tear, pierce

sloppy *adj.* careless, lax, untidy, messy, disorderly
slope *n.* incline, grade, slant, inclination
slouch *v.* slump, droop, bend, stoop
slovenly *adj.* messy, careless, sloppy, disorderly, disheveled, bedraggled, untidy, slipshod
slow *adj.* LEISURELY: gradual, deliberate, lethargic; DENSE: dull, stupid
sluggish *adj.* languid, lethargic, indolent, slothful
slumber *v.* sleep, rest, nap, doze, snooze
slump *n.* decrease, drop, depression, setback, decline
sly *adj.* cunning, wily, deceitful, deceptive, tricky, artful, shifty, evasive, shrewd, elusive, clever, calculating, treacherous
small *adj.* SELFISH: stingy, mean, petty; INCONSEQUENTIAL: little, insignificant, trivial, unimportant
smart *adj.* CLEVER: intelligent, keen, penetrating, alert, bright; STYLISH: sharp, dashing, neat, elegant
smash *v.* break, shatter, crush, pound, destroy, wreck, demolish, ruin
smear *v.* SLANDER: libel, sully, slur; SMUDGE: daub, plaster, spread, apply
smell *n.* odor, aroma, fragrance, scent, stench, stink
smile *v.* grin, smirk, beam, laugh
smirk *n.* sneer, leer, grimace
smoky *adj.* hazy, foggy, smoggy, dingy, frosted, filmy
smooth *adj.* EVEN: level, flat, flush, polished, sleek, uniform; SUAVE: glib, polite, courteous
smother *v.* suffocate, stifle, asphyxiate, strangle, subdue, suppress
smudge *n.* smear, blot, blur, stain, blemish, streak

smug *adj.* conceited, egotistical, satisfied
smutty *adj.* pornographic, lewd, indecent, obscene, vulgar, suggestive, raunchy
snare *v.* catch, entangle, trap, trick, lure
snatch *v.* grab, pluck, seize, steal, filch, swipe, take
sneak *v.* lurk, prowl, creep, slink, steal, skulk
sneer *v.* criticize, deride, ridicule, scoff, gibe, taunt
snide *adj.* underhanded, sarcastic, derogatory, insinuating, vicious, nasty, mean, malicious
snip *v.* clip, pare, cut, lop, nip, slice, slit
snivel *v.* weep, whine, bawl, bemoan, blubber
snobbery *n.* contempt, arrogance, insolence
snobbish *adj.* condescending, patronizing
snub *n.* insult, affront, slight, slur, rebuke
snug *adj.* comfortable, cozy, secure, safe
snuggle *v.* cuddle, nestle, nuzzle, burrow, hug
soak *v.* steep, saturate, douse, permeate, infuse
sob *v.* cry, moan, weep, wail, lament, whimper, bewail
sober *adj.* serious, solemn, subdued, restrained, sedate, composed, rational, reasonable, sound, somber
social *adj.* genial, pleasant, polite, civil, pleasant
society *n.* **ORGANIZATION:** fellowship, association, brotherhood, fraternity, club; **CULTURE:** community, civilization, people, nation
soft *adj.* malleable, pliant, yielding, fluffy
sojourn *n.* stay, visit, stopover, vacation, abide
solace *v.* comfort, console, soothe, cheer, relieve, alleviate, assuage, allay, soften, mitigate

sole *adj.* one, single, lone, exclusive, individual, unique, unshared

solemn *adj.* sacred, grave, serious, grim, imposing, thoughtful, dignified, somber

solemnize *v.* commemorate, celebrate, honor, hallow

solicit *v.* supplicate, beg, implore, urge, request, ask, inquire, question, proposition

solicitation *n.* request, petition, appeal

solicitor *n.* attorney, petitioner, supplicant

solicitous *adj.* concerned, anxious, heedful, kind, devoted, tender, loving, thoughtful

solid *adj.* whole, unbroken, firm, substantial, sound, hard, stable, dense, stout

solidify *v.* harden, crystallize, set, coagulate, congeal

solitary *adj.* single, sole, individual, singular, isolated, lonely, remote, separate

solitude *n.* isolation, seclusion, privacy

solution *n.* answer, resolution, conclusion, explanation, settlement

solve *v.* answer, resolve, explain, decipher, decode

somber *adj.* dull, gloomy, dark, dim, drab, dismal, depressing, dreary, melancholy

sonorous *adj.* resonant, reverberating, vibrant

sooty *adj.* blackened, dirty, grimy, dingy, filthy

soothe *v.* calm, comfort, ease, quiet, refresh, soften, alleviate, assuage, mitigate, pacify

soothsayer *n.* prognosticator, diviner, oracle, prophet, astrologer, seer, mystic

sophisticated *adj.* worldly, refined, cultured

sorcery *n.* magic, witchcraft, alchemy, enchantment

sordid *adj.* vile, dirty, squalid, foul, low, base, abject

sore *adj.* sensitive, raw, tender, painful, inflamed

sorrow *n.* grief, affliction, anguish, remorse, misery, sadness, woe, trouble, affliction

sorrow *v.* grieve, mourn, weep, lament, deplore

sorry *adj.* regretful, repentant, apologetic

sort *v.* order, arrange, classify, distribute, assort

soul *n.* spirit, essence, ghost, being

sound *adj.* safe, whole, healthy, strong, complete, vigorous, stable, sensible, rational, sane, hale

sound *n.* tone, noise, vibration, resonance, intonation

source *n.* origin, beginning, inception, cause, root

souvenir *n.* keepsake, token, memento, relic, trophy

sow *v.* scatter, disseminate, disperse, plant

space *n.* room, area, gap, expanse, distance, interval

spacious *adj.* roomy, capacious, large, ample, commodious, vast, huge, voluminous, extensive

span *n.* distance, measure, length, extent, stretch

span *v.* cross, traverse, reach, connect, link, bridge

spare *adj.* **LEAN:** thin, gaunt, slight, emaciated; **EXTRA:** excess, additional

sparkle *v.* glitter, gleam, twinkle, glisten, shine

sparse *adj.* meager, inadequate, scanty, thin, spare

spasm *n.* convulsion, fit, contortion, seizure

spatter *v.* splash, slosh, spray, shower, speckle

speak *v* talk, articulate, say, utter, lecture, address

special *adj.* specific, certain, particular, designated, unique, distinctive, uncommon, unusual

specialist *n.* expert, professional, authority

specie *n.* coin, money, currency

species *n.* type, kind, class, breed, variety, category

specific *adj.* precise, particular, distinct, explicit

specify *v.* stipulate, designate, cite, name, define

specimen *n.* sample, example, model, type, pattern

specious *adj.* deceptive, misleading, false

speck *n.* bit, particle, trace, grain, iota

spectacle *n.* sight, show, demonstration, wonder

spectacular *adj.* amazing, marvelous, impressive, sensational, dramatic, splendid, striking, fabulous

spectator *n.* onlooker, observer, witness, bystander

specter *n.* ghost, spook, spirit, phantom, apparition

spectrum *n.* range, scale, sweep, extent

speculate *v.* **CONSIDER:** theorize, contemplate, consider, infer; **RISK:** gamble, venture, chance

speech *n.* language, oration, communication

speed *v.* hasten, hurry, expedite, precipitate

speedy *adj.* quick, fast, hasty, brisk, swift, hurried

spend *v.* give, waste, disburse, dissipate, deplete

sphere *n.* **GLOBE:**, orb, shell, planet; **DOMAIN:** province realm

spill *v.* slop, splash, drop, flow

spin *v.* turn, rotate, twirl, whirl, gyrate

spindle *n.* shaft, beam, axle, arbor

spirit *n.* **GHOST:** apparition, phantom,

specter; **VITALITY:** vivacity, vigor, zeal, ardor; **SIGNIFICANCE:** sense, meaning

spite *n.* malice, malevolence, rancor

spiteful *adj.* vindictive, malicious, cruel, malevolent

splash *v.* spatter, douse, spray, swash

spleen *n.* anger, petulance, wrath, rancor

splendid *adj.* grand, magnificent, impressive, dazzling

splendor *n.* glory, magnificence, grandeur

splice *v.* join, implant, unite, graft

splinter *v.* crumble, shatter, break, fracture, smash

split *v.* divide, sever, break, separate, cleave

spoil *v.* decay, ruin, damage, decompose, putrefy

sponsor *n.* patron, mentor, supporter, backer

spontaneous *adj.* impromptu, impulsive, natural

sporadic *adj.* occasional, infrequent, scattered

spot *n.* **STAIN:** blot, blemish; **LOCATION:** locale, site

spout *v.* pour, discharge, emit, flow, spill, gush

sprawl *v.* recline, lounge, relax, slouch

sprightly *adj.* lively, frisky, nimble, animated, agile

spring *v.* bound, leap, issue, jump, hop, vault

sprinkle *v.* disperse, distribute, scatter, spatter

sprint *v.* run, race, zip, dash, tear

sprout *v.* germinate, bud, burgeon, grow, develop

spry *adj.* nimble, agile, active, vigorous, animated, brisk, lively, quick, energetic

spur *v.* urge, incite, induce, provoke, goad, press

spurious *adj.* false, fake, deceptive, phony, feigned

spurn *v.* reject, shun, slight, snub, scorn, disdain

spurt *v.* burst, gush, spout, issue, spring

spy *v.* see, discover, glimpse

squabble *v.* wrangle, quarrel, bicker, argue, feud

squalid *adj.* filthy, foul, dirty, unclean, seedy

squalor *n.* filth, poverty, misery

squander *v.* waste, dissipate, expend, lavish, misuse

square *adj.* fair, just, honest, straight, level, true

squeamish *adj.* queasy, modest, prudish, finicky

squeeze *v.* compress, crush, squash, press

squelch *v.* subdue, crush, squash, suppress, thwart

squirm *v.* wriggle, writhe, fidget, twist, shift

stab *n.* wound, cut, puncture, thrust

stabilize *v.* steady, secure, brace, poise

stable *adj.* fixed, firm, steady, sturdy, enduring, perpetual, steadfast, sound, reliable, solid

staff *n.* personnel, employees, crew, cast

stage *n.* platform, dais, scaffold

stagger *v.* **WEAVE:** falter, waver; **ASTONISH:** astound, amaze, dumbfound, shock, surprise

stagnant *adj.* inert, stale, dirty, filthy, fetid

stagnate *v.* decay, rot, decompose, taint

staid *adj.* steady, sober, sedate, quiet, solemn

stale *adj.* dry, trite, common, dull, humdrum

stalk *v.* hunt, track, chase, pursue

stall *v.* delay, obstruct, hamper, hinder, impede

stalwart *adj.* stout, sturdy, strong, rugged, robust, vigorous, bold, gallant, steadfast, formidable

stamina *n.* endurance, strength, vigor, vitality, power

stammer *v.* sputter, falter, stumble, hesitate, stutter

stand *n.* position, attitude, belief, opinion

stand *v.* endure, resist, oppose, confront, withstand

standard *n.* **MODEL:** measure, gauge, example; **BANNER:** symbol, flag, pennant

staple *adj.* basic, necessary, essential, fundamental

stare *v.* gaze, gawk, gape, glare, watch

stark *adj.* simple, desolate, dreary, grim, harsh

start *n.* beginning, onset, origin, outset, initiation

start *v.* initiate, begin, commence, establish

startle *v.* surprise, alarm, scare, frighten, disturb

state *n.* condition, situation, status, circumstance, position, standing, station

state *v.* recite, declare, pronounce, assert, affirm

statement *n.* declaration, allegation, assertion, remark, report, account

stately *adj.* majestic, dignified, regal, elegant, grand

static *adj.* immobile, stationary, fixed, rigid

station *n.* rank, standing, position

stationary *adj.* fixed, static, permanent, rooted, stable

statue *n.* sculpture, bust, image, icon, figurine

stature *n.* height, bulk, build, status, standing

status *n.* state, condition, position, rank, standing

statute *n.* law, decree, act, bill, rule, ordinance, edict

stay *n.* prop, support, brace, prop

stay *v.* remain, continue, wait, linger, pause, detain, hinder, suspend, curb

steadfast *adj.* resolute, unwavering, constant, faithful, dependable, firm

steal *v.* rob, thieve, filch, pilfer, swindle, embezzle

steep *adj.* precipitous, sheer, abrupt

steeple *n.* spire, tower, minaret

steer *v.* guide, direct, pilot, conduct, lead, navigate

stellar *adj.* remarkable, phenomenal, outstanding

stereotype *v.* classify, categorize, typecast, label

sterling *adj.* genuine, flawless, noble, perfect, excellent, superior, exceptional

stern *adj.* severe, rigid, hard, strict, austere, rigorous

stiff *adj.* rigid, formal, inflexible, firm, stubborn, obstinate, unyielding, formal, uncompromising, severe

stiffen *v.* harden, congeal, thicken, coagulate

stifle *v.* suppress, repress, restrain, stop

stigma *n.* disgrace, shame, blemish, infamy, blot, stain

stigmatize *v.* disgrace, discredit, dishonor, defame, taint, shame, brand, humiliate

still *adj.* silent, motionless, inert, stationary, calm, serene, hushed, tranquil

still *v.* silence, hush, calm, soothe, stop, stall, arrest

stilted *adj.* awkward, affected, unnatural, strained, contrived, artificial, labored, stiff

stimulate *v.* excite, arouse, rouse, activate, provoke

stingy *adj.* niggardly, miserly, tight, close-fisted

stint *v.* limit, confine, restrict, restrain

stipulate *v.* specify, determine, designate, indicate

stipulation *n.* prerequisite, condition, qualification, term, requirement, clause

stir *n.* tumult, bustle, excitement, commotion, disorder, uproar, furor, agitation, fuss

stir *v.* agitate, rouse, excite, incite, provoke, stimulate

stock *v.* store, supply, hoard, equip, fill, furnish

stockpile *n.* reserve, supply, deposit, hoard, store

stoic *n.* impassive, apathetic, indifferent, nonchalant, composed, poised

stolid *adj.* impassive, unemotional, dispassionate, indifferent, imperturbable

stoop *v.* bend, bow, crouch

stop *v.* halt, end, terminate, discontinue, arrest, restrain, hinder, impede, prevent, thwart

store *v.* hoard, gather, collect, stash, stockpile

storm *n.* tempest, blizzard, gale, squall, commotion, turmoil, outbreak, disturbance

stormy *adj.* tempestuous, wild, blustering, tumultuous, raging, turbulent, boisterous

story *n.* **TALE:** anecdote, yarn, parable, fable, legend, report, account; **LEVEL:** floor, landing

stout *adj.* **PLUMP:** portly, heavy, bulky, corpulent; **RESOLUTE:** brave, courageous, bold, fearless, dauntless, hardy, indomitable, strong, robust

straggler *n.* dawdler, lingerer, laggard, slowpoke

straight *adj.* direct, honest, fair, just, virtuous, open

straighten *v.* adjust, align, rectify, correct

strain *n.* effort, exertion, force, pressure, anxiety, stress

strait *n.* difficulty, distress, predicament, plight

strange *adj.* unusual, abnormal, bizarre, peculiar, outlandish, extraordinary, unfamiliar

stranger *n.* foreigner, alien, outsider
stratagem *n.* trick, deception, ruse, wile, scheme, plan, contrivance, device
strategy *n.* tactics, scheme, system, approach
stray *v.* wander, drift, roam, deviate, digress
stream *n.* flow, emit, issue, pour, run
streamer *n.* flag, banner, pennant, standard, ensign
strength *n.* power, force, might
strengthen *v.* fortify, reinforce, restore, invigorate
strenuous *adj.* vigorous, spirited, laborious
stress *n.* emphasis, weight, significance, accent
stretch *n.* expanse, range, reach, extent
strew *v.* scatter, spread, disseminate, broadcast
strict *adj.* demanding, exacting, rigid, inflexible
strident *adj.* raucous, shrill, harsh, piercing, grating
strife *n.* conflict, fight, discord, clash
strike *v.* **HIT:** slap, cuff; **UNEARTH:** find, uncover
stringent *adj.* strict, harsh, severe
stripling *n.* youth, child, lad, lass, youngster
strive *v.* endeavor, attempt, compete, contend
stroll *v.* walk, saunter, meander, wander, roam
strong *adj.* muscular, potent, solid, impregnable
struggle *n.* battle, clash, conflict, exertion, endeavor
struggle *v.* grapple, contend, strive, toil, labor
stubborn *adj.* obstinate, headstrong, stiff, resolute, inflexible, intractable
student *n.* pupil, scholar, disciple, apprentice

study *v.* investigate, analyze, scrutinize, examine, ponder, consider, reflect

stun *v.* shock, confound, amaze, astonish, astound, bewilder, stupefy

stupendous *adj.* amazing, astounding, marvelous, extraordinary, incredible, spectacular, wondrous

stupid *adj.* dull, boring, tedious, vapid, tiresome, foolish, absurd, inane, senseless

stupor *n.* daze, trance, numbness, lethargy

sturdy *adj.* robust, rugged, stalwart, strong, strapping, muscular, firm, indomitable, stout

stutter *v.* stammer, stumble, falter

stylish *adj.* fashionable, chic, smart, modish

suave *adj.* sophisticated, smooth, cultured, worldly

subdue *v.* defeat, conquer, overpower, tame

subjective *adj.* biased, prejudiced, individual

subjugate *v.* conquer, enslave, subdue, defeat

sublime *adj.* lofty, inspiring, imposing, majestic

submerge *v.* immerse, engulf, plunge, sink

submission *n.* surrender, resignation, compliance

submit *v.* ACCEDE: comply, obey; SUGGEST: volunteer, propose, present, tender

subordinate *adj.* inferior, lower, junior, subservient

subscribe *v.* support, donate, authorize, sanction

subsequent *adj.* following, ensuing, succeeding, later

subservient *adj.* subordinate, servile, deferential

subside *v.* decline, dwindle, diminish, lessen, wane

subsidize *v.* support, sponsor, fund, back

subsidy *n.* endowment, allowance, grant, bequest
substance *n.* object, element, essence, basis, meaning, import, gist, significance
substantial *adj.* plentiful, abundant, ample, considerable, wealthy affluent, influential, valuable
substantiate *v.* verify, authenticate, confirm, validate, prove, corroborate, attest
substitute *adj.* alternative, surrogate, tentative
subterfuge *n.* ploy, scheme, stratagem, device, expedient, deceit, deception
subtle *adj.* delicate, understated, refined, elusive, deceptive, inferred, insinuated, artful, insidious
subtract *v.* deduct, decrease, diminish, lessen, lower
succeed *v.* **FLOURISH:** thrive, prevail, triumph; **REPLACE:** supersede
success *n.* achievement, mastery, victory, attainment
successful *adj.* triumphant, flourishing, thriving
succession *n.* sequence, order, continuation
succinct *adj.* brief, concise, terse, abbreviated
succor *n.* aid, help, sustenance, assistance
succumb *v.* submit, concede, relent, capitulate, collapse, fail
sudden *adj.* abrupt, quick, unexpected, impromptu
suffer *v.* endure, tolerate, bear, undergo, agonize
sufficient *adj.* plenty, ample, enough
suffuse *v.* saturate, pervade, soak, impregnate
suggest *v.* propose, submit, imply, insinuate
suit *v.* satisfy, please, gratify, shape, accommodate

suitor *n.* wooer, admirer, gallant, beau
sulk *v.* pout, scowl, frown, glower
sullen *adj.* moody, morose, gloomy, somber
sully *v.* shame, dishonor, stain, taint, tarnish, blemish, defile, corrupt, besmirch
sultry *adj.* sweltering, muggy, humid, sticky
summary *n.* condensation, digest, abridgment, brief
summit *n.* peak, pinnacle, apex, crown, culmination
summon *v.* call, invite, invoke, request, petition
sumptuous *adj.* luxurious, elegant, lavish, opulent
sundry *adj.* various, several, divers
superb *adj.* outstanding, exquisite, grand, magnificent, luxurious
supersede *v.* replace, supplant, succeed
supervise *v.* superintend, chaperon, manage, control
supervision *n.* management, guidance, surveillance
supplant *v.* replace, displace, succeed, supersede
supple *adj.* elastic, pliable, limber
supplement *n.* addition, subsidiary, extension
supplement *v.* augment, enhance, fortify
supplicate *v.* implore, beseech, beg, entreat
supply *v.* equip, stock, replenish
support *n.* AID: assistance, help, relief, succor; BRACE: prop, column, buttress, strut
suppose *v.* assume, infer, presume, believe, think
suppress *v.* OVERPOWER: repress, curb, quell, crush; CONCEAL: bury, cover
supreme *adj.* preeminent, superior, greatest
supremacy *n.* dominion, dominance, preeminence

sure *adj.* trusty, reliable, infallible, certain, safe, solid, precise, accurate, unerring, inevitable
surface *n.* rise, appear, emerge
surge *v.* gush, rush, pour, rise, heave
surly *adj.* cantankerous, rude, irritable, sullen, hostile
surmise *v.* speculate, guess, infer, imagine, suppose
surmount *v.* conquer, transcend, hurdle, overcome
surpass *v.* exceed, transcend, excel
surplus *n.* excess, abundance, remainder, residue
surprise *n.* astonishment, amazement, shock, wonder
surprise *v.* astound, bewilder, dumbfound, startle
surrender *v.* submit, abandon, capitulate, yield
surreptitious *adj.* furtive, clandestine, stealthy
surrogate *adj.* substitute, backup, alternative
surround *v.* encompass, enclose, circle
survey *v.* scrutinize, scan, examine, inspect, observe
survive *v.* endure, persist, remain, continue
suspect *v.* **DISTRUST:** mistrust, doubt; **BELIEVE:** suppose, imagine, conjecture
suspend *v.* postpone, delay, defer, interrupt
suspense *n.* apprehension, anxiety
suspension *n.* delay, deferment, postponement
suspicion *n.* skepticism, misgiving, mistrust, cynicism, notion, impression
suspicious *adj.* **DUBIOUS:** shady, untrustworthy, doubtful; **WARY:** skeptical
sustenance *n.* food, nourishment, provisions
swagger *v.* strut, prance, boast, brag, gloat

swallow *v.* drink, eat, gulp, consume, devour
swamp *n.* bayou, marsh, mire, morass, slough
swarm *n.* horde, mass, flock, multitude, host
sway *n.* dominion, dominance, control, influence
swear *v.* **PROMISE:** declare, testify, affirm; **BLASPHEME:** damn, curse
sweet *adj.* luscious, aromatic, fragrant, clean, fresh, melodious, harmonious
swell *v.* increase, inflate, bloat, bulge, grow
swift *adj.* fast, rapid, expeditious, fleet, prompt, quick
swig *v.* drink, swallow, quaff, gulp, guzzle
swindle *v.* trick, deceive, dupe, defraud, victimize
swing *v.* hang, dangle, flap, oscillate, wave
switch *v.* swap, trade, exchange, replace, substitute
sycophant *n.* flatterer, flunky, parasite, toady
symbol *n.* character, letter, numeral, representation
symbolize *v.* signify, connote, mean, represent
sympathetic *adj.* considerate, compassionate
sympathize *v.* commiserate, console, pity
sympathy *n.* compassion, understanding, warmth, consolation, solace, comfort
symptom *n.* clue, trait, characteristic, feature, sign
synchronize *v.* accommodate, adjust, attune
syndicate *n.* coalition, alliance, company, association
syndicate *v.* affiliate, connect, consolidate, merge
synopsis *n.* summary, abridgment, condensation
system *n.* strategy, plan, scheme, method

systematic *adj.* methodical, orderly, precise, regular

tabloid *n.* newspaper, periodical, publication
taboo *adj.* forbidden, banned, prohibited
tacit *adj.* implied, understood, assumed, inferred
taciturn *adj.* reserved, quiet
tact *n.* subtlety, discretion, finesse, style
tactics *n.* scheme, stratagem, procedure, system
tailor *v.* customize, adapt, adjust
taint *v.* corrupt, infect, defile, contaminate
take *v.* obtain, get, procure, seize, grasp, capture, adopt, select, accept, choose, pick
tale *n.* **YARN:** narrative, account; **FALSEHOOD:** fib, lie
talent *n.* aptitude, genius, gift
talisman *n.* amulet, charm
talk *n.* conversation, dialogue, speech
talk *v.* converse, speak, discuss, gossip
talkative *adj.* loquacious, chatty, garrulous, gabby
tall *adj.* towering, high, big, rangy, lanky
tally *n.* count, reckoning, sum, calculation
tame *adj.* docile, gentle, obedient
tamper *v.* change, alter, meddle, damage
tangible *adj.* material, corporeal, tactile, discernible, evident, actual, real, genuine
tantalize *v.* tease, provoke, torment, frustrate, vex
tantamount *adj.* equivalent, parallel, identical
tape *n.* bind, wrap, seal, mend
tarnish *n.* blemish, blot, stain, taint
tarnish *v.* defame, disgrace embarrass
tarry *v.* stall, linger, loiter, dally, dawdle, stay
task *n.* job, labor, assignment, duty, chore

taste *n.* partiality, liking, bias, preference
taste *v.* sample, try, sip, savor, relish
taunt *v.* insult, jeer, mock, provoke
tavern *n.* bar, saloon, pub, cafe, inn, lodge, hostelry
tax *n.* levy, assessment, tariff, toll, duty, obligation
teach *v.* instruct, inform, train, enlighten, guide
tear *v.* rip, split, sever, cleave, rend
tease *v.* annoy, taunt, torment, harass, irritate, vex
technique *n.* METHOD: procedure, system, approach, methodology; ABILITY: skill, aptitude, knack
tedious *adj.* monotonous, tiresome, dull, boring
tell *v.* recount, describe, report, speak, mention, explain, reveal, declare, divulge
temper *n.* disposition, temperament, humor, composure, poise
temper *v.* soothe, pacify, calm, mollify
temperament *n.* disposition, attitude, mood, emotion
temperance *n.* restraint, sobriety, abstinence
temperate *adj.* calm, composed, cool, reasonable
tempestuous *adj.* stormy, raging, tumultuous
temporary *adj.* transitory, fleeting, interim
tenable *adj.* defensible, justifiable
tenacious *adj.* resolute, persistent, obstinate
tenant *n.* renter, leaseholder, inhabitant
tend *v.* guard, protect, keep, manage
tendency *n.* inclination, partiality, bias, penchant
tender *adj.* DELICATE: fragile, frail; COMPASSIONATE: sympathetic, kindhearted considerate

tenet *n.* belief, conviction, dogma, creed, doctrine
tenor *n.* drift, trend, tone, course
tense *adj.* taut, nervous, strained, agitated, drawn
tension *n.* pressure, strain, stress, unease
tentative *adj.* provisional, probationary, experimental, indefinite
tenuous *adj.* fine, narrow, insubstantial, flimsy, feeble
terminal *adj.* boundary, limit, extremity
terminate *v.* complete, conclude, eliminate, cancel
termination *n.* close, finish, cessation, completion
terminology *n.* vocabulary, language, jargon
terminus *n.* extremity, objective, conclusion
terrible *adj.* frightful, appalling, dreadful, horrible, horrendous, disastrous, disturbing, extreme
terrific *adj.* splendid, marvelous, wonderful, outstanding, super
terrify *v.* terrorize, appall, paralyze, horrify, frighten
territory *n.* area, region, dominion
terror *n.* fright, horror, alarm, dismay, consternation
terse *adj.* brief, succinct, concise, precise, curt
test *n.* inspection, experiment, examination, quiz
testify *v.* swear, certify, demonstrate, indicate, argue
testimony *n.* statement, declaration, confirmation, testament, affidavit
testy *adj.* irritable, cranky, grouchy, edgy, short–tempered, touchy, peevish
thank *v.* acknowledge, appreciate, recognize, credit
thaw *v.* warm, melt, dissolve, liquefy
theft *n.* burglary, robbery, thievery, looting

theology *n.* religion, faith, belief, scripture, dogma, convictions, creed

theorem *n.* principle, hypothesis, postulate, premise

theory *n.* conjecture, speculation, rationale, explanation, view, conception, outlook

theoretical *adj.* abstract, academic, hypothetical

theorize *v.* speculate, postulate, presume, suppose

therapeutic *adj.* restorative, curative, recuperative, remedial, corrective

thesis *n.* opinion, contention, argument, assumption, assertion, hypothesis

thick *adj.* abundant, dense, packed, crowded

thicken *v.* jell, congeal, stiffen, harden, intensify

thin *adj.* lean, gaunt, scanty, meager

thin *v.* dilute, weaken, reduce

think *v.* contemplate meditate, consider, remember, recall, recollect, believe, suppose

thirst *n.* longing, desire, yearning, eagerness

thorough *adj.* total, meticulous, precise, painstaking

thoroughfare *n.* artery, highway, expressway, boulevard, concourse, freeway

thought *v.* concept, conviction, notion, opinion, theory, hypothesis, supposition

thoughtful *adj.* considerate, caring, attentive, concerned, discreet, tender

threadbare *adj.* worn, shabby, tattered, frayed, seedy

threat *n.* risk, hazard, danger, jeopardy, menace

threaten *v.* endanger, menace, terrorize, scare

threshold *n.* start, beginning, outset, commencement

thrift *n.* economy, husbandry, conservation
thrifty *adj.* frugal, sparing, provident
thrill *n.* excitement, stimulation
thrill *v.* delight, electrify, rouse
thrive *v.* flourish, succeed, increase, grow
throb *v.* pulse, pound, thump, pulsate
throng *n.* mass, multitude, horde, swarm, host, assemblage, crowd
through *adj.* completed, done, finished
throw *v.* fling, hurl, pitch, heave, toss
thrust *v.* shove, plunge, jab, push
tidings *n.* news, information, gossip
tidy *adj.* neat, orderly, spruce, trim
tie *n.* **ROPE:** band, strap, cord, **NECKTIE:** bow, scarf, cravat, choker, **CONNECTION:** relation, bond, link, knot, **STANDOFF:** draw, deadlock, stalemate
tie *v.* fasten, secure attach, connect, join, link
tier *n.* line, row, array, bank
tiff *n.* quarrel, dispute, disagreement, scrap, spat
tighten *v.* squeeze, compress, constrict, clench
tilt *n.* tip, list, slant, incline, slope, angle, pitch
time *n.* **AGE:** epoch, generation, cycle; **INTERVAL:** duration, span; **RHYTHM:** tempo, beat, cadence
timely *adj.* auspicious, propitious, favorable, prompt
timetable *n.* schedule, program, calendar, agenda
timid *adj.* shy, retiring, fearful, withdrawn, reticent, indecisive, vacillating
timorous *adj.* timid, fearful, apprehensive, anxious, scared, afraid
tinge *n.* trace, hint, trifle, dab, nuance

tinker *v.* dabble, putter, potter, trifle

tiny *adj.* small, diminutive, minute, microscopic

tip *n.* PEAK: pinnacle, summit; GRATUITY: compensation, consideration; ADVICE: pointer, hint, clue

tirade *n.* harangue, denunciation, outburst

tire *v.* exhaust, fatigue, drain, irk, bore

title *n.* DESIGNATION: name, appellation, epithet; CLAIM: interest, holding, ownership

titter *v.* laugh, giggle, snicker, chuckle

toil *v.* labor, work, strive, slave, sweat

token *adj.* nominal, superficial, minimal

token *n.* sign, emblem, mark

tolerable *adj.* ENDURABLE: bearable, sufferable; ADEQUATE: decent, average

tolerance *n.* forbearance, impartiality, magnanimity

tolerant *adj.* unprejudiced, moderate

tolerate *v.* SUFFER: abide, accept, bear; ALLOW: oblige, indulge

tomb *n.* grave, vault, crypt, sepulcher, mausoleum

tool *n.* implement, appliance, gadget, utensil

top *n.* pinnacle, crest, summit, zenith, crown

topical *adj.* local, isolated, provincial, regional

topple *v.* fall, tumble, collapse, overturn, upset

torment *n.* anguish, suffering, distress, misery

torment *v.* distress, vex, afflict, annoy, tease, harass, irritate, pester, provoke, needle

torpid *adj.* inactive, inert, lethargic, sluggish, motionless, dormant, hibernating

torpor *n.* idleness, inactivity, indolence, sluggishness

torrent *n.* cloudburst, deluge, flood
tortuous *adj.* winding serpentine, twisted, snaky, crooked, bent
toss *v.* throw, fling, pitch, cast, hurl, chuck
total *adj.* entire, utter, whole, gross
totter *v.* stumble, falter, weave, reel, lurch
tough *adj.* rugged, hardy, sturdy, durable, hardy, unyielding, incorrigible
tourist *n.* visitor, sightseer, wayfarer
tournament *n.* competition, rivalry, contest, match
tousle *v.* dishevel, disarray, ruffle, muss
tout *v.* vaunt, plug, promote, herald, extol
town *n.* community, municipality, village, hamlet
toxic *adj.* poisonous, deadly, lethal, virulent
trace *n.* vestige, indication, hint
track *v.* hunt, trail, pursue, trace
tractable *adj.* docile, compliant, pliable, flexible
trade *n.* vocation, profession, livelihood, craft
trade *v.* exchange, swap, barter, buy, sell
tragedy *n.* disaster, calamity, catastrophe, affliction, suffering, tribulation
tragic *adj.* disastrous, dreadful, distressing
train *v.* tutor, teach, enlighten, inform, instruct, educate, guide
trait *n.* characteristic, quality, property, attribute, mannerism, habit
tramp *n.* hobo, vagabond, vagrant, gypsy
tramp *v.* roam, rove, hike, tromp, march
tranquil *adj.* peaceful, serene, placid, still, pleasant
tranquillity *n.* quiet, calm, serenity
transform *v.* alter, transfigure, convert, commute
transgress *n.* infringe, violate, trespass

transient *adj.* brief, transitory, passing, fleeting

translate *v.* reword, explain, interpret, decipher

translucent *adj.* transparent, clear

transmit *v.* transfer, send, convey, dispatch

transparent *adj.* lucid, translucent, diaphanous, clear, sheer

transpose *v.* switch, swap, exchange, transfer

trap *n.* snare, trick, stratagem, maneuver, artifice

traumatic *adj.* alarming, upsetting, frightful

travel *v.* journey, tour, roam, expedition, excursion

travesty *n.* parody, satire, spoof burlesque, lampoon, caricature, farce

treacherous *adj.* unfaithful, deceitful, deceptive, insidious, disloyal, treasonous, difficult, unstable

treatise *n.* dissertation, thesis, essay, discourse

treaty *n.* agreement, settlement, covenant, pact

tremble *v.* shiver, quiver, shake

tremendous *adj.* colossal, huge, immense

tribulation *n.* distress, suffering, hardship

tribute *n.* accolade, homage, recognition, applause

trick *n.* deception, artifice, ruse

trim *adj.* neat, orderly, tidy, groomed, natty

trinket *n.* bauble, adornment, decoration, ornament

trip *n.* voyage, excursion, jaunt, pilgrimage

trite *adj.* ordinary, commonplace, hackneyed, stale

triumph *v.* prevail, conquer, overwhelm, overpower

trivial *adj.* insignificant, inconsequential, unimportant, irrelevant, frivolous

troll *v.* goblin, gremlin, hobgoblin, demon
trophy *n.* award, citation, medal
trot *v.* canter, jog, lope, amble
trouble *n.* calamity, distress, misfortune, tribulation
trouble *v.* distress, harass, harry, irritate, pester
troublesome *adj.* pesky, bothersome, trying, perplexing, galling, burdensome, disturbing
trough *n.* channel, furrow, rut, crater, ditch
truce *n.* armistice, reprieve, amnesty
truculent *adj.* fierce, mean, malevolent, pugnacious, belligerent, contentious, hostile
true *adj.* real, genuine, truthful, undistorted, authentic, just, honest, faithful, reliable
trunk *n.* chest, strongbox, coffer, case
trust *n.* confidence, dependence, reliance, faith
try *v.* endeavor, strive, test, examine
tryst *n.* meeting, rendezvous, assignation
tumble *v.* fall, slip, descend, decline, drop
tumor *n.* growth, cyst, polyp, melanoma, sarcoma
tumult *n.* disorder, commotion, turmoil, melee, agitation
tumultuous *adj.* riotous, violent, restive, uneasy, boisterous, disorderly, obstreperous
turbulent *adj.* violent, blustery, disorderly
turbulence *n.* commotion, excitement, uproar, tumult, disturbance
turmoil *n.* chaos, commotion, disorder, tumult, turbulence, uproar
turn *v.* **ROTATE:** spin, gyrate; **CONVERT:** transform, change, alter, transmute,
turpitude *n.* depravity, baseness, perversion, vileness, evil, sinfulness, corruption

tutor *n.* instructor, trainer, teacher

tweak *v.* nip, pinch, grasp, squeeze, twist

twine *n.* rope, cord, strand, string, braid

twinge *n.* twitch, tingle, spasm, crick, stitch, throb

twinkle *v.* shimmer, glitter, flicker, glint, glimmer

twirl *v.* twist, gyrate, turn, rotate, pivot

type *n.* kind, class, breed, group, family, genus

typical *adj.* characteristic, representative, ideal

typify *v.* represent, personify, epitomize, exemplify

tyrannical *adj.* oppressive, despotic, arbitrary, domineering, unjust, cruel

tyro *n.* amateur, novice, apprentice, neophyte

ubiquity *n.* prevalence, pervasiveness, commonness, omnipresence, universality

ugly *adj.* homely, unsightly, displeasing, monstrous, objectionable, nasty

ulcer *n.* abscess, infection, boil

ulterior *adj.* concealed, shrouded, obscured

ultimate *adj.* extreme, final, decisive, concluding, eventual, maximum, utmost, preeminent

ultimatum *n.* warning, mandate, demand, order

unaffected *adj.* NATURAL: simple, sincere, genuine, real, artless; UNMOVED: indifferent, unemotional, unresponsive, disinterested

unassuming *adj.* modest, unpretentious, humble, simple, plain, diffident

unauthorized *adj.* unsanctioned, prohibited, illicit, forbidden, banned

unbalanced *adj.* unstable, maladjusted, biased, untrustworthy, treacherous

unbearable *adj.* intolerable, insufferable, obnoxious
unbecoming *adj.* inappropriate, unsuitable, indecent, unseemly, rough, improper, unfit
unbiased *adj.* impartial, objective, neutral, unprejudiced, tolerant, disinterested
unbounded *adj.* **IMMENSE:** endless, vast; **UNCONFINED:** free, unbridled, unfettered
uncanny *adj.* strange, odd, weird, mysterious, eerie
unceasing *adj.* continual, incessant, chronic, perpetual, persistent
uncivilized *adj.* primitive, barbarous, crude, uncouth
unclean *adj.* dirty, grimy, soiled, squalid, foul, vile, impure, defiled, adulterated, profaned
uncommon *adj.* exceptional, extraordinary, unique, remarkable, rare, scarce
uncompromising *adj.* obstinate, inflexible, unyielding, immovable, steadfast,
unconditional *adj.* absolute, certain, unrestricted
unconscionable *adj.* unscrupulous, unprincipled, wicked, wanton, dishonest, unholy
unconscious *adj.* senseless, oblivious, benumbed
uncouth *adj.* rude, ill-mannered, vulgar, crass
uncover *v.* reveal, expose, disclose, unearth
undaunted *adj.* fearless, courageous, valiant, intrepid, audacious
underestimate *v.* misjudge, miscalculate, slight
undergo *v.* endure, tolerate, suffer, bear, abide
underhanded *adj.* sly, furtive, deceitful, dishonest, traitorous, unscrupulous

undermine *v.* weaken, erode, corrode, decay, threaten

underrate *v.* devaluate, lessen, downgrade, depreciate

understand *v.* comprehend, grasp, perceive, discern, interpret, hear, accept, conclude

understanding *adj.* sympathetic, accepting, tolerant

understanding *n.* comprehension, grasp, awareness

undervalue *v.* minimize, cheapen, misjudge, belittle, discredit, underrate

underwrite *v.* guarantee, support, endorse

undetermined *adj.* dubious, obscure, enigmatic, doubtful, unsettled

undo *v.* cancel, efface, erase, expunge, obliterate

undress *n.* disrobe, undrape, shed, peel

undulate *v.* wave, surge, heave, flap, pulsate, billow

unduly *adj.* excessively, inordinately, exceedingly

undying *adj.* eternal, permanent, everlasting, unceasing

uneasy *adj.* restless, perplexed, troubled, apprehensive, fidgety, nervous, jittery, uncomfortable

unencumbered *adj.* free, unobstructed, unhampered, unhindered, unfettered

unequal *adj.* disparate, unlike, uneven, odd

unequaled *adj.* incomparable, matchless, unparalleled, distinct, peerless, special

unequivocal *adj.* definite, unmistakable, incontestable, evident, absolute, explicit, clear, plain

unerring *adj.* accurate, exact, precise, perfect, correct, definite, unfailing, infallible

uneven *adj.* jagged, coarse, rugged, serrated, intermittent, spasmodic, irregular, rough

unfailing *adj.* certain, absolute, sure, reliable, surefire, dependable

unfair *adj.* unjust, prejudiced, discriminatory, biased, inequitable, despotic, wrongful, arbitrary

unfaltering *adj.* steadfast, resolute, untiring, unfailing, unflagging, tireless, persistent, firm

unfathomable *adj.* incomprehensible, enigmatic, mysterious, inscrutable, profound, baffling, puzzling

unfeeling *adj.* callous, merciless, unsympathetic, cold-hearted, hard, brutal, cruel

unfeigned *adj.* genuine, real, natural, unaffected, truthful, candid, sincere

unflagging *adj.* tireless, unrelenting, persisting, assiduous, devoted, consistent

unfold *v.* evolve, reveal, show, unravel, unearth, resolve, open, extend, expand

unfortunate *adj.* unlucky, inept, hapless, doomed, cursed, ill–fated

unfounded *adj.* baseless, groundless, unsupported, unsound, erroneous, untrue

unfurl *v.* unfold, open, uncoil, extend

ungovernable *adj.* uncontrollable, headstrong, unruly

unguarded *adj.* open, undefended, unprotected, incautious

unguent *n.* ointment, salve, lotion, balm, poultice, dressing

uniform *adj.* regular, routine, normal, unwavering, invariable, consistent, steady

uniformity *n.* regularity, similarity, accord, order, concord

unify *v.* combine, integrate, consolidate, compact, concentrate, arrange, blend, integrate, synthesize

unimpeachable *adj.* irrefutable, obvious, unassailable, conclusive, adequate

unintentional *adj.* involuntary, accidental, inadvertent, unconscious, unplanned

union *n.* coalition, merger, alliance, association, confederacy, order, league, brotherhood, society, matrimony

unique *adj.* singular, particular, peerless, unrivaled, unequaled, matchless, unusual, uncommon, odd, peculiar, rare

unit *n.* element, constituent, component, part, section, piece, member

unite *v.* combine, join, link, couple, connect, associate, incorporate, blend, consolidate, compound, fuse, weld, marry, join

unity *n.* union, harmony, agreement, concert, unison, concord, rapport, congruity

universal *adj.* general, widespread, extensive, entire, whole, sweeping

universe *n.* cosmos, world, totality

unjust *adj.* unfair, partial, prejudiced, biased, inequitable, shabby, undeserved, unjustified, unmerited

unkempt *adj.* disorderly, disheveled, untidy, messy, tousled

unkind *adj.* cruel, harsh, unfeeling, callous, cold-hearted, hard, brutal, heartless

unlettered *adj.* untaught, ignorant, uneducated, illiterate, unenlightened, untutored

unlike *adj.* different, dissimilar, incompatible, mismatched, disparate, divergent, diverse

unlimited *adj.* boundless, infinite, immense, vast, extensive, endless, unconstrained, unrestricted, total, complete, totalitarian

unmanageable *adj.* ungovernable, unruly,

difficult, uncooperative, stubborn, obstinate, balky, rebellious, uncontrollable, wild, irrepressible

unmoved *adj.* determined, decided, solid, unshaken, unaffected, collected, firm, steadfast, indifferent, resolute, unemotional

unnerve *v.* upset, unsettle, fluster, disarm, discourage, aggravate, disconcert, trouble, rattle

unparalleled *adj.* uncommon, rare, singular, unequaled, unrivaled, unique, peerless, matchless

unprecedented *adj.* unparalleled, unique, unequal, unusual, uncommon, untoward

unprincipled *adj.* amoral, corrupt, unethical, wanton, unscrupulous, dishonest

unqualified *adj.* incompetent, unskilled, unable, inept, untrained, unsatisfactory, unsuitable, incapable, ineligible

unravel *v.* explain, elucidate, clarify, justify, resolve, interpret, solve, untangle, unwind, disengage

unremitting *n.* constant, ceaseless, endless, incessant, constant, perpetual, unending, continuous,

unrest *n.* agitation, disquiet, trouble, disturbance, bickering, crisis, turbulence

unscathed *adj.* unharmed, safe, unimpaired, sound, uninjured

unseemly *adj.* indecent, improper, unbecoming, inappropriate, wrong, incorrect,

unsettle *v.* confuse, disturb, upset, perturb, bother, trouble, fluster, ruffle, rattle

unsightly *adj.* unattractive, homely, plain, disagreeable, repulsive, hideous

unsophisticated *adj.* naive, provincial, callow, unrefined, simple, coarse, crude, harsh, vulgar, artless, guileless, ingenuous, natural, genuine

unspeakable *adj.* unutterable, indescribable, astonishing, incredible, offensive, abusive, nasty, repulsive, coarse, odious, ineffable

untiring *adj.* inexhaustible, constant, powerful, resolute, strong, unflagging

unveil *v.* reveal, show, expose, divulge, announce

upbraid *v.* censure, scold, chide, admonish, reproach, reprove, berate, condemn

upheaval *n.* eruption, earthquake, volcano, blowup, outbreak, explosion, outburst

uphold *v.* maintain, support, champion, sustain, endorse, sanction, bolster, help

uppermost *adj.* topmost, foremost, highest, predominant, supreme, loftiest

upright *adj.* upstanding, honest, good, outstanding, moral, ethical, principled, just, righteous, pure, true

uprising *n.* revolt, insurrection, rebellion, revolution, demonstration, skirmish

uproar *n.* disturbance, clamor, commotion, fracas, furor, hubbub, melee

uproarious *adj.* hilarious, funny, noisy, tumultuous, turbulent, frenzied, confused, disorderly

uproot *v.* remove, transport, liquidate, excavate, extirpate, eradicate, eliminate, dislodge

upset *adj.* irritated, worried, uneasy, disturbed, troubled, aggravated, concerned, perturbed, unsettled, disconcerted

upset *v.* capsize, overturn, upend, topple, founder, invert, flip

upshot *n.* outcome, consequence, conclusion, result

upstart *n.* opportunist, pretender, snob, phony, fraud, rogue, impostor

urban *adj.* city, metropolitan, municipal

urbane *adj.* suave, poised, polished, refined, elegant, gracious, courteous

urchin *n.* waif, stray, foundling, orphan, ragamuffin, child, infant

urge *n.* drive, desire, impulse, craving, passion, push, influence, stimulus, impulse

urge *v.* drive, impel, press, spur, incite, goad, stimulate, implore, beg, beseech, entreat, persuade, induce, advise, advocate, recommend

urgent *adj.* pressing, compelling, demanding, driving, forcing, imperative, anxious, insistent, earnest

urgency *n.* seriousness, need, insistence, gravity, exigency, emergency, crisis, necessity

usable *adj.* useful, employable, applicable, functional

usage *n.* custom, practice, acceptance, convention, habit, fashion, form

use *n.* application, help, habit, custom

use *v.* employ, utilize, operate, apply, exploit

useful *adj.* beneficial, helpful, serviceable, effective, practical, functional, handy

usual *adj.* common, customary, familiar

usurp *v.* capture, commandeer, appropriate, assume

utensil *n.* instrument, device, implement, gadget

utility *n.* usefulness, value, advantage

utilize *v.* use, employ, exploit, operate

utmost *adj.* ultimate, maximum, maximal, entire, greatest, undiminished, unlimited

utopian *adj.* idealistic, ideological, visionary, perfect, ideal, fanciful, theoretical

utter *adj.* complete, entire, total, unconditional, unqualified, thorough

utter *v.* speak, articulate, vocalize, voice, say, remark, express, proclaim, state

utterance *n.* assertion, declaration, enunciation, proclamation, pronouncement

vacant *adj.* empty, uninhabited, abandoned, deserted, expressionless, vacuous, vapid

vacate *v.* leave, abandon, depart, quit

vacation *n.* holiday, furlough, respite, sabbatical

vaccinate *v.* immunize, inoculate, inject

vacillate *v.* waver, hesitate, fluctuate, alternate, sway

vacuum *n.* void, emptiness, vacuity, nothingness

vagary *n.* caprice, whim, urge, notion, impulse, fancy, quirk, eccentricity

vagrant *n.* beggar, tramp, hobo, idler, loafer, rascal

vague *adj.* obscure, indistinct, indefinite, imprecise, unspecified, uncertain, loose, unclear

vain *adj.* **FUTILE:** unavailing, fruitless, ineffective, inefficient, hollow; **CONCEITED:** egotistical, arrogant, proud, narcissistic

valet *n.* manservant, attendant, butler, steward

valiant *adj.* valorous, brave, bold, courageous, intrepid, stouthearted, fearless, chivalrous

valid *adj.* logical, well–founded, sensible, sound, convincing, authoritative, legal, lawful

valley *n.* glen, dale, hollow, basin, lowland, vale

valor *n.* bravery, courage, boldness, spirit

valorous *adj.* brave, valiant, courageous, fearless

valuable *adj.* expensive, precious, rare, priceless, useful, beneficial, profitable, serviceable
value *n.* worth, importance, cost, price, significance
value *v.* appraise, assess, estimate, evaluate, judge, reckon, weigh, consider, rate
vandalism *n.* defacement, damage, mutilation, disfiguration, marring, spoiling
vanguard *n.* forefront, leaders, precursors, spearhead
vanish *v.* disappear, depart, evaporate, fade, dissolve
vanity *n.* conceit, pretension, self–esteem, pride, folly
vanquish *v.* conquer, overwhelm, subdue, overpower, defeat, suppress, quell, subjugate, quash, crush
vapid *adj.* dull, lifeless, insipid, uninteresting, tiresome, spiritless, vacuous, prosaic, mundane
vapor *n.* fog, haze, mist, gas, smog, condensation
vaporize *v.* evaporate, vanish, dissolve, disappear
variable *adj.* fluctuating, inconstant, wavering
variance *n.* difference, divergence, discrepancy, incongruity, disagreement, discord
variation *n.* alteration, modification, deviation, difference, discrepancy, diversity, dissimilarity, irregularity, inequality, aberration, departure
variety *n.* category, group, classification, division
various *adj.* miscellaneous, assorted, divers, diverse, diversified, varied, sundry
varnish *v.* embellish, disguise, mask, veil, falsify
vary *v.* change, alter, modify, diversify, deviate, differ, fluctuate, alternate
vast *adj.* boundless,

large, limitless, unbounded, extensive, immense, widespread

vat *n.* container, keg, barrel, cask, tub

vault *n.* crypt, tomb, mausoleum, sepulcher

vault *v.* jump, hurdle, bound, leap, spring

vaunt *v.* boast, gloat, brag, strut, swagger, flaunt

veer *v.* swerve, deviate, diverge, curve, deflect

vehement *adj.* fervent, impassioned

vehemence *n.* ardor, eagerness, energy, enthusiasm, passion, zeal, spirit

vehicle *n.* conveyance, transportation, medium, means, agency, instrumentality

veil *v.* conceal, mask, cover, shroud, cloud, obscure

velocity *n.* speed, swiftness, dispatch, quickness

venal *adj.* corrupt, unscrupulous, treacherous, mercenary, dishonorable, corruptible

vend *v.* sell, merchandise, market, retail

veneer *n.* facing, cover, coating, surfacing

venerable *adj.* esteemed, revered, distinguished, honorable, ancient, respected

venerate *v.* admire, worship, revere, esteem, respect

vengeance *n.* revenge, retaliation, retribution

vengeful *adj.* vindictive, unforgiving, unrelenting, spiteful, rancorous, malicious

venial *adj.* excusable, justifiable, forgivable

venom *n.* bitterness, virulence, malice anger, contempt, spitefulness, malevolence, hate

vent *v.* express, air, assert, verbalize, articulate, expound, release, unleash, discharge

venture *n.* undertaking, enterprise, investment, speculation, endeavor, attempt

venture *v.* chance, wager, risk, gamble, hazard, dare, plunge, imperil, jeopardize, endanger, hazard

veracious *adj.* truthful, accurate, precise, honest, sincere, trustworthy, righteous

veracity *n.* truth honesty, sincerity, accuracy, precision, exactness, correctness

verandah *n.* terrace, porch, deck, patio, courtyard

verbal *adj.* oral, spoken, stated

verbose *adj.* wordy, windy, loquacious, tedious, garrulous, talkative, chatty

verdant *adj.* green, flourishing, thriving, dense, lush

verdict *n.* decision, judgment, ruling, finding, adjudication, decree, determination, sentence

verify *v.* confirm, prove, authenticate, corroborate, substantiate, validate

verification *n.* evidence, proof, validation, documentation, support, confirmation

veritable *adj.* real, genuine, actual, positive, true, virtual, authentic

vernacular *adj.* native, indigenous, regional, informal, colloquial, everyday, ordinary, familiar

vernacular *n.* dialect, argot, jargon, idiom

versatile *adj.* flexible, pliable, adaptable, tractable, docile, pliant, yielding

versatility *n.* flexibility, pliancy, agility, compliance, adaptability, amenity, amiability

versed *adj.* experienced, seasoned, competent, adept, capable, skilled, practiced, trained

version *n.* rendition, interpretation, rendition

vertical *adj.* erect, upright, perpendicular, plumb

vestibule *n.* foyer, hallway, entry, lobby

vestige *n.* trace, indication, shred, fragment, remainder, hint, suggestion

veteran *adj.* experienced, skilled, seasoned, versed

veto *v.* reject, discard, eliminate, refuse, void, nullify, invalidate, forbid, dismiss

vex *v.* annoy, harass, irk, bother, disturb, irritate, plague, torment, agitate

viaduct *n.* bridge, overpass, trestle

vibrate *v.* shake, flutter, tremble, quiver, undulate, fluctuate, oscillate, reverberate

vicarious *adj.* substituted, delegated, sympathetic

vice *n.* wickedness, corruption, evil, depravity, immorality, depravity, iniquity, malignancy

vicinity *n* area, locality, neighborhood, environment, proximity, nearness

vicious *adj.* base, degenerate, vile, depraved, reprehensible, malicious, malevolent, malignant, unruly

victim *n.* casualty, dupe, gull, prey

victor *n.* winner, champion, conqueror

victory *n.* triumph, conquest, success, achievement

victorious *adj.* triumphant, successful

vie *v.* compete, oppose, contend, clash, rival, strive

view *n.* scene, sight, spectacle, vision, glimpse, aspect, object, purpose, intention, description, notion, opinion, judgment, assessment

view *v.* observe, regard, behold, survey, witness, inspect, examine, study, scrutinize

vigil *n.* watchfulness, wakefulness, surveillance

vigilant *adj.* watchful, alert, observant, attentive, careful, wary

vigor *n.* vitality, stamina, strength power, potency, energy, endurance, soundness
vile *adj.* evil depraved, wretched, repulsive, contemptible, revolting, disgusting, offensive, vulgar
vilify *v.* malign, slander, slur, defame
village *n.* town, community, hamlet, municipality
villain *n.* miscreant, cad, rascal, rogue, scoundrel
vindicate *v.* exonerate, acquit, absolve, clear, defend, justify, support, uphold, corroborate, assert
vindictive *adj.* vengeful, spiteful, unforgiving
vintage *adj.* classic, choice, old, excellent
violate *v.* breach, infringe, transgress, trespass
violation *n.* transgression infringement, breach, defilement, debasement, assault, outrage
violent *adj.* intense, fierce, furious, rough, vicious, brutal, barbarous, savage, fierce
virgin *n.* pure, undefiled, unsullied, unadulterated, unmixed, fresh, unspoiled
virile *adj.* vibrant, strong, forceful, vigorous, robust
virtue *n.* integrity, temperance, purity, decency
virtuous *adj.* moral, ethical, honest, noble, right, pure, chaste
virulent *adj.* **LETHAL:** malignant, venomous, poisonous; **HATEFUL:** bitter, malicious, antagonistic
virus *n.* infection, disease, germ, microbe
visa *n.* endorsement, permit, authorization
visage *n.* countenance, appearance, aspect
viscous *adj.* sticky, thick, sticky, gummy
visible *adj.* discernible, perceptible, perceivable, obvious, apparent, clear, evident, conspicuous

visibility *n.* distinctness, perceptibility, prominence
vision *n.* **PERCEPTION:** sight, understanding, discernment, intuition; **CONCEPT:** image, imagination, view, **HALLUCINATION:** apparition, ghost, phantom
visit *n.* call, appointment, interview, talk, sojourn
visitor *n.* guest, caller, company
visor *n.* shield, sunshade, bill, peak
vista *n.* view, perspective, prospect, outlook
visual *adj.* visible, perceptible, obvious; ocular
vital *adj.* **ESSENTIAL:** necessary, important, critical, requisite; **VIGOROUS:** lively, energetic, active
vivacious *adj.* lively, animated, brisk, spirited, sprightly, energetic, spry
vivid *adj.* **BRIGHT:** shining, intense, lucid, lively, spirited, energetic, vivacious, realistic, picturesque, distinct, graphic, striking, clear, discernible
vocabulary *n.* lexicon, glossary, dictionary
vocal *adj.* **UTTERED:** spoken, oral, articulated, expressed, verbalized; **OUTSPOKEN:** open, honest, assertive, candid, blunt
vocation *n.* occupation, trade, profession, business, pursuit, calling
vociferous *adj.* noisy, boisterous, uproarious, blatant
vogue *n.* fashion, style, custom, trend, fad, popularity
voice *n.* expression, utterance, assertion, declaration, preference, opinion, say, vote, view
void *adj.* useless, empty, barren, destitute, vacant, abandoned, unoccupied
void *n.* nothingness, emptiness, space, vacuum

volatile *adj.* explosive, unstable, fickle, erratic, passing, transient, frivolous

volition *n.* will, choosing, preference, choice, election, discretion, determination

voluble *adj.* talkative, loquacious, fluent, articulate, verbose, wordy, garrulous

volume *n.* **EDITION:** book, manuscript; **MASS:** size, magnitude, bulk; **LOUDNESS:** intensity, strength

voluntary *adj.* willing, disposed, inclined, prone, deliberate, intended, intentional, planned, willful

volunteer *v.* offer, extend, render, submit, proffer, tender, propose, suggest, recommend

voluptuous *adj.* sensual, indulgent, carnal, erotic, lustful, licentious

voracious *adj.* greedy, insatiable, ravenous, hungry, rapacious, grasping

vote *v.* elect, choose, enact, legislate, select, decide

vouch *v.* certify, attest, swear, state, assure

vow *n.* promise, pledge, covenant, contract

vow *v.* swear, promise, assure, attest, certify, affirm

voyage *n.* journey, excursion, trip, tour

vulgar *adj.* coarse tasteless, gross, crude, unrefined

vulgarity *n* obscenity, rudeness, indelicacy, coarseness, crassness, impropriety, immodesty

vulnerable *adj.* unprotected, unguarded, defenseless, exposed, susceptible, unsafe

waft *v.* float, hover, drift, skim flit flutter

wage *v.* conduct, undertake, pursue

wages *n.* pay, compensation, stipend, remuneration

wager *v.* bet, stake, risk, gamble, speculate, hazard

waif *n.* stray, foundling, orphan, urchin, ragamuffin

wail *v.* lament, bemoan, sob, whine, mourn

wait *v.* abide, delay, linger, remain, tarry, stay

waive *v.* forgo, sacrifice, relinquish, renounce, resign, postpone, defer

wake *v.* arouse, rise, awaken, stir, rouse, call, prod, activate, provoke, stimulate, motivate, kindle

walk *n.* path, lane, passageway, promenade

wan *adj.* pallid, sickly, pale, pasty, ashen, blanched

wand *n.* baton, staff, stick, scepter

wander *v.* roam, drift, ramble, meander, rove, range, stroll, saunter, digress, stray, shift, veer

wane *v.* diminish, subside, abate, decline, weaken, dwindle, decrease, fade, sink, fail

want *n.* **NECESSITY:** requirement, demand, lack, deficiency, inadequacy, **POVERTY:** impoverishment, indigence, privation, need

want *v.* desire, crave, covet, fancy

wanton *adj.* **MALICIOUS:** hateful, spiteful, unruly, willful, reckless; **LEWD:** lascivious, lustful, dissolute

ward *n.* **DEPENDENT:** child, minor, orphan; **DISTRICT:** territory, precinct, parish

warden *n.* guard, jailer, guardian, caretaker, custodian, watchman

warm *adj.* gracious, amiable, pleasant, kind, intimate, amicable, sympathetic, close

warn *v.* caution, advise, admonish, counsel, forewarn, alert inform, apprise

warrant *n.* guarantee insurance, assurance, pledge, certificate, authorization commission, license, permit, order, writ

warrant *v.* certify, approve, authorize, sanction
wary *adj.* alert, cautious, circumspect, vigilant, watchful
wash *v.* clean, cleanse, scrub, swab, bathe
waste *n.* **DEVASTATION:** ruin, blight, destruction; **TRASH:** garbage, debris, refuse, rubbish; **SQUANDER:** consume, expend, misuse, dissipate
watch *v.* observe, view, see, regard, scrutinize, inspect, guard, patrol, protect
watchful *adj.* vigilant, alert, careful, mindful, attentive, observant, wary
waterlogged *adj.* soaked, sodden, sopping, saturated
waver *v.* fluctuate, vacillate, hesitate
wax *v.* increase, grow, enlarge, expand, flourish
way *n.* method, style, technique, system
waylay *v.* ambush, assail, lurk, trap
weak *adj.* delicate, dainty, feeble, puny, infirm, powerless, flimsy, slight, wobbly
wealth *n.* riches, affluence, assets, abundance
wear *n.* deterioration, erosion, fraying, fatigue
weary *adj.* tired, exhausted, drained, fatigued, spent
weary *v.* harass, annoy, bother, badger, pester, irk, vex, distress, harry, torment
weep *v.* cry, sob, whimper, bawl, moan, wail, lament
weigh *v.* consider, contemplate, ponder, study
weight *n.* **MASS:** density, heft, heaviness, tonnage; **SIGNIFICANCE:** import, importance, gravity, consequence, influence
weird *adj.* mysterious, eerie, spooky, uncanny, unnatural, ghostly, puzzling, arcane

welcome *adj.* appreciated, desirable, delightful

welcome *v.* greet, salute, hail, embrace

weld *v.* join, connect, bind, bond

well *adj.* healthy, strong, hardy, robust, fit, sound

wet *v.* soak, drench, saturate, dampen, douse

wheedle *v.* coax, wangle, entreat, appeal, beg, cajole

whereabouts *n.* location, position, situation, locale, place, spot, site

whet *v.* sharpen, hone, strop, file, grind

whim *n.* impulse, inclination, urge, impulse, desire, craving, caprice, whimsy, notion, fancy, quirk

whimper *v.* cry, whine, sniffle, snivel, weep

whimsical *adj.* capricious, fanciful, playful, impulsive

whine *v.* cry, complain, grumble, snivel, whimper

whip *v.* beat, lash, flog, scourge, switch, punish

whirl *n.* revolve, rotate, spin, gyrate

whittle *v.* form, fashion, sculpt, carve, chisel, shape

whole *adj.* entire, unbroken, undivided, complete

wholesome *adj.* nourishing, healthy, nutritious, beneficial, advantageous, good

whoop *v.* holler, howl, shout, cheer, scream, yell

wicked *adj.* evil, depraved, immoral, nefarious

wide *adj.* extensive, comprehensive, universal

widen *v.* broaden, increase, expand, extend, spread, extend, enlarge, augment, stretch

width *n.* breadth, expanse, amplitude, scope

wield *v.* handle, utilize, operate, use, control, manage

wild *adj.* untamed, uncivilized, unrestrained

will *n.* **COMMAND:** decree, order, bidding, **DECISION:** choice, determination, **DESIRE:** purpose, pleasure, fancy, wish

will *v.* **COMMAND:** order, decree, proclaim, direct; **BEQUEATH:** grant, give, leave

willful *adj.* **DELIBERATE:** intended, meant, voluntary, willed; **STUBBORN:** obstinate, headstrong, inflexible, adamant, resolute

wilt *v.* droop, wither, shrivel, decay, slump

wily *adj.* deceitful, artful, cunning, sly, crafty, treacherous

win *v.* **TRIUMPH:** prevail; **ACHIEVE:** secure, persuade, influence, convert

wind *v.* curve, twist, swerve, snake, meander, curl, twist, twine, encircle

windfall *n.* blessing, godsend, boon, bonanza

winning *adj.* **ENGAGING:** captivating, charming, pleasant, likable, dazzling, winsome; **VICTORIOUS:** triumphant, conquering, successful

winnings *n.* accumulation, profits, gain

winnow *v.* sift, separate, sieve, extract

winsome *adj.* winning, beautiful, charming, captivating, lovely, cute, comely, engaging, delightful

wisdom *n.* sagacity, understanding, discretion, insight, tact, diplomacy, intelligence, knowledge

wise *adj.* intelligent, scholarly, learned, educated, sagacious, rational, sensible, prudent, insightful, discerning, smart

wish *n.* desire, craving, inclination, aspiration, goal

wish *v.* **CRAVE:** yearn, want, need; **DIRECT:** order, bid, instruct; **REQUEST:** beg, , entreat, solicit

wistful *adj.* melancholy, sentimental, nostalgic, plaintive

wit *n.* intellect, reason, sagacity, sense, wisdom

witch *n.* sorceress, enchantress, hag, crone

witchcraft *n.* sorcery, wizardry, divination

withdraw *v.* retract, revoke, recant

wither *v.* shrivel, wilt, shrink, atrophy, languish

withhold *v.* repress, restrain, check, retain

withstand *v.* oppose, defy, confront, resist, endure

witness *n.* spectator, bystander, onlooker, eyewitness

witness *v.* observe, see, watch, perceive, notice

witticism *n.* quip, jest, pun, gag, joke, wisecrack

witty *adj.* humorous, amusing, bright, keen, droll

wizard *n.* magician, conjurer, soothsayer, sorcerer

wizened *adj.* withered, shriveled, dry, dehydrated

woe *n.* sorrow, anguish, grief, misery, agony

woeful *adj.* mournful, sad, sorrowful, doleful

wonder *n.* amazement, astonishment, awe

wonder *v.* QUESTION: ponder, speculate, doubt; MARVEL: gape, stare

wonderful *adj.* extraordinary, marvelous, astounding, awesome, remarkable, startling, excellent, superb

wondrous *adj.* amazing, astonishing, striking, astounding, extraordinary, miraculous

word *n.* pledge, promise, guarantee, assurance

work *n.* labor, enterprise, undertaking, profession, business, occupation

work *v.* labor, toil, accomplish, perform, produce

world *n.* earth, globe, planet, realm, sphere, domain, kingdom, province, environment

worldly *adj.* sophisticated, urbane, suave

worry *n.* anxiety, apprehension, fear, disquiet, misgiving, uneasiness

worry *v.* **FRET:** care, fuss; **IRRITATE:** torment, bother, disturb, harass, trouble, pester, plague

worship *n.* adoration, devotion, reverence, veneration

worship *v.* esteem, revere, venerate, glorify, respect

worst *adj.* poorest, lowest

worth *n.* value, importance, quality, excellence

worthy *adj.* deserving, commendable, estimable, noble, excellent, exemplary

wound *v.* injure, harm, hurt, lacerate

wrap *v.* enfold, envelop, swathe, bandage, swaddle

wrath *n.* anger, fury, ire, irritation, resentment

wreak *v.* perpetrate, do, perform, commit

wreath *n.* garland, bouquet, decoration

wreathe *v.* curl, entwine, encircle

wreck *v.* destroy, demolish, ruin, shatter, spoil, raze

wreckage *n.* remains, debris, wreck, flotsam

wretch *n.* miscreant, rogue, villain, rascal, brute

wretched *adj.* miserable, woeful, dejected, depressed, forlorn, unhappy, contemptible, pitiful, sorry, vile

wriggle *v.* wiggle, squirm, writhe, worm, twist

wrinkle *n.* fold, crease, pucker, furrow, ridge

writ *n.* law, decree, order, edict

write *v.* inscribe, scrawl, sign, compose, record

writing *n.* penmanship, hand, lettering, calligraphy

writhe *v.* squirm, contort, agonize, thrash, flail
wrong *adj.* immoral, evil, false, inaccurate, improper
wrong *v.* harm, abuse, oppress, maltreat, dishonor
wrongful *adj.* unlawful, criminal, illegal, illicit

yard *n.* tract, area, enclosure, patch, courtyard, lot, plot, square
yardstick *n.* measure, guide, gauge, scale, model, norm, standard
yarn *n.* tale, anecdote, alibi, fabrication
yearning *n.* longing, craving, desire, want, wish
yell *v.* cheer, root, shout, call, holler, scream
yellow *adj.* cowardly, timid, scared, timorous, craven
yen *n.* longing, yearning, desire, urge, craving
yield *v.* surrender, abdicate, cede, concede, resign, grant, acquiesce, give
yoke *n.* couple, harness, join, link, attach, connect
young *adj.* immature, juvenile, adolescent, youthful, inexperienced, green
youth *n.* immaturity, adolescence, minority

zany *adj.* crazy, funny, silly, nonsensical, wacky
zeal *n.* enthusiasm, fervor, passion, spirit, ardor
zealot *n.* fanatic, devotee, partisan
zealous *adj.* enthusiastic, eager, fervent, passionate, spirited, ardent, earnest
zenith *n.* top, peak, crest, elevation
zephyr *n.* breeze, draft, wind
zest *n.* relish, enthusiasm, gusto, enjoyment, delight